The Campus History Series

UNIVERSITY OF CALIFORNIA, DAVIS

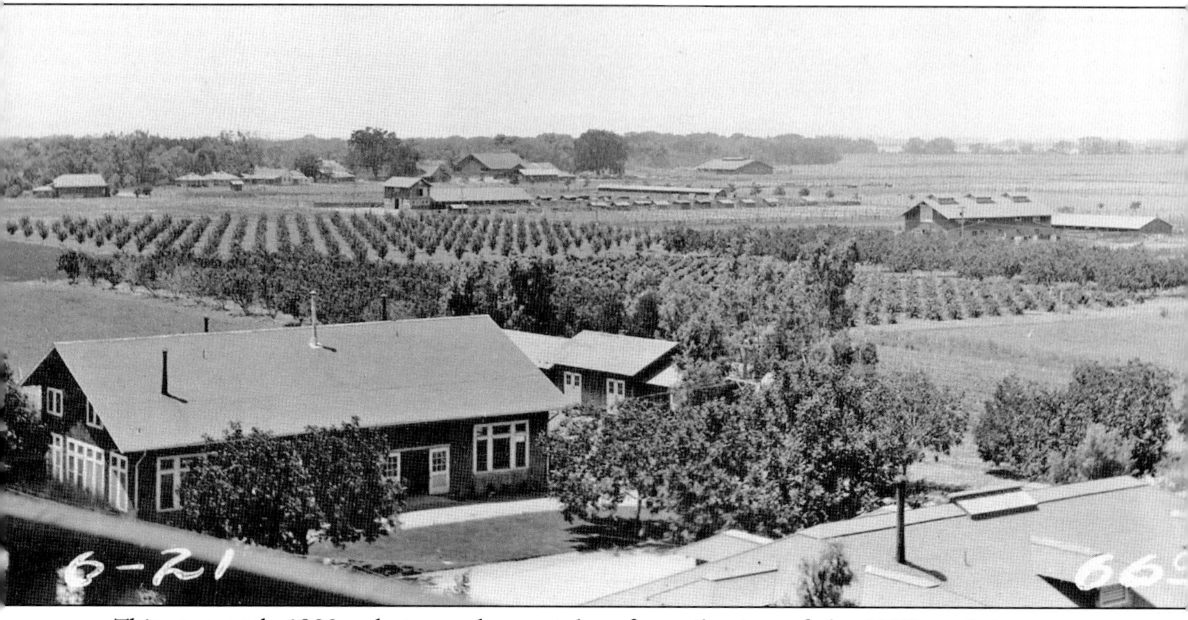

This rare early-1920s photograph was taken from the top of the 1908 tank house tower and shows the farm side of the campus. Barns abound, and rudimentary sheds with brown-shingle siding dot the southward view. Riparian vegetation along Putah Creek defines the horizon. (UC Davis University Library Department of Special Collections.)

On the Cover: Students in the 1930s examine the characteristics of grape varieties. They are in a 1909 building situated west of the main campus—the Viticulture Field Laboratory—set among vineyards and orchards. Researchers in the disciplines of viticulture and enology used increasingly sophisticated approaches and instruments over the decades to improve grape cultivation and wine quality. (UC Davis University Library Department of Special Collections.)

On the Back Cover: In 1940, the California Aggie Band struts its stuff. Band founder Price Gittinger directs, and the drum majorette is Mary Jane Gilhooley. In a few more years, the band was praised by the *Cal Aggie* as "every bit as good as Berkeley's." (UC Davis University Library Department of Special Collections.)

The Campus History Series

UNIVERSITY OF CALIFORNIA, DAVIS

DENNIS DINGEMANS AND ANN F. SCHEURING

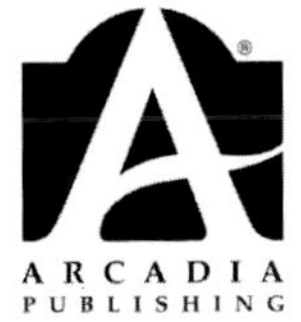

ISBN 978-0-7385-9699-0

Published by Arcadia Publishing
Charleston, South Carolina

Printed in the United States of America

Library of Congress Catalog Card Number: 2012943380

For all general information, please contact Arcadia Publishing:
Telephone 843-853-2070
Fax 843-853-0044
E-mail sales@arcadiapublishing.com
For customer service and orders:
Toll-Free 1-888-313-2665

Visit us on the Internet at www.arcadiapublishing.com

This book is dedicated to all the university's librarians—past, present, and future—whose service to education and research is indispensable.

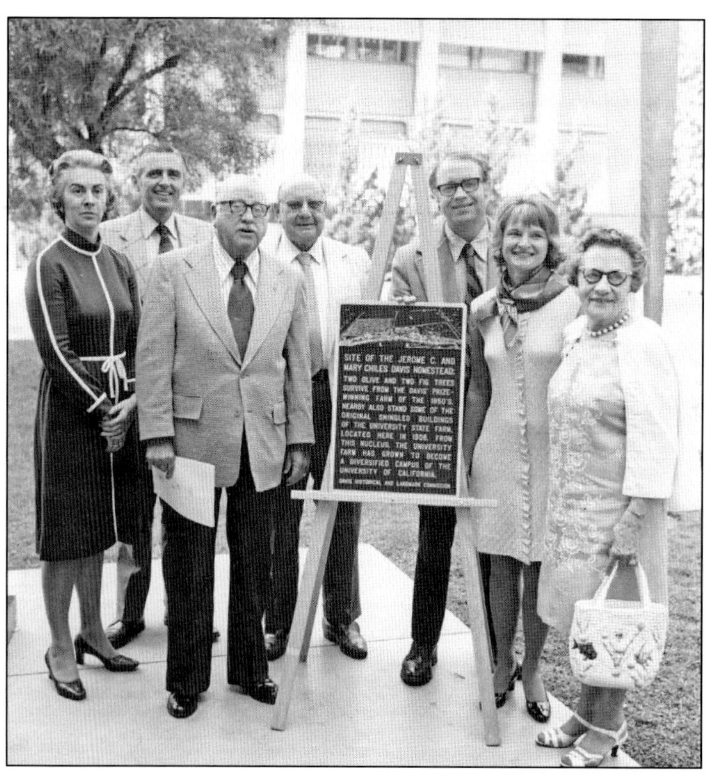

Yolo County Historical Society leaders join top UC Davis executives in 1972 in dedicating a plaque commemorating the Jerome Davis farm, which gave the town its name and the campus its territory. In the back row from left to right are Chancellor James Meyer, Chancellor Emeritus Emil Mrak, and registrar Maynard Skinner. Olive and fig trees in front of Olson Hall survived from the Davis orchards of the 1850s. (Yolo County Archives.)

CONTENTS

ACKNOWLEDGMENTS

The UC Davis University Library Department of Special Collections (SCL) is the greatest single resource for studying the history of the campus and finding images that illustrate it. We are grateful for SCL's open door, which we went through many times during the six months we worked on this book. Within its walls, we found a half dozen genial librarians and other assistants who quickly adopted our project and helped us through to its culmination. In particular, we appreciate the assistance of university archivist John Skarstad, the person most responsible for assembling the treasure trove.

The other sources that provided us with images are listed here, and the letter codes appearing at the end of each caption identify the image as having come from that source. The Hattie Weber Museum of Davis, under director emeritus Jim Becket, let us use dozens of its items (HWM). John Lofland, this college town's preeminent historian (and author of two Arcadia books about Davis) was generous with his time and his collection (JL). The Associated Students of the University of California at Davis gave us permission to reproduce images scanned from their yearbooks *Agricola* or *El Rodeo* (YB). The Bohart Museum of Entomology allowed us to use a charming photograph of its founder (BME). The California National Primate Research Center gave us two images (CPB). Mark Honbo of Intercollegiate Athletics provided many, and we used one (ICA). The Women's Center on campus contributed an image (WC). The former pomology department has miraculously retained its professional photographers' 100 years of work (PD). From the Herbarium in Plant Sciences, we received several images (PSH). The UC Davis Arboretum also opened its scrapbooks to us (PCA). Prof. Richard Walters (RW) and librarian Axel Borg (AB) gave us pictures of themselves with their work. Tom Rost allowed us to use his unit's marvelous portrait of Katherine Esau (TR). The Gibson House Museum (GHM) and the Yolo County Archives (YCA) opened their files to us. The Bodega Marine Laboratory (BML) allowed us to use one of its photographs. The UC Davis Medical Center permitted use of an air view (MC). Jeanne Olmo contributed an image of her dad (JO). The Ogasawaras provided postcard views of the World War II campus scene (FKO). The C.M. Rick Tomato Genetics Resource Center (RTG) provided us with the wonderful picture that ends this book. Two images come from author Dennis Dingemans (DJD).

INTRODUCTION

The University of California, Davis campus lies in the heart of California close to Sacramento, the state capital, and nearly in the middle of the state's great Central Valley. In many ways, the campus itself functions as a kind of heart for the region, beating strongly through the years, both as an educational resource for students of all backgrounds and as a research powerhouse supporting and encouraging our economy and well-being. With a long tradition of outreach, UC Davis continues to pour its energies into public service.

More than a century old, UC Davis has developed from modest beginnings into a nationally and internationally respected institution, richly diverse in its offerings and activities. The campus is the second in the University of California system; it was founded to establish the University Farm for Berkeley's thriving College of Agriculture. In 1905, the state legislature passed the University Farm Bill to provide funding for the selection and purchase of appropriate land, and after lengthy review of more than 70 proposals, the State Farm Commission decided on the Davis site in 1906. The first Farm School students were officially enrolled in 1908, with Berkeley students arriving to join them for a semester or two of "practical education." Specialized short courses in agriculture were also offered to the public from the beginning.

Through the following decades, the agricultural programs at Davis became increasingly sophisticated as scientific knowledge increased, enhancing the reputation of the University of California in their own way. By the close of the 1930s, the campus was known as the College of Agriculture at Davis, which included four-year degree work as well as the two-year program tailored for farm students.

After World War II, as the University of California underwent tremendous expansion, UC Davis was transformed into an independent campus, growing steadily in its offerings and reputation. Widely recognized for its strengths in the biological sciences, the campus also encouraged a flowering of other disciplines, including the liberal arts. After opening its long-awaited School of Veterinary Medicine in 1948, UC Davis established other new graduate programs and professional schools, including its College of Letters and Science in 1951, College of Engineering in 1962, School of Law in 1964, and School of Medicine in 1966. Physically, the campus also expanded into satellite research facilities situated in sites across California from the coast to the inland mountains.

UC Davis has long been known for its wholesome campus life, tree-shaded grounds, and loyal alumni. Mirroring campus growth, the city of Davis is a pleasant example of a small college town. Undergraduate student life still retains its traditional friendliness, even as enrollments have grown and academic programs have become more rigorous. Students are encouraged to think in terms of public service, not only in their own communities but worldwide. Friendships formed here often last a lifetime.

In choosing the illustrations for this book as part of the Arcadia Campus History Series, we have looked for images to represent milestones and highlights of institutional development. As an album of historical photographs, the volume focuses on the past and not on current issues. We have attempted to assemble a variety of illustrations from group portraits to candid action shots; individuals are included only as they have been recognized as leaders in campus administration or in their disciplinary fields.

Chapters 1 through 4 are organized along chronological lines to illustrate the periods of campus development. Chapter 1 focuses on the University Farm years, 1906 through 1921, when the student body was small and programs were designed to give Farm School students and Berkeley undergraduates practical experience. Chapter 2 shows campus evolution toward a more science-based curriculum, as well as toward specific professional training in fields such as the dairy industry or agricultural engineering. Chapter 3 looks at the post–World War II years when UC Davis began to become a true university with the founding of the School of Veterinary Medicine and the Colleges of Engineering and Letters and Science. Chapter 4 includes the development of other new professional schools, the continuing evolution of programs, and changing extracurricular activities.

Chapters 5 through 8 take a thematic approach. Chapter 5 looks at student life and traditions over the years. Chapter 6 includes a variety of photographs capturing moments in ever-popular sports and recreation. Chapter 7 celebrates Picnic Day along with the development of the arboretum. Chapter 8 selectively shows UC Davis regional and global connections, from international students and visitors on campus to world-class research collections.

UC Davis is still making history every day as it meets societal changes and challenges, and its heart beats on strongly. The university now offers interdisciplinary graduate studies and more than 100 undergraduate majors in four colleges. It houses six professional schools, has more than 32,000 students, more than 2,500 faculty and more than 21,000 staff members, plus an annual research budget exceeding $684 million, a comprehensive health system, and 13 designated research centers. The teaching, research, and public service carried on here help the state of California in myriad ways and help transform the world.

It has been a privilege and a pleasure to work on this book. Both of us as authors have long been fascinated with the history of UC Davis, one as a longtime faculty member in the Department of Geography and the other as a writer and editor for a lengthy list of UC-sponsored publications. Though both of us were already well versed in campus history, we learned a great deal in our collection process, and we found inspiration too. Over the years, UC Davis and its many thousands of faculty, staff, and alumni have truly served all of us well.

One

The University Farm Years

1906–1921

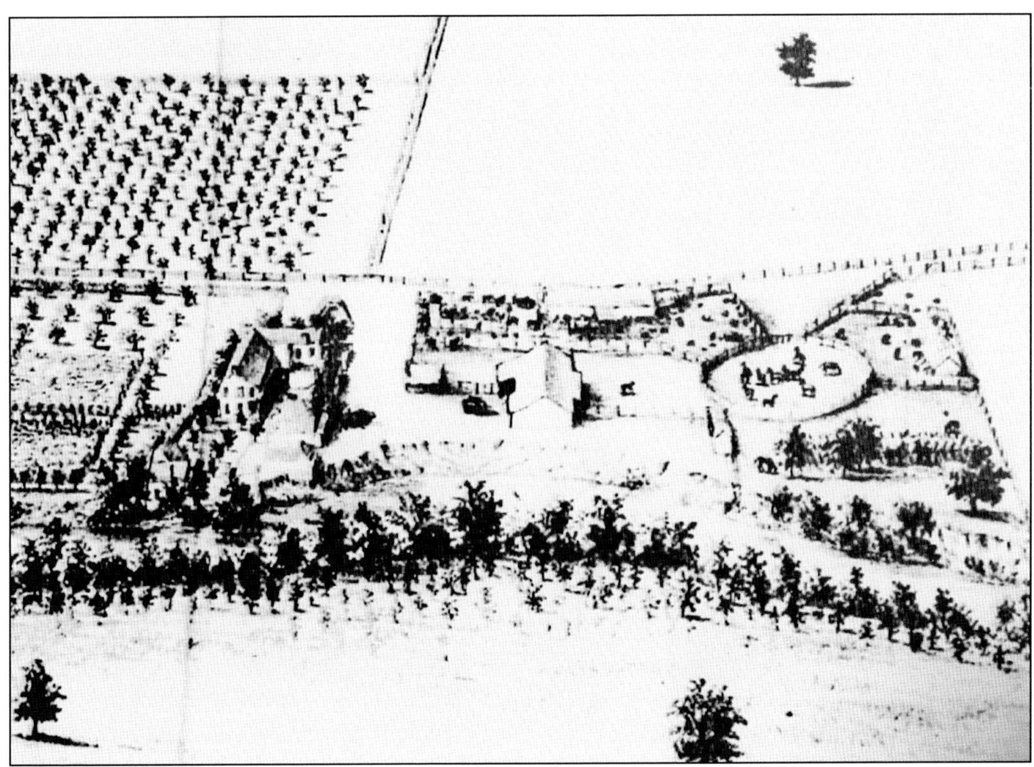

In the mid-1850s, pioneer settler Jerome Davis established a prize-winning livestock farm along the bank of Putah Creek in Yolo County. Half a century later, this property, with its rich alluvial soils and ready access to water, would become part of the University Farm, an adjunct of the University of California's thriving College of Agriculture at Berkeley. A memorial marker near Olson Hall in the center of campus commemorates the selection of this site out of more than 70 offered across the state. (HWM.)

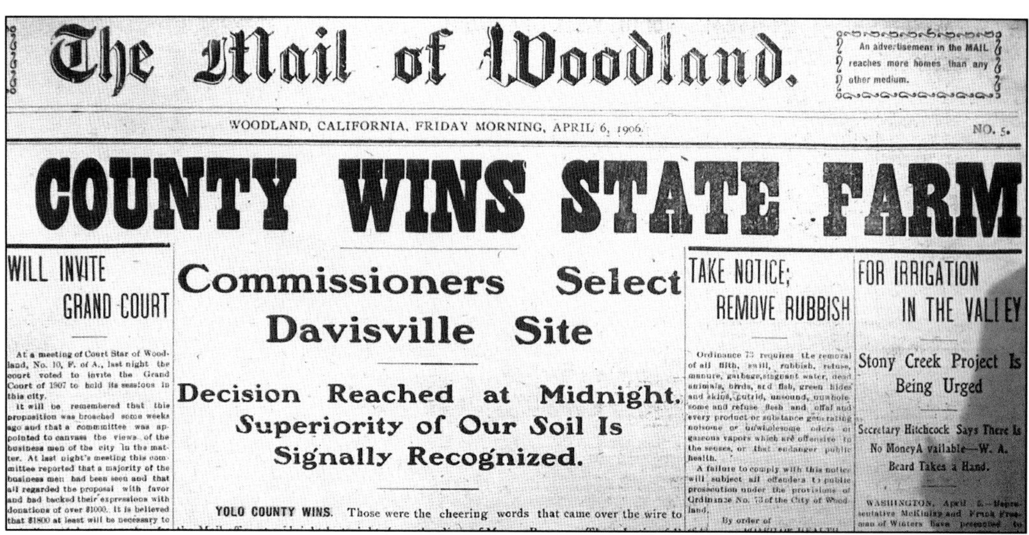

The Mail of Woodland.

An advertisement in the MAIL reaches more homes than any other medium.

WOODLAND, CALIFORNIA, FRIDAY MORNING, APRIL 6, 1906. NO. 5.

COUNTY WINS STATE FARM

WILL INVITE GRAND COURT

At a meeting of Court Star of Woodland, No. 10, F. of A., last night the court voted to invite the Grand Court of 1907 to hold its sessions in this city.

It will be remembered that this proposition was broached some weeks ago and that a committee was appointed to canvass the views of the business men of the city in the matter. At last night's meeting this committee reported that a majority of the business men had been seen and that all regarded the proposal with favor and had backed their expressions with donations of over $1000. It is believed that $1800 at least will be necessary to

Commissioners Select Davisville Site

Decision Reached at Midnight. Superiority of Our Soil Is Signally Recognized.

YOLO COUNTY WINS. Those were the cheering words that came over the wire to

TAKE NOTICE; REMOVE RUBBISH

Ordinance 73 requires the removal of all filth, swill, rubbish, refuse, manure, garbage, stagnant water, dead animals, birds, and fish, green hides and skins, putrid, unsound, unwholesome and refuse flesh and offal and every product or substance generating noisome or unwholesome odors or gaseous vapors which are offensive to the senses, or that endanger public health.

A failure to comply with this notice will subject all offenders to public prosecution under the provisions of Ordinance No. 73 of the City of Woodland.

By order of

FOR IRRIGATION IN THE VALLEY

Stony Creek Project Is Being Urged

Secretary Hitchcock Says There Is No MoneyA vailable—W. A. Beard Takes a Hand.

WASHINGTON, April 5.—Representative McKinlay and Frank Freeman of Winters have presented to

The University Farm Bill of 1905 created a State Farm Commission entrusted with evaluating proposed sites for the University Farm. Yolo County citizens offered several properties in various locations. Supporters of Woodland, the county seat, hoped to win the prize, promoting several hundred acres on that city's south side, but the 778-acre tract near Davisville, a much smaller town, was finally chosen by virtue of its winning combination of soils, water, and enthusiastic local citizen campaign. (HWM.)

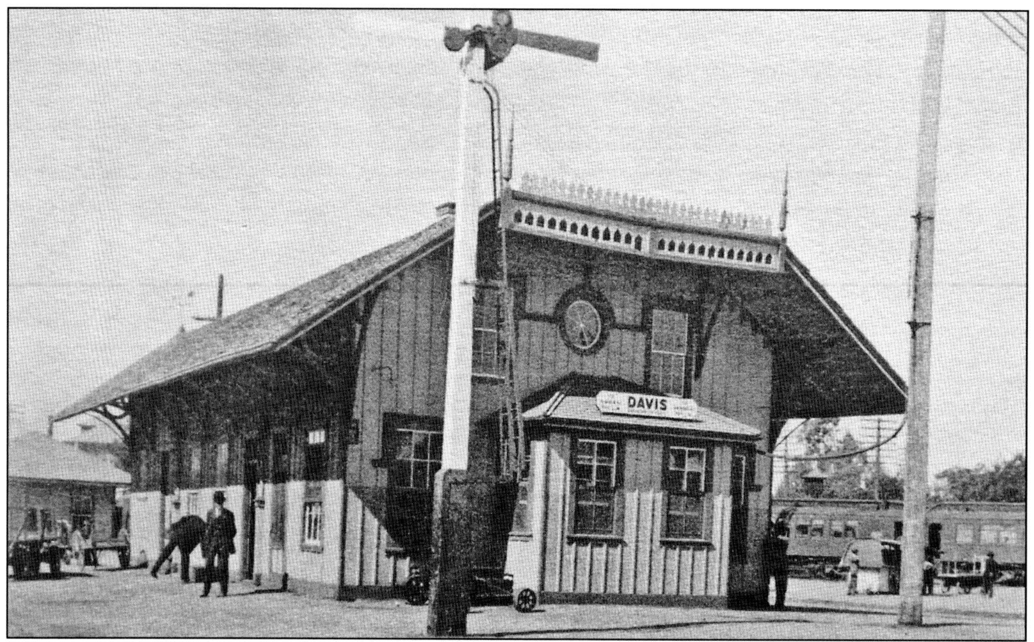

Two other major reasons for selecting the Davisville site were its proximity to Sacramento, the state capital, and its convenient station on the main line of the Southern Pacific transcontinental railroad. This simple wood-frame building at Davisville—renamed Davis in 1907 to avoid confusion with Danville—was replaced in 1913 with a Spanish mission–style depot. The station has continued over the years to serve travelers to and from the UC Davis campus. (HWM.)

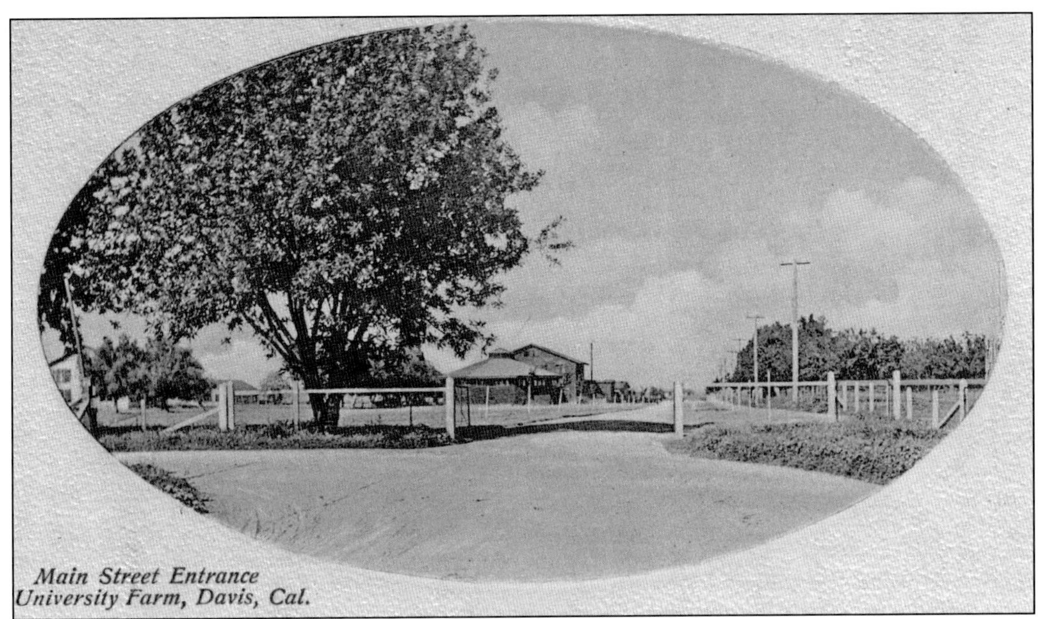

The modest east entry to the University Farm initially consisted of this road leading to the livestock judging pavilion and creamery building. Constructed in 1907, these were the first buildings on campus, erected for use in the animal husbandry programs that would be a hallmark of Farm School instruction. Cottages were also built for the University Farm director and the creamery manager. (JL.)

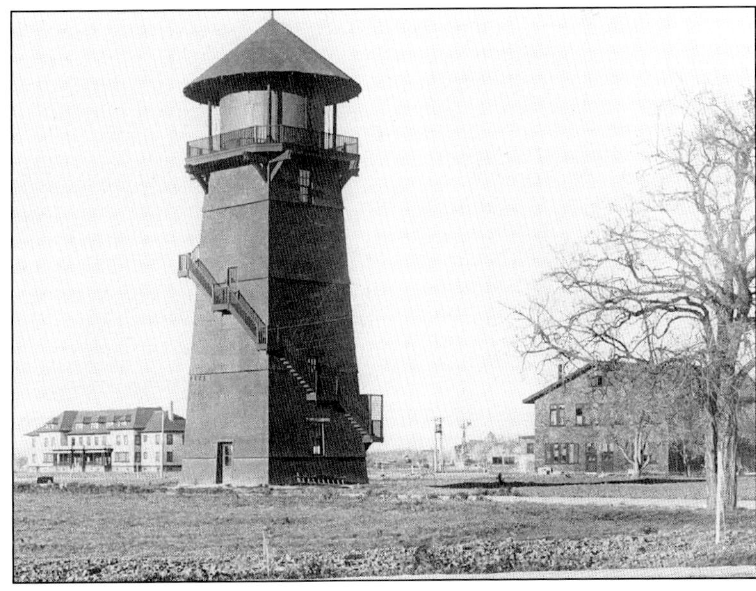

An imposing water tower that supplies the needs of the new campus overlooks construction of the first buildings, somewhat delayed by the demands of reconstruction in the Bay Area after the San Francisco earthquake of 1906. Included in the background just to the left of the tower is North Hall, the first dormitory (1908). To the right is the creamery. (HWM.)

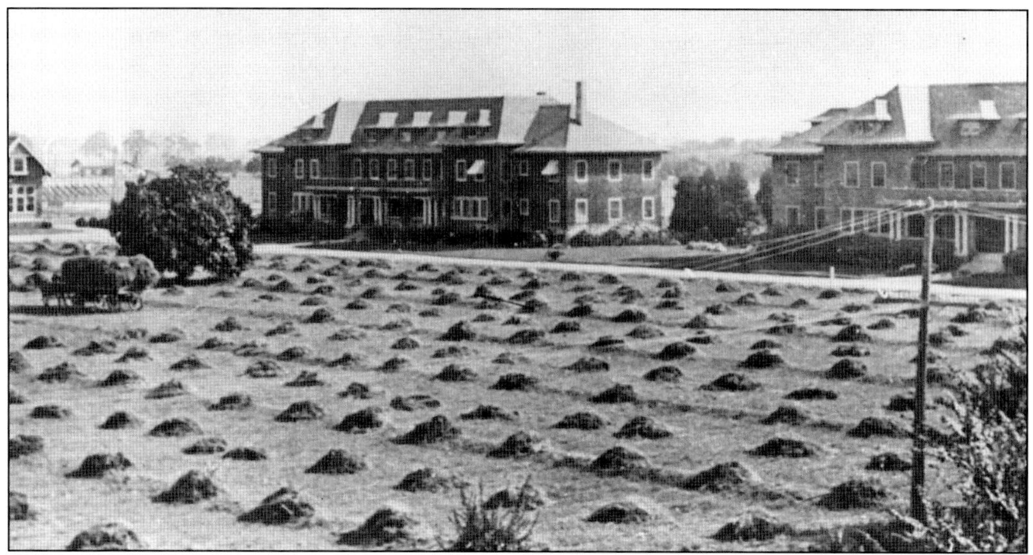

Two large student dormitories built between 1908 and 1912 were called simply North Hall (center) and South Hall. The wood-shingled buildings were designed with upper-story gabled windows for ventilation and large veranda porches for shelter from the weather. For years, the large quadrangle in front was planted to farm crops, not only for campus use but also as an example of good cultivation. Haystacks decorate the vista here, destined eventually for the animal barns. (PD.)

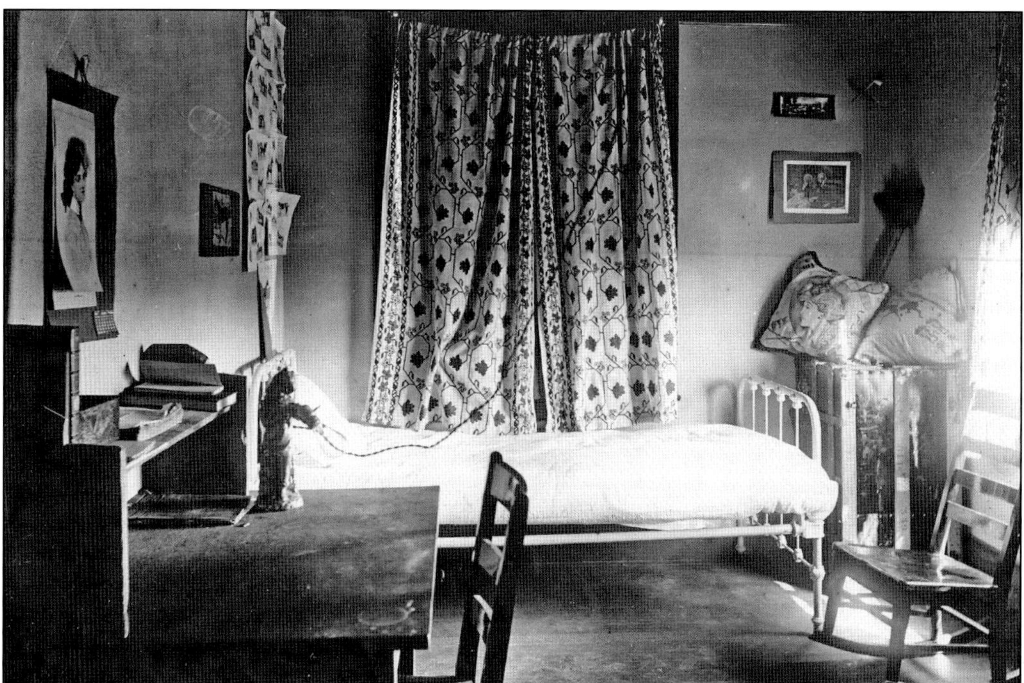

A typical student dormitory room included a simple bed and desk, as well as personalized touches including curtains, pillows, and pictures on the wall. The wiring in this room would certainly not meet today's standards. (SCL.)

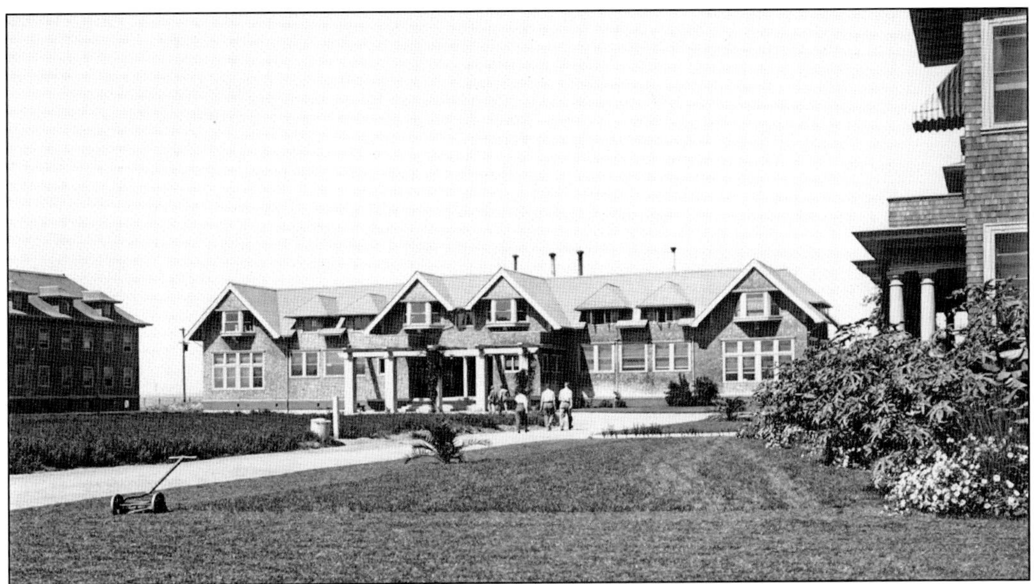

East Hall, built in 1909 close to the North Hall dormitory, included the all-important kitchen and dining hall for students, staff, and visitors. One side also served as a small infirmary of three beds supervised by a resident nurse who treated minor injuries or ailments. The infirmary later expanded to 20 beds on the second floor, remaining there until 1948. (SCL.)

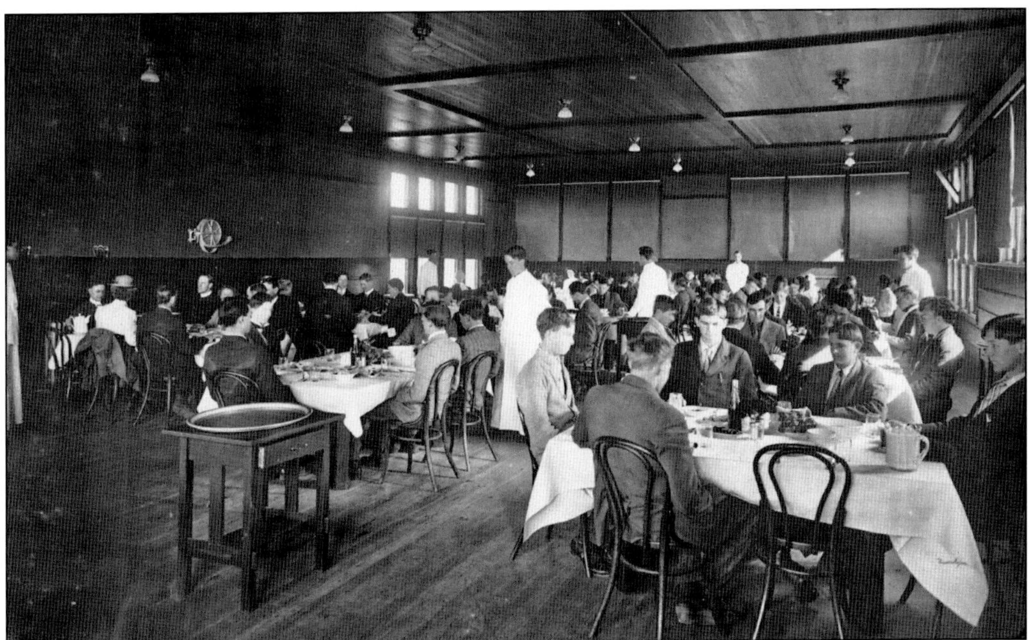

Meals were served family style in the dining hall by student waiters who learned to balance big trays. Mealtimes were important social gathering times for students who spent much of their day out on the farm. (SCL.)

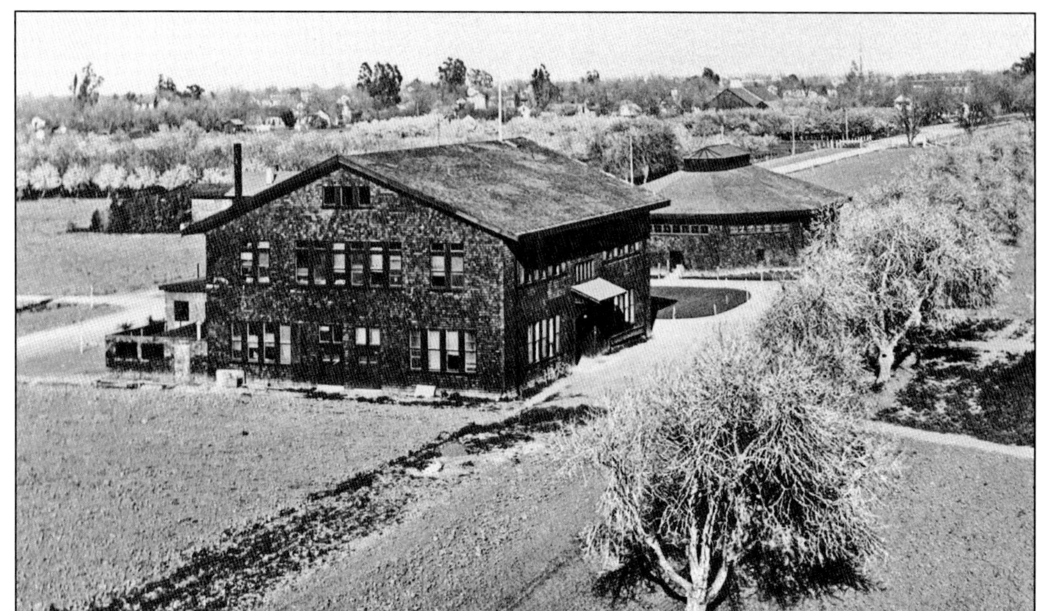

The two-story creamery contained a commercial-size dairy plant, a laboratory, offices, and classrooms, while the octagonal judging pavilion doubled as a lecture and demonstration hall. The creamery was one of the busiest buildings on campus, processing and shipping milk and other products from the university herd. This photograph, taken from the water tower, shows the creamery, the pavilion, and the entry to campus with the town beyond. (HWM.)

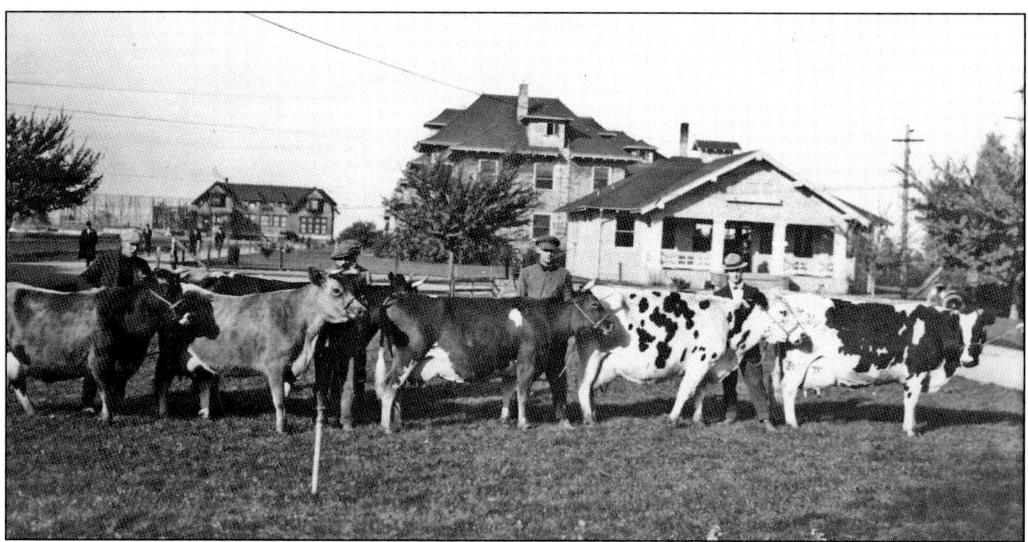

Farm animals were part of daily life on the University Farm, moved as needed for instruction. These dairy cows pictured in front of the manager's cottage and the side of South Hall, with East Hall in the background, were probably gathered for an event at the livestock pavilion. The shingled cottage, built in 1914, has served many uses over the years, including the administration of cooperative extension on campus. It became the Cross-Cultural Center in 1992. (SCL.)

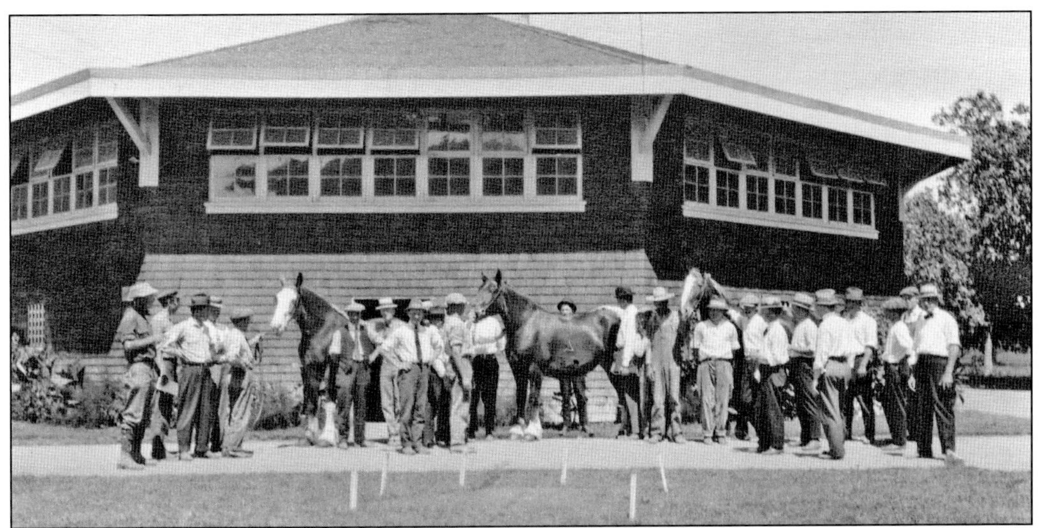

The livestock judging pavilion was used constantly as a place for students to learn how to distinguish breeds and evaluate quality animals. This class is gathered around several workhorses, still a crucial source of power and primary means of transportation in rural areas. Early on, the University Farm became known for its horses, encouraging California farmers and ranchers to obtain the best breeds and provide competent care. (SCL.)

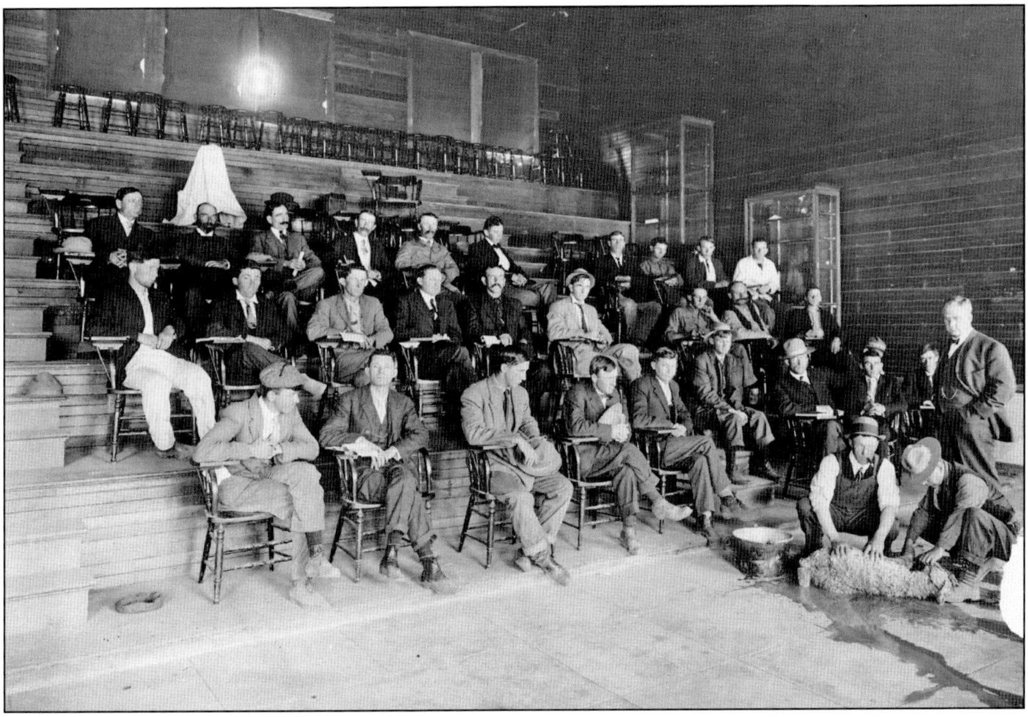

Instruction was given inside the livestock pavilion to both resident and short-course students. Here, a group seated on risers views a demonstration on how to wash a sheep's fleece. The 500-seat pavilion was moved and converted many years later into the Wyatt Pavilion Theatre, a theater-in-the-round housing dramatic productions and musical performances. (SCL.)

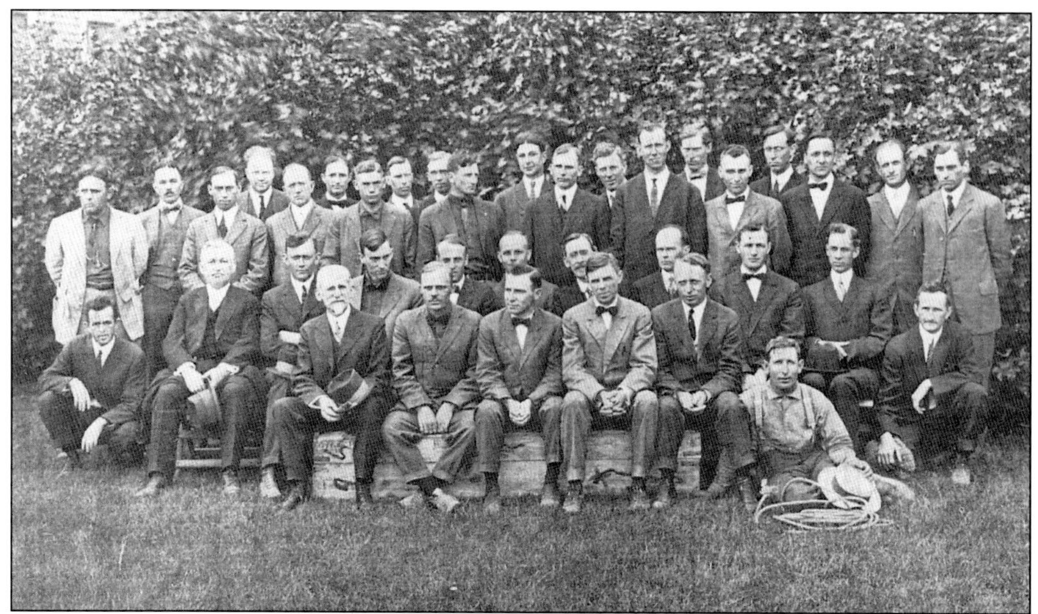

The University Farm faculty, pictured here in the 1915 student yearbook, sat for its formal portrait by a commercial photographer. Some of the academic faculty seen here commuted to Davis from Berkeley by train, an easy trip of little more than an hour. Some of the resident staff had long careers at Davis and are memorialized in various ways on campus today. (YB, HWM.)

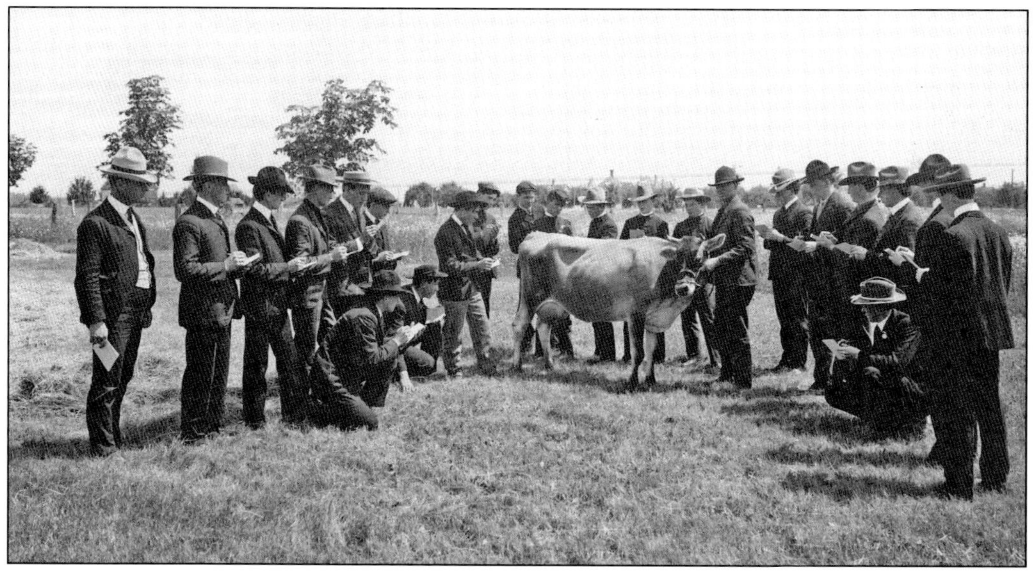

University Farm students learned to judge the fine points of animal breeding and development and soon began to compete in regional and national livestock judging expositions, such as the Panama Pacific International Exposition and the Chicago International Livestock Exposition. University Farm animals sent to these shows brought home many awards, and so did the students who showed them. (SCL.)

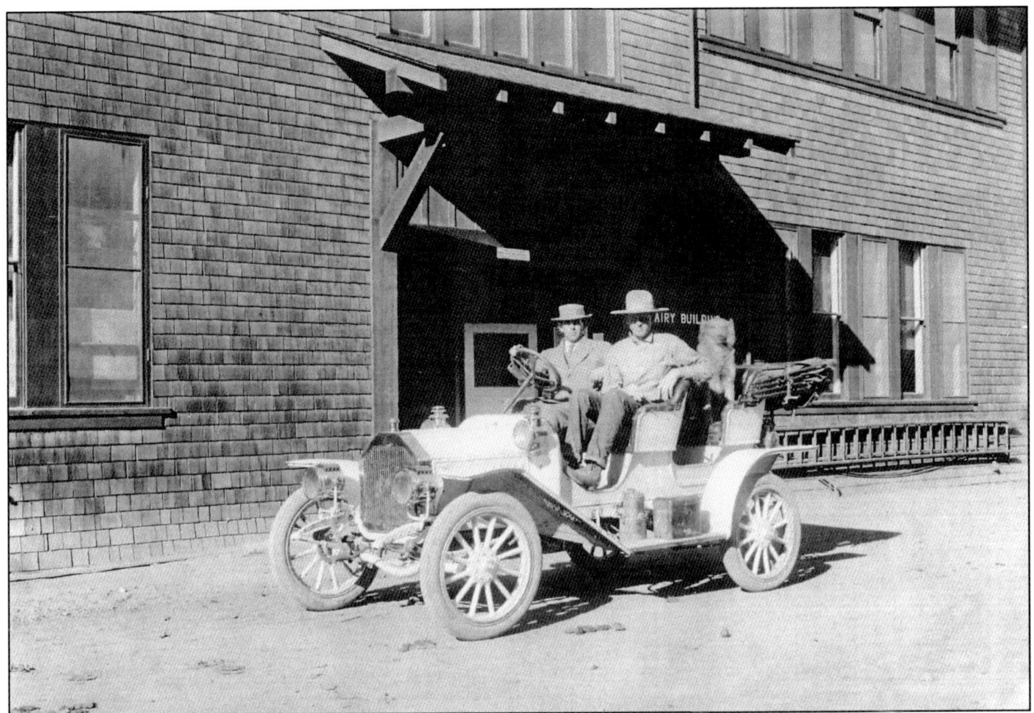

The university purchased its first automobile—a Model T without a starter—in 1913 for the use of Leroy Anderson, the farm superintendent. Up until then, he had been using horses to get around the campus. In this photograph, farm manager John Rogers and assistant to the superintendent Roger Roberts are pictured in front of the creamery building. (HWM.)

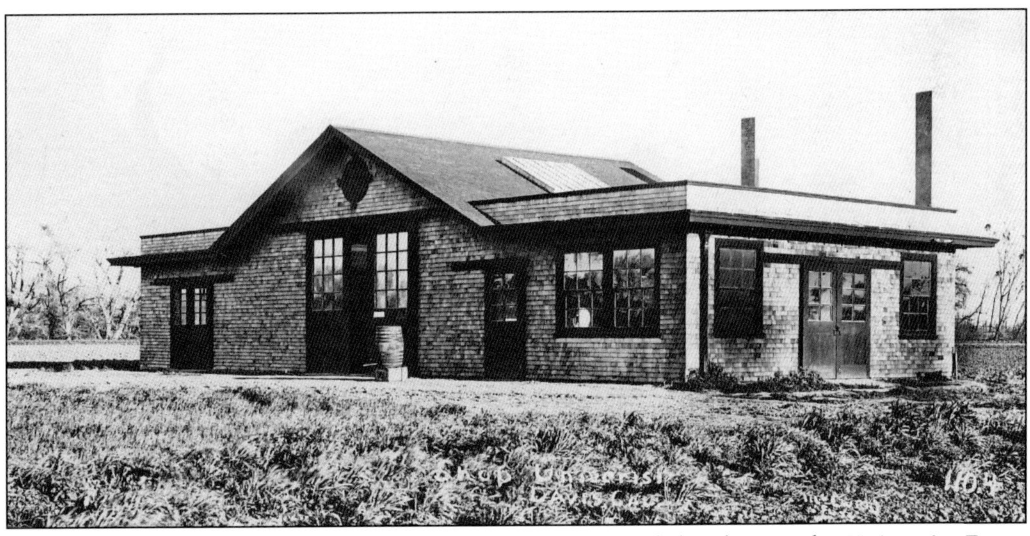

Every farm needs a shop for machinery maintenance, and the shop at the University Farm, built around 1915, was intended to serve as a model for visiting farmers and students hoping to go home with new ideas for their family operations. Its rustic wood-shingled vernacular design complemented other campus buildings constructed in the same style. (YCA.)

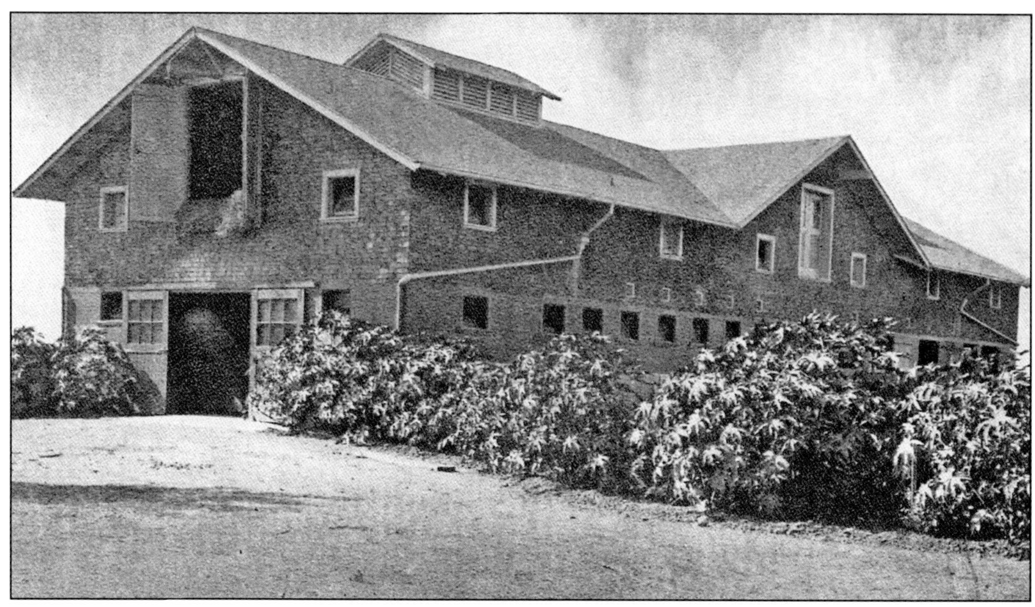

For nearly 40 years, the big horse barn across the road from the dairy barn housed the workhorses used on the farm as well as the riding horses used by staff. Not until after World War II was the structure demolished and the animals moved to an outlying area. The site of the horse barn was used for construction of the School of Veterinary Medicine, which celebrated its ground-breaking ceremony in 1948. (JL.)

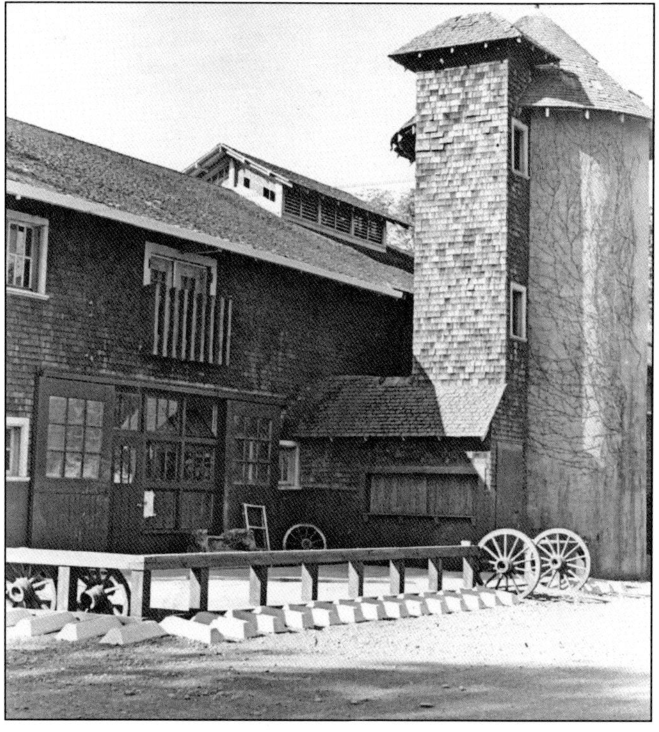

The iconic dairy barn with its attached silo occupied a prominent position on campus and was the site of much daily activity from feeding to milking. The structure was intended to serve as a model for the dairy industry, utilizing up-to-date equipment and stressing hygiene and efficiency. Its brown-shingled style echoed other barns and farm buildings. This photograph shows the barn and silo after later conversion to student uses, including bicycle parking. (HWM.)

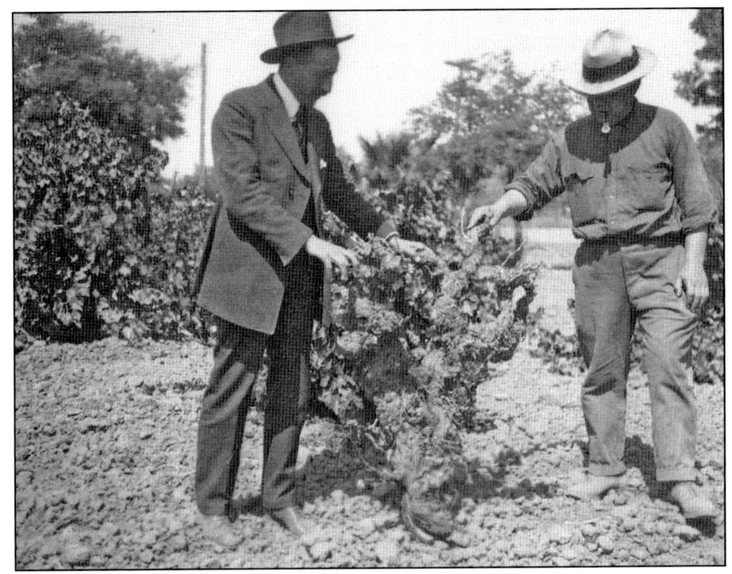

Vineyards were planted at the University Farm, with Prof. Frederic Bioletti of Berkeley in charge of variety selection and cultivation. Here, an unidentified visitor examines a planting with Frederick Flossfeder, the vineyard manager on the right. Although the Volstead Act in 1919 was to prohibit commercial winemaking for 14 years, the UC Davis viticulture program later became world famous. (SCL.)

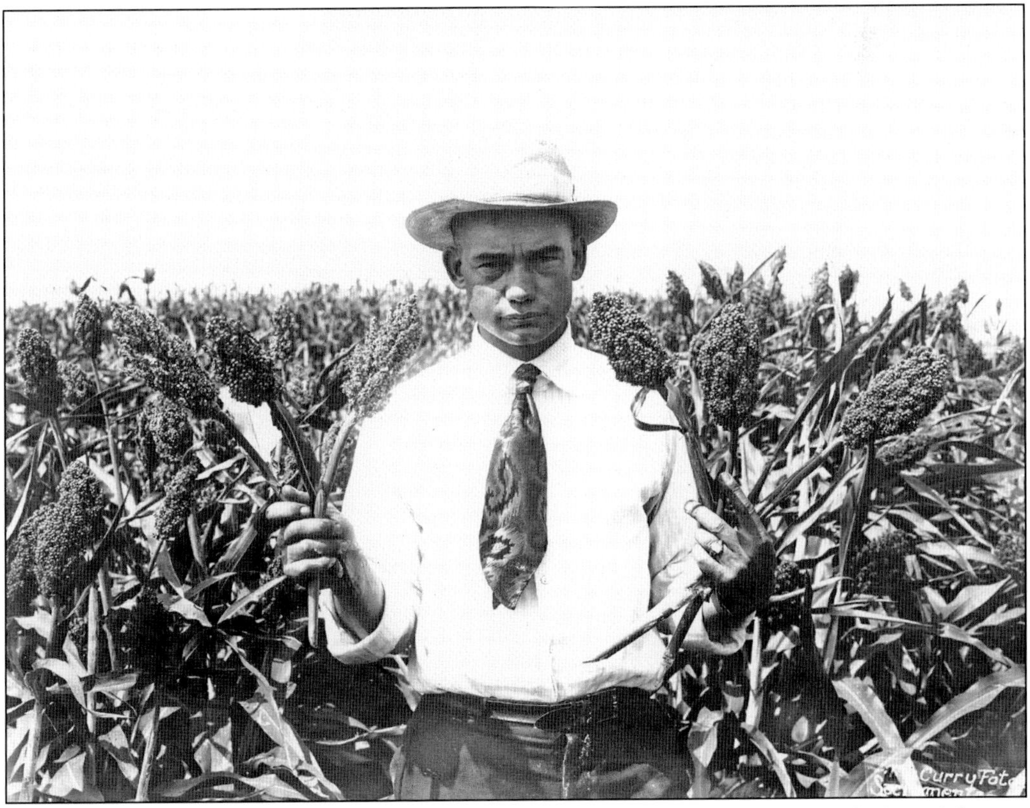

Thomas Tavernetti, standing in a field of millet in 1917, came to Davis in 1913 straight out of University of California, Berkeley. As an assistant to the directors of the University Farm from 1913 to 1930, Tavernetti was a competent and popular staff member, supporting and encouraging improvements in research and teaching. After his early death, his admirers commemorated him with the Tavernetti Bell, which is still traditionally rung after Aggie football victories. (SCL.)

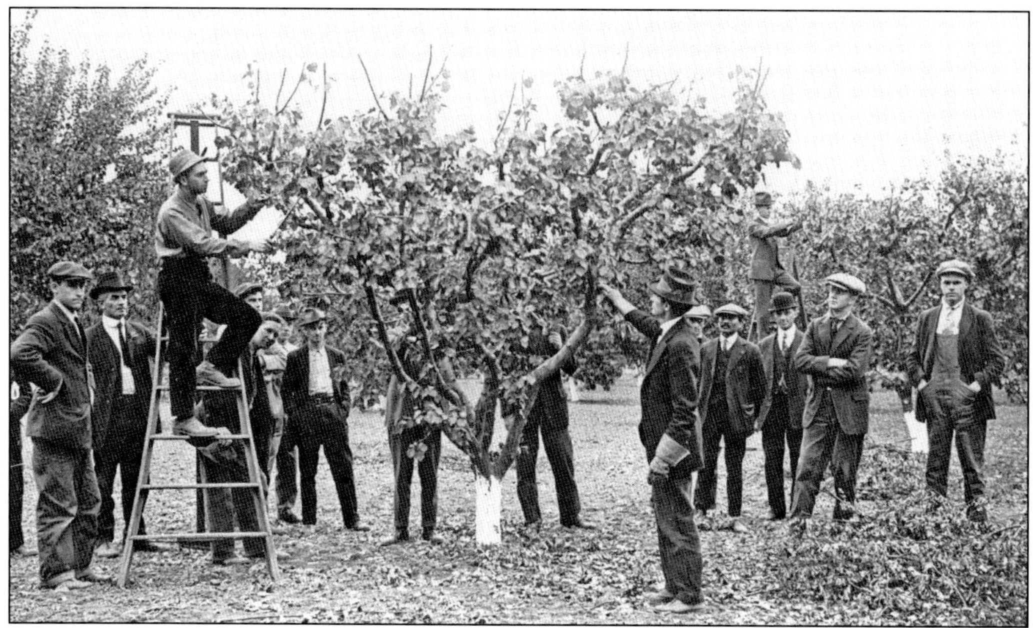

During this period, as irrigation made new crops feasible, many farmers began planting fruit orchards. Many orchard crops were planted experimentally on the University Farm in response to the great need for information on desirable varieties and best techniques for cultivation. Pomology specialists here show visitors how to prune for the health of the trees and the quality of the crop. (PD.)

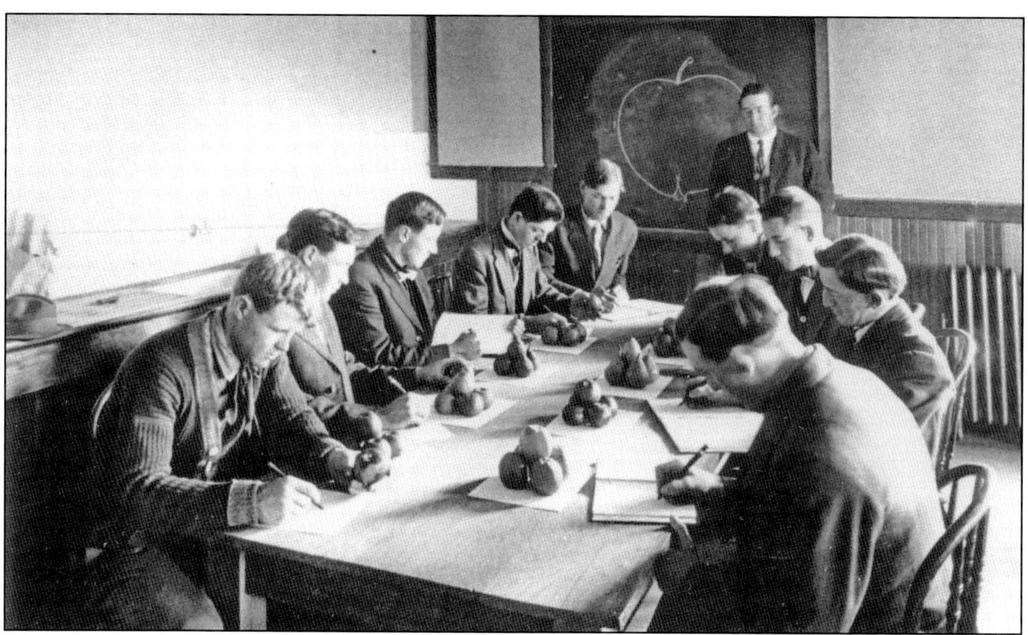

Students learned to judge the differences between fruit varieties by hands-on evaluation of crops like these apples, as well as peaches, plums, grapes, and other important fruits. This was serious business, as some of them might later earn their livings by orchard management. The challenge for the instructor was collecting all the fruit. (HWM.)

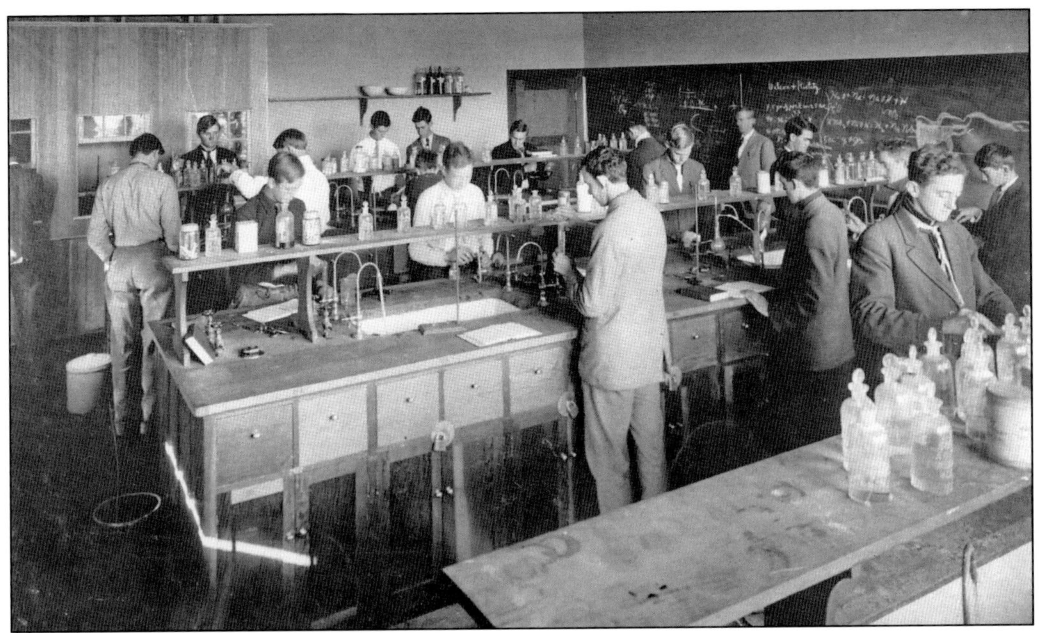

Laboratory work was part of the curriculum also, where students could learn basic chemistry and how it might apply in farming. From its earliest days, College of Agriculture work in agricultural chemistry was of great help to California farmers. An emerging problem in some farming districts, for example, was the salinization of soils resulting from early irrigation efforts. Chemical analysis could help determine the degree of the problem and the efficacy of various countermeasures. (SCL.)

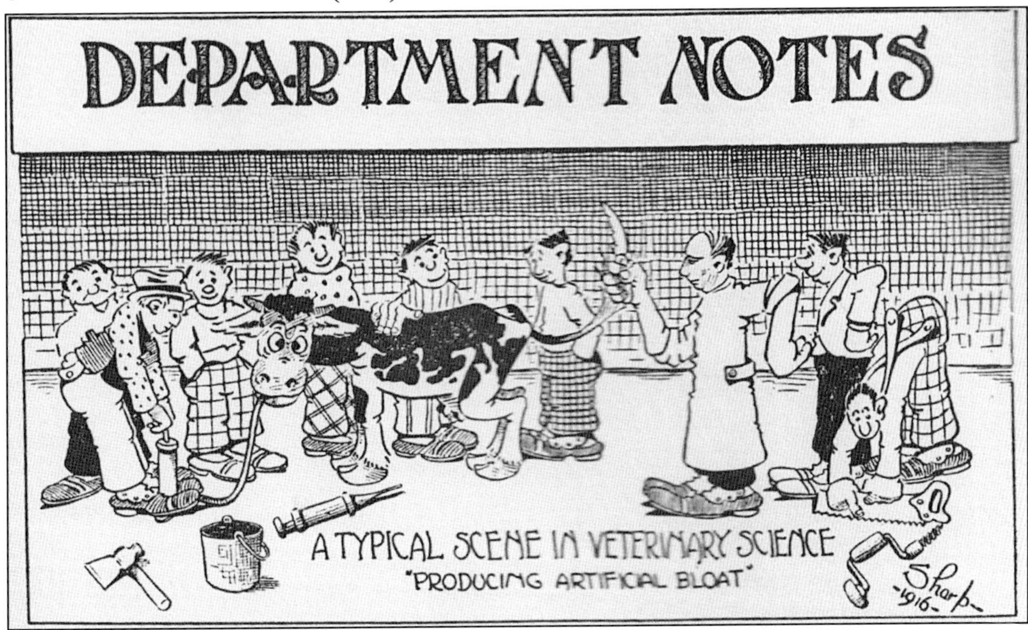

Some of the early student yearbooks had very talented staff artists. This deftly executed cartoon in the 1916 *Agricola* shows activities in veterinary science; however, bloat in dairy cows was no joke, as it could bring death, so students needed to learn how to deal with it. (YB, HWM.)

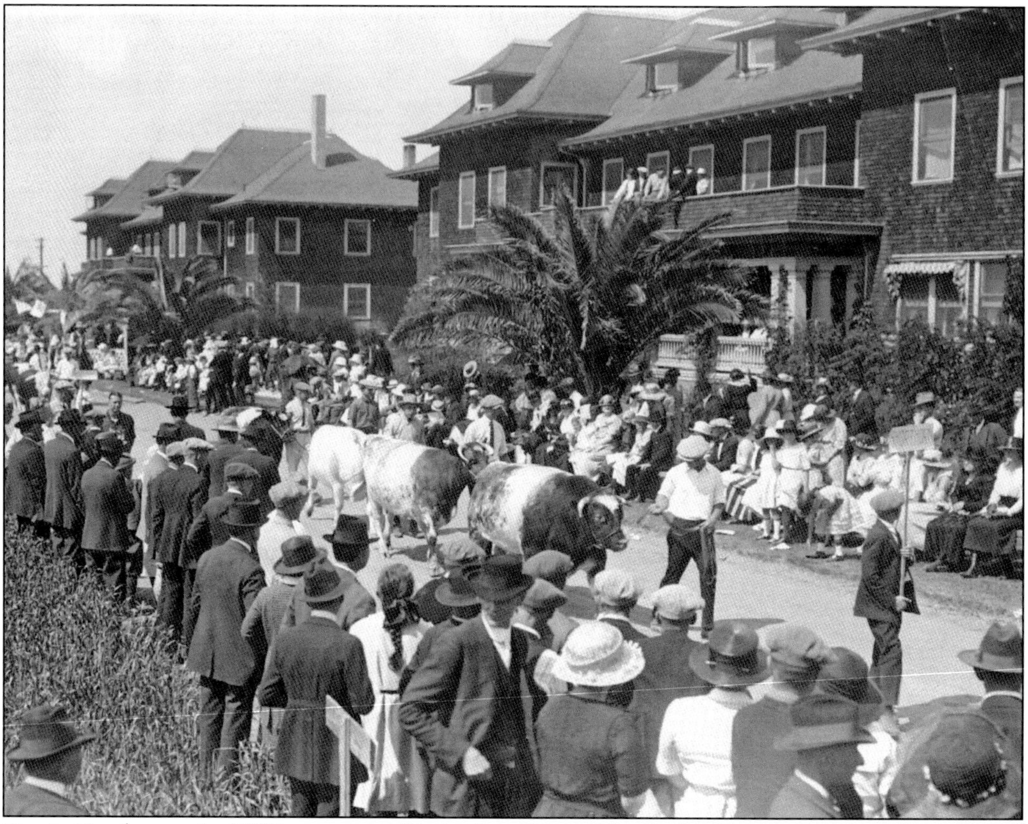

Picnic Day began in 1908 as a way of bringing the public to the University Farm for a day of celebration. It became an annual spring event, and thousands of visitors soon came each year to the campus to see what students and staff were doing. Picnic Day parades became popular displays of campus pride, like this one showing some of the prize livestock on the farm in 1920. (YCA.)

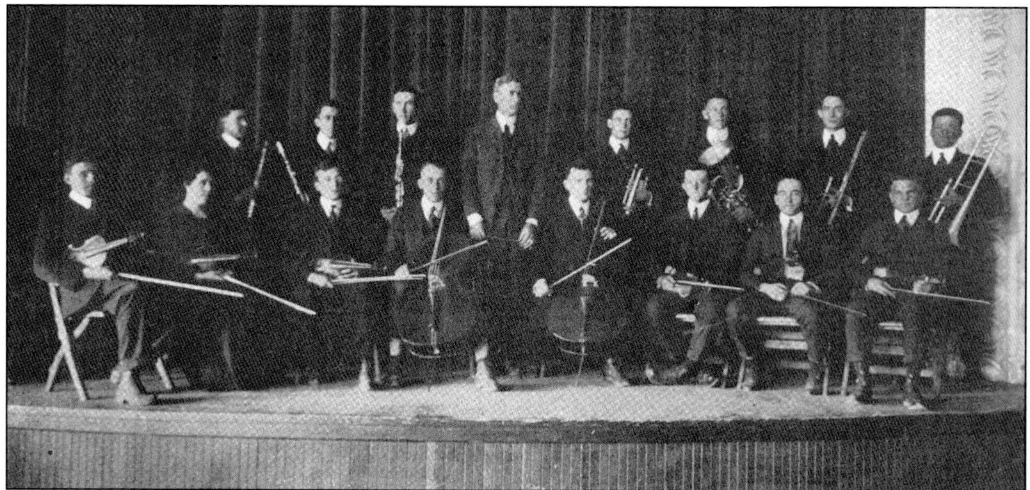

Early on, the University Farm Orchestra was organized to perform occasional campus concerts. This orchestra, pictured in the 1917 student yearbook, included Farm School students and possibly a faculty wife and townspeople. (YB, HWM.)

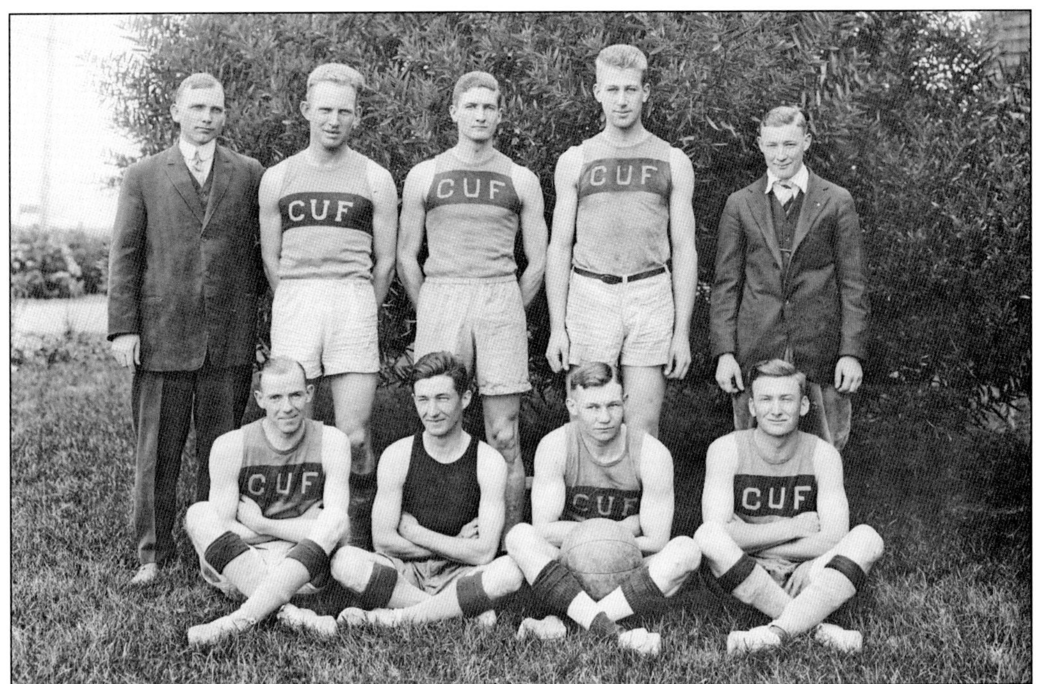

California University Farm (CUF) teams soon competed in tournaments with neighboring schools. This basketball team includes Babe Slater, second from right in back row, who participated in almost every organized sport and later earned a reputation as a champion athlete. In 1924, he was captain of the Olympic gold medal–winning rugby team. (SCL.)

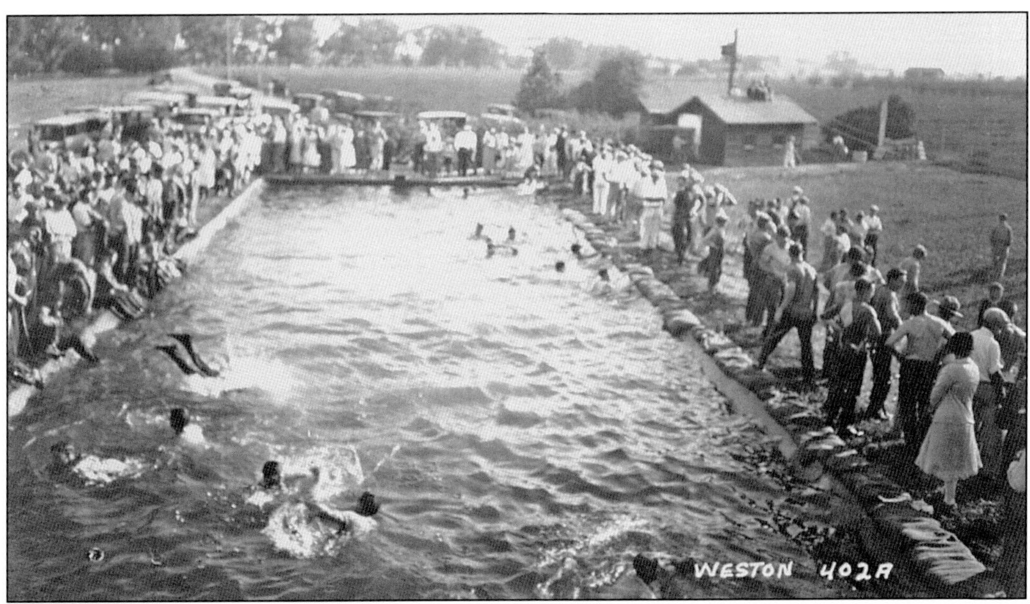

Boys will be boys, and the tank rush started as a mischievous way of letting off steam. In this very popular annual event, the goal was for upperclassmen to throw freshmen into the campus reservoir. Students demonstrated great enthusiasm for the task, and spectators loved it. The event was discontinued in 1929, when it was ruled too rough. (SCL.)

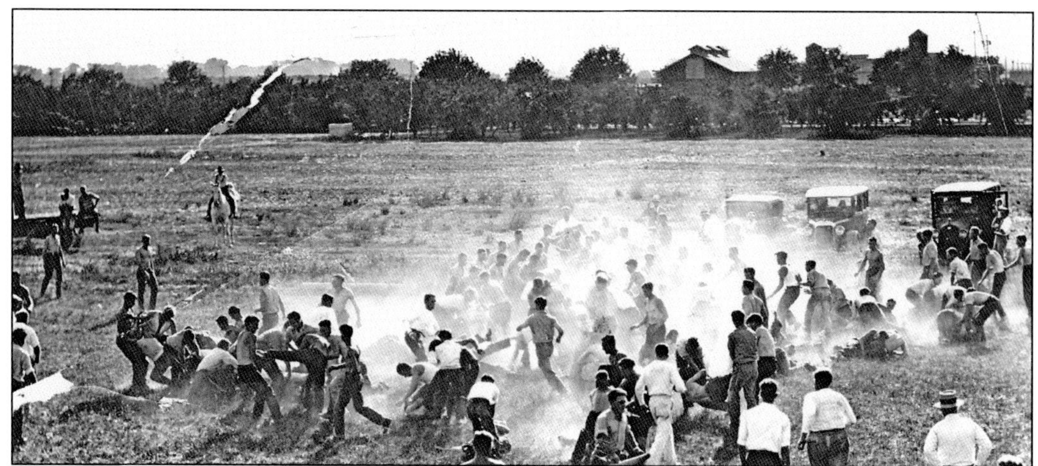

Another beloved masculine pastime was the "frosh-soph brawl," an organized, good-natured struggle on the quad held near the end of the year. Weapons were minimal, and tactics were occasionally ragged, but competition was fierce. (JL.)

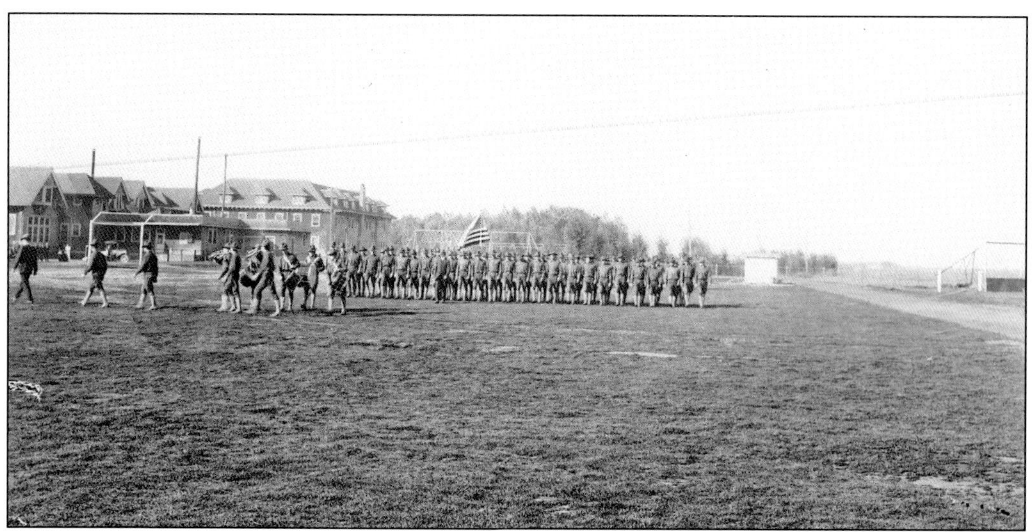

In April 1917, the United States officially entered the European war against Germany. Military training was required for all students, and three University Farm companies were organized. Daily drills instilled discipline and prepared students for possible service in the Army. Here, recruits march on the quad in front of the dormitories. During the war, student enrollments fell dramatically. (SCL.)

Two

The College of Agriculture at Davis 1922–1945

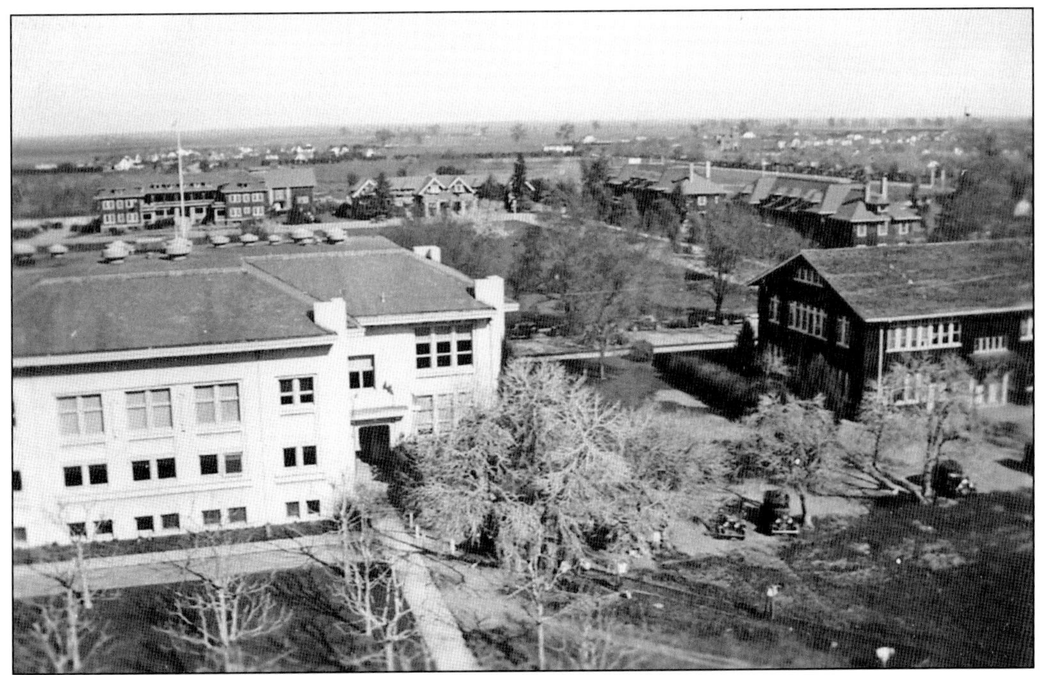

This aerial view of the quad was taken in the 1920s from the water tower behind the classroom-library building. Clockwise around the quad are West Hall, East Hall, North Hall, and South Hall. Immediately to the right of the classroom building is the original creamery. (SCL.)

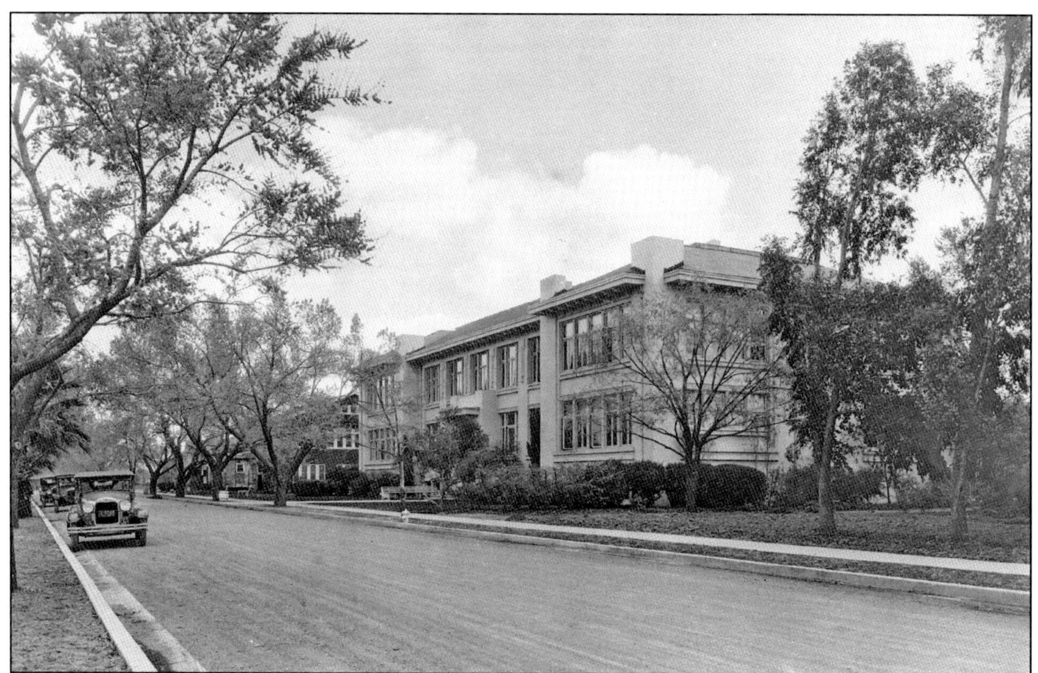

This photograph of the classroom-library building, shot for a 1930s promotional booklet about the University Farm, shows well-developed landscaping and a paved street—progress over the years as the campus matured. The classroom building, constructed around 1920, served students and staff for 20 years before it was torn down to make way for a new, larger library in 1940. (SCL.)

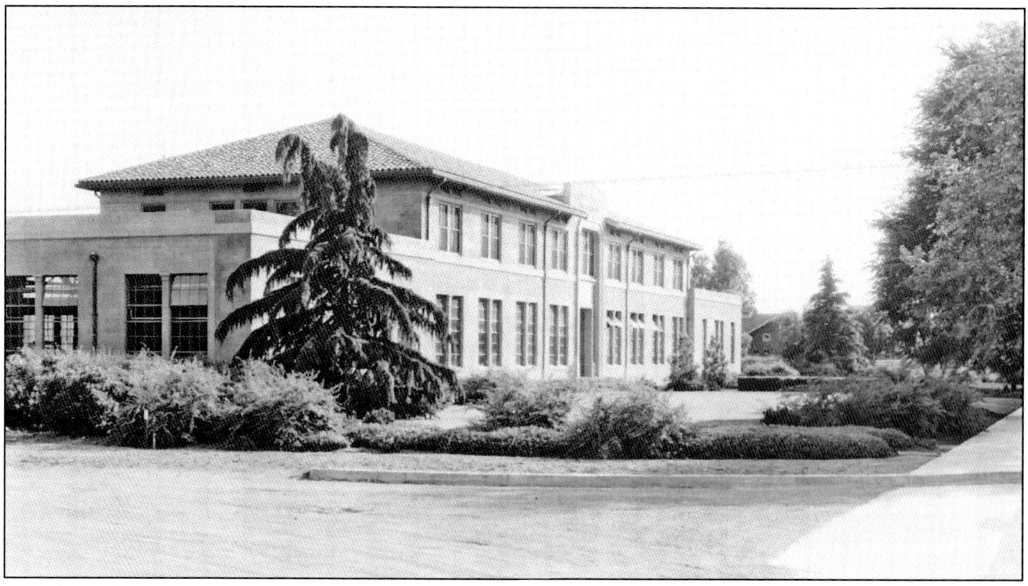

Another photograph shows the agricultural engineering building, completed in 1927 just off the quad. During the 1930s, the Davis campus supported one of the foremost agricultural engineering programs in the nation, producing many technical innovations, and the building was considered top-notch in its day. Later, it was Walker Hall after Harry B. Walker, longtime chair of the division. (SCL.)

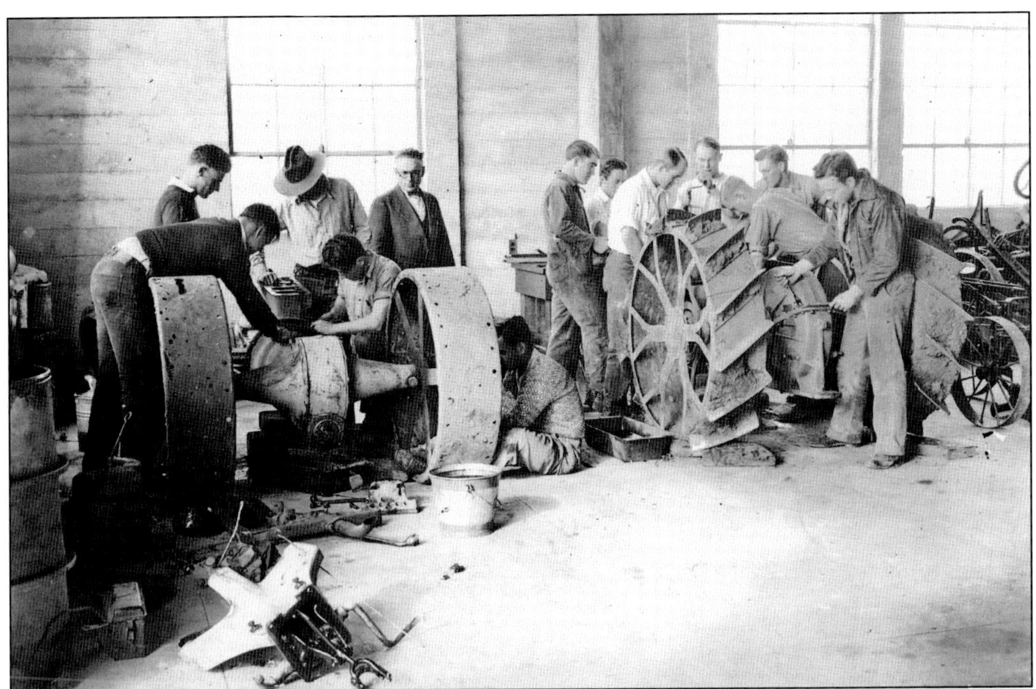

In the 1920s, the horsepower of tractors rapidly replaced the horsepower of animals, and farmers purchased machinery as soon as they could afford it. In the workshops of the engineering building, the two-year non-degree students received valuable training in machinery maintenance and repair. Classroom instruction also focused on the principles of mechanical design for those inventive young men who wanted to build their own machines. (SCL.)

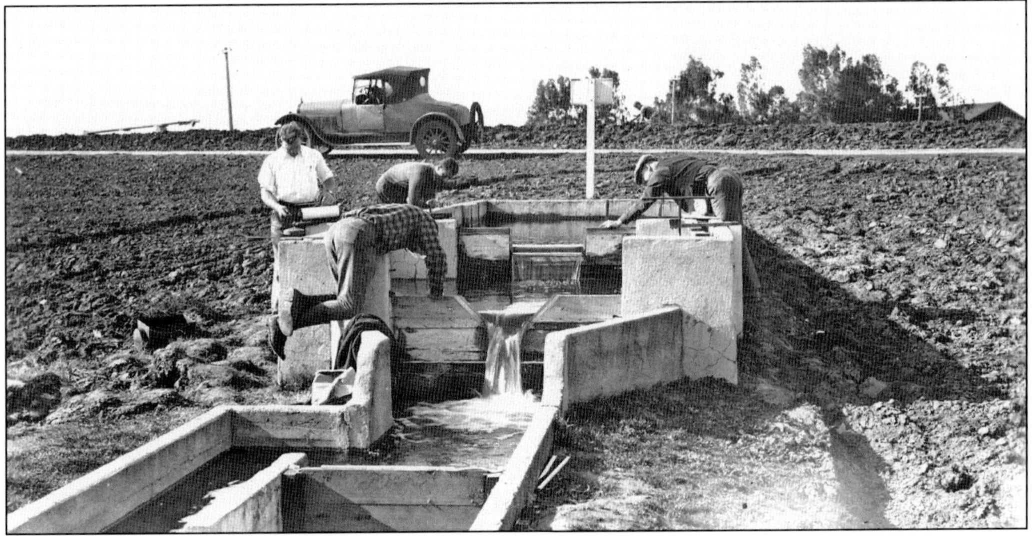

Another important unit on campus was the division of irrigation, offering instruction in the design, construction, and maintenance of irrigation systems for both two-year and degree students. Faculty and staff actively experimented with varying designs for pumps, measuring devices, and conveyance and sprinkling systems. Learning how to move water more effectively and efficiently has continued to be an important goal in engineering studies. (SCL.)

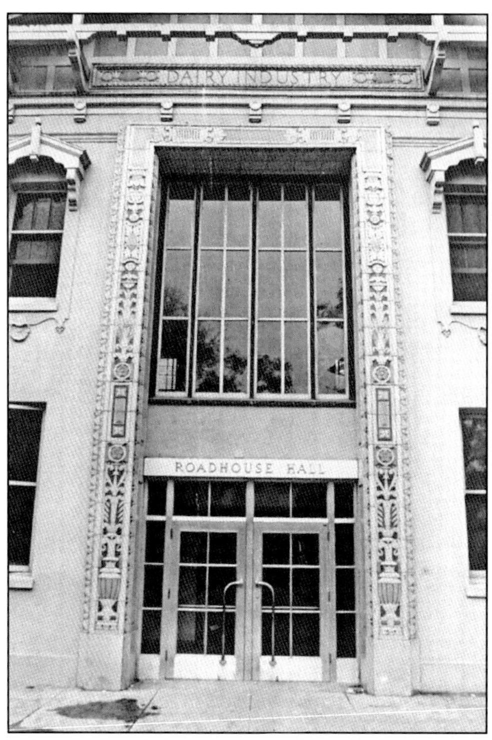

A new dairy-industry building opened in 1922, replacing the old wood-shingled creamery with a modern processing facility. Its architecture featured the period's typical decorative concrete relief borders around doorways and windows. The building was later named Roadhouse Hall in honor of Chester L. Roadhouse, head of the dairy division from 1917 through 1944. (SCL.)

In this highly staged photograph, short-course dairy students practice making ice cream in the well-equipped creamery, where hygienic standards were strictly enforced. Chester Roadhouse, in the lab coat on the stairs, directs the action. (SCL.)

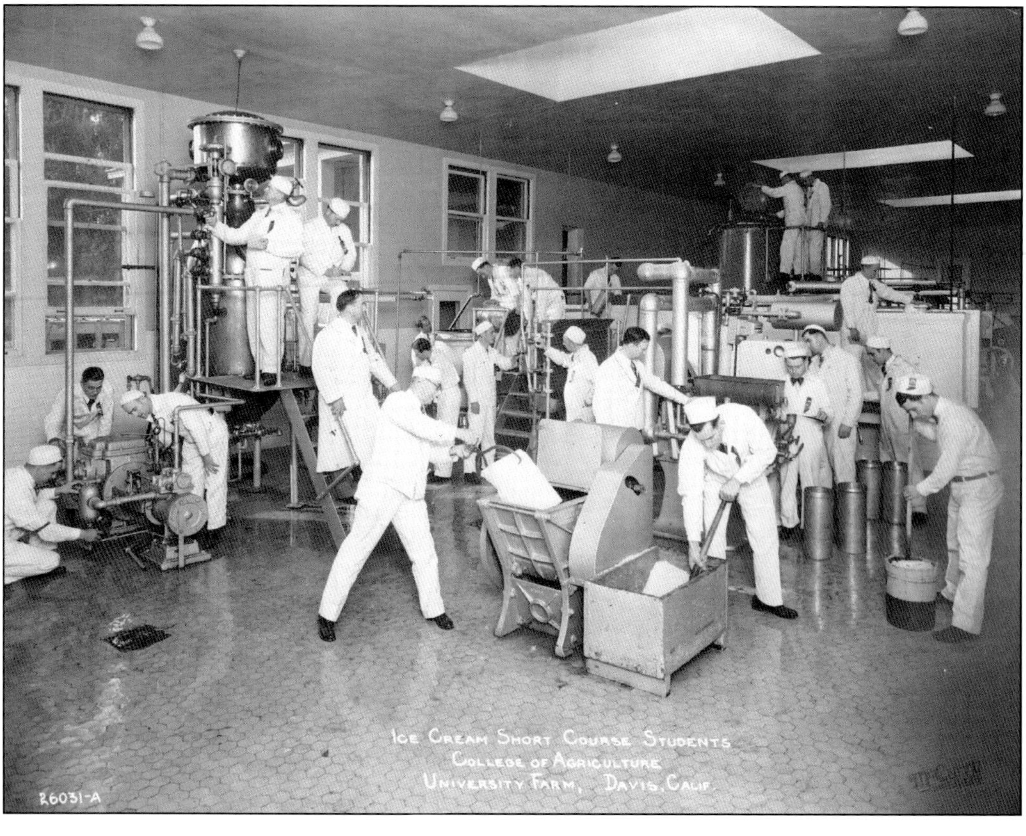

During the depression, when jobs were scarce, the dairy industry remained relatively stable, and trained dairymen were in demand. At UC Davis, the dairy program had strong enrollments in both the two-year resident school and short courses. In 1937 and 1938, more than half the students in the small student body were dairy majors. The university's archives contain many pictures of short-course students who learned very practical skills, like running this milk bottling line. (SCL.)

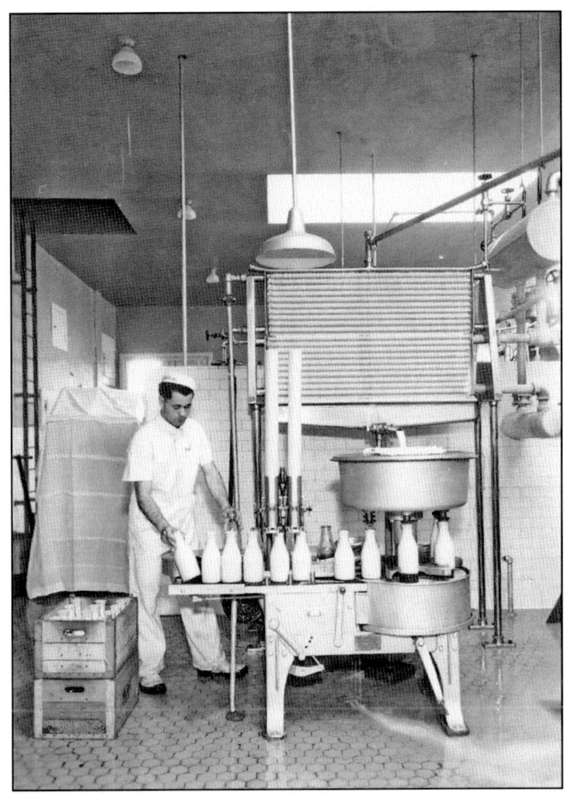

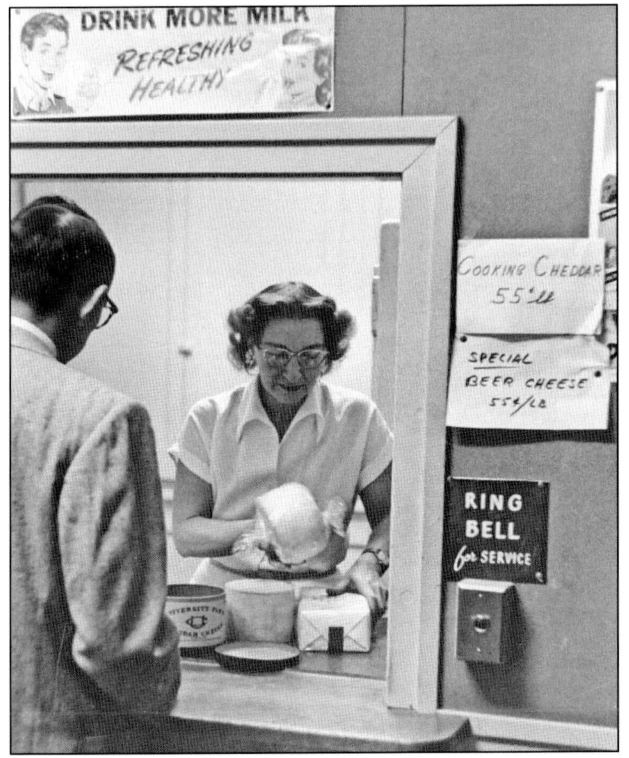

For many years, until well after World War II, the dairy division at Davis operated a retail window where staff, students, and the public could buy products manufactured in the program. Milk, butter, and ice cream were sold, and cheese was particularly popular. Buyers knew the products would be fresh and of high quality. (SCL.)

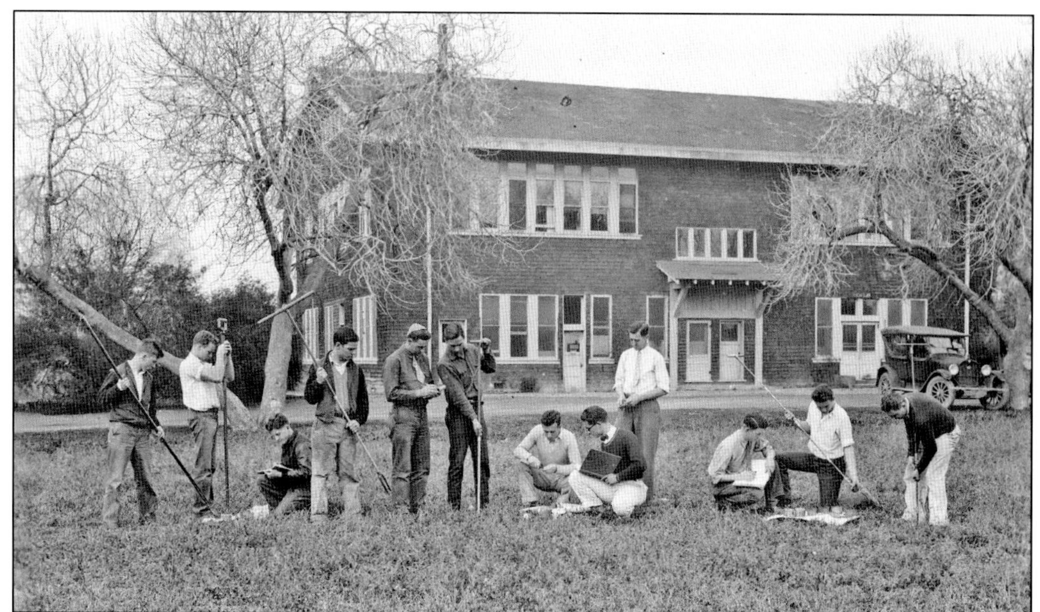

Students practice using soil probes to gather soil samples for testing in the laboratory. The College of Agriculture at Berkeley had a reputation for excellence in soil studies, attracting students from many regions. Hands-on work at Davis offered valuable supplemental experience to academic instruction. (SCL.)

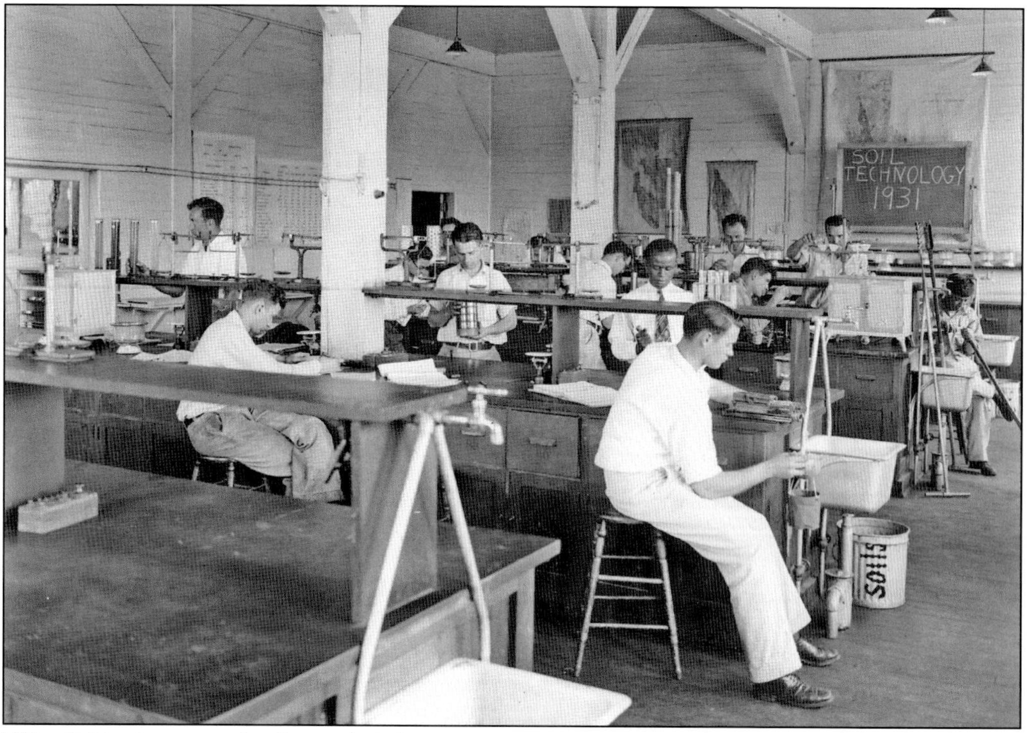

This 1931 photograph of a soils laboratory shows students concentrating on the physical properties of soil samples, using screens and other devices to classify them. Because the soils of California are highly diverse, such studies had great practicality. (SCL.)

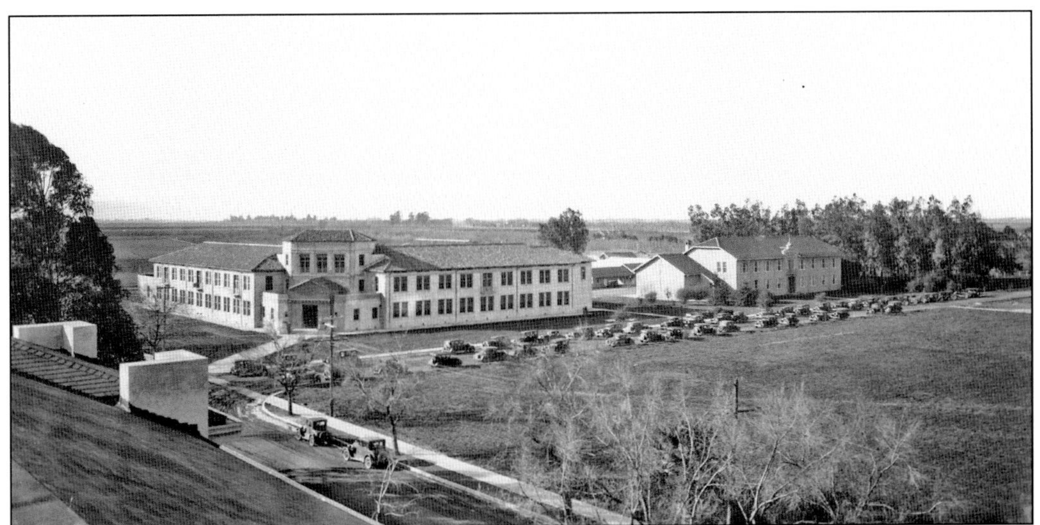

Cars are parked along the quad in front of the animal science building, completed in 1928 on the corner across from the agricultural engineering building. To the right is the horticulture building, constructed in 1922, with its greenhouse behind. The animal science building was later named Hart Hall in honor of George H. Hart, chair of the department for 22 years. Hart, a veterinarian, strongly encouraged the departmental shift in focus from animal husbandry to animal science. (SCL.)

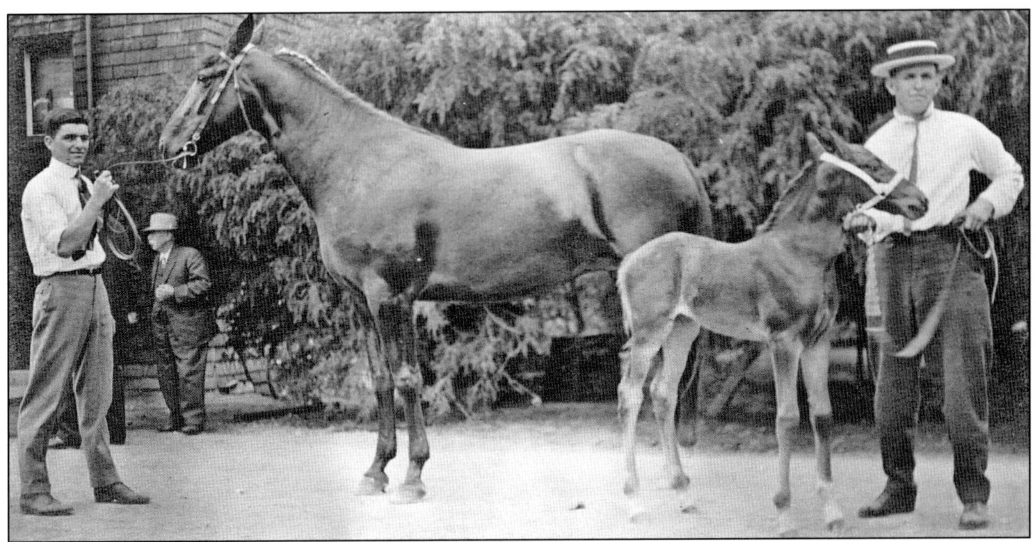

All through the interwar period, horses were a huge part of campus life. Students here show a champion mare with her foal. University Farm animals regularly won competitions until about 1929, when the campus decided to place less emphasis on championship animals and more on the development of the biological sciences in relation to animal health and reproduction. (SCL.)

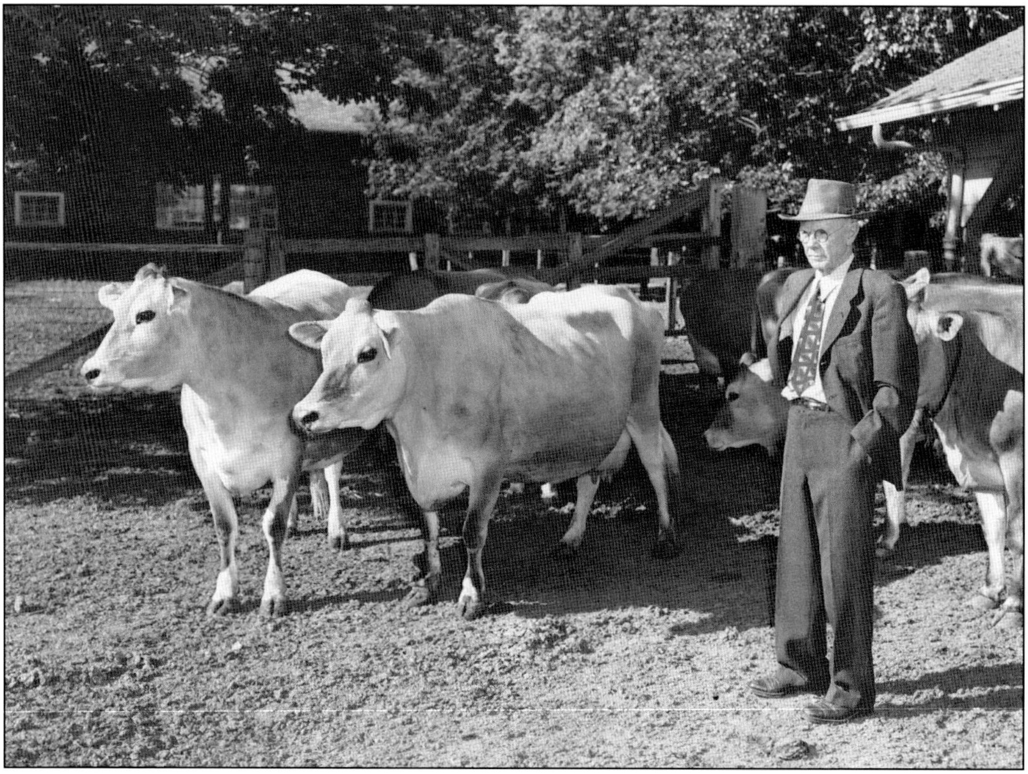

William M. Regan arrived on the Davis campus in 1922 to help perfect the dairy breeding program, bringing with him his own herd of 30 purebred Jersey dairy cows to form the nucleus of the University Farm herd. Regan conducted the first large-scale inbreeding experiments with dairy cattle and was instrumental in organizing the California Purebred Dairy Cattle Association. Regan's wife, Susan, served as dean of women at Davis for many years. (SCL.)

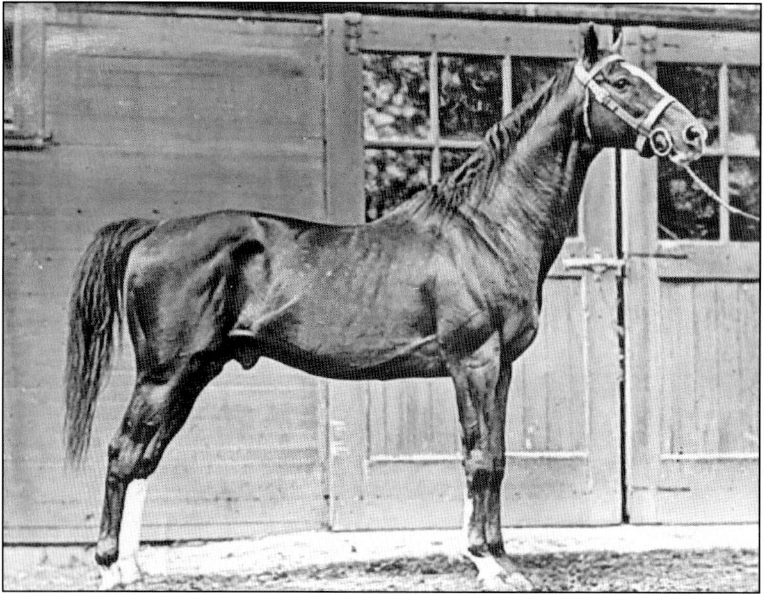

This handsome stallion named Gunrock later became the symbol of the UC Davis campus for his great breeding and strength. Brought to the campus by the US Army as a stud intended to sire good cavalry horses, Gunrock eventually serviced some 400 mares brought in from across California. Students allowed to ride him considered it a great honor. (HWM.)

University Farm judging teams won many trophies during the 1920s, participating in major national expositions with great success. These young men don their best attire for this ceremonial photograph; however, this is not what they wore in the livestock ring. (SCL.)

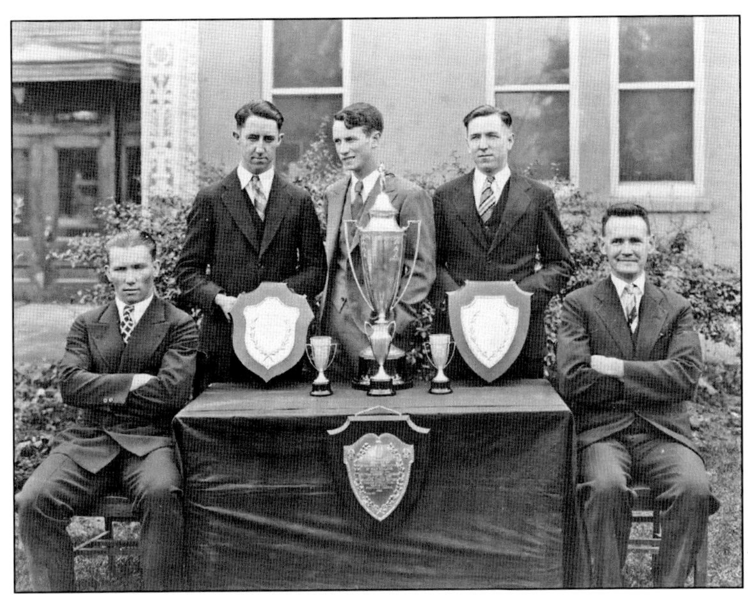

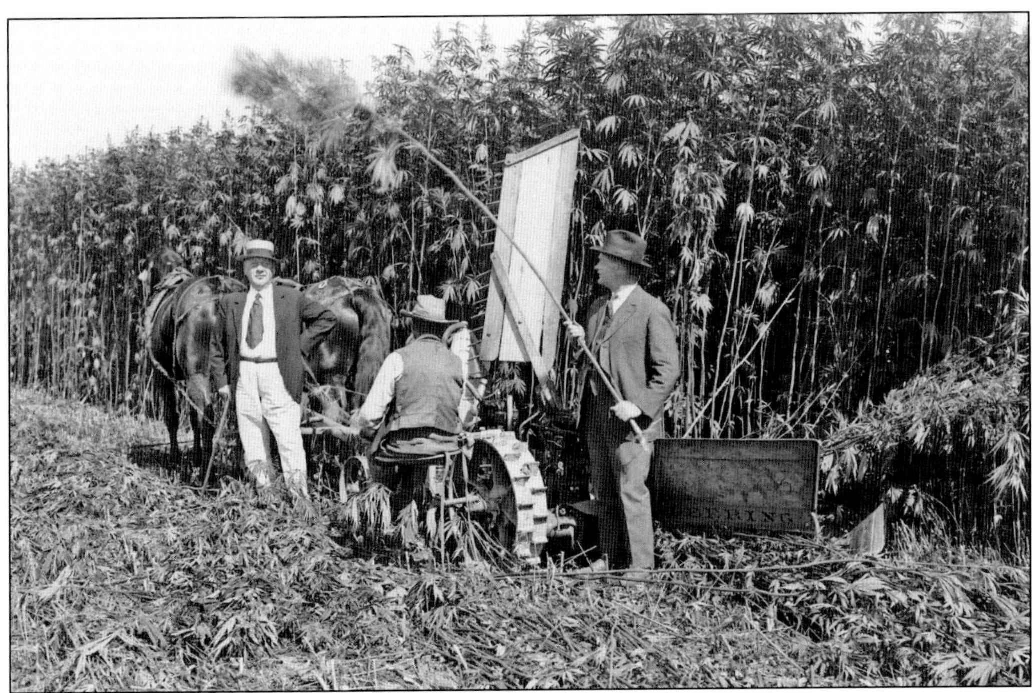

This 1919 photograph shows one of the experimental crops planted at Davis during the interwar period. Hemp is a fiber crop used for making textiles, paper, and other industrial products. Industrial hemp grows rapidly and produces large biomass. It also has food uses, but because of its association with marijuana, its commercial cultivation in the United States is currently restricted. During World War II, the "Hemp for Victory" program encouraged production. (SCL.)

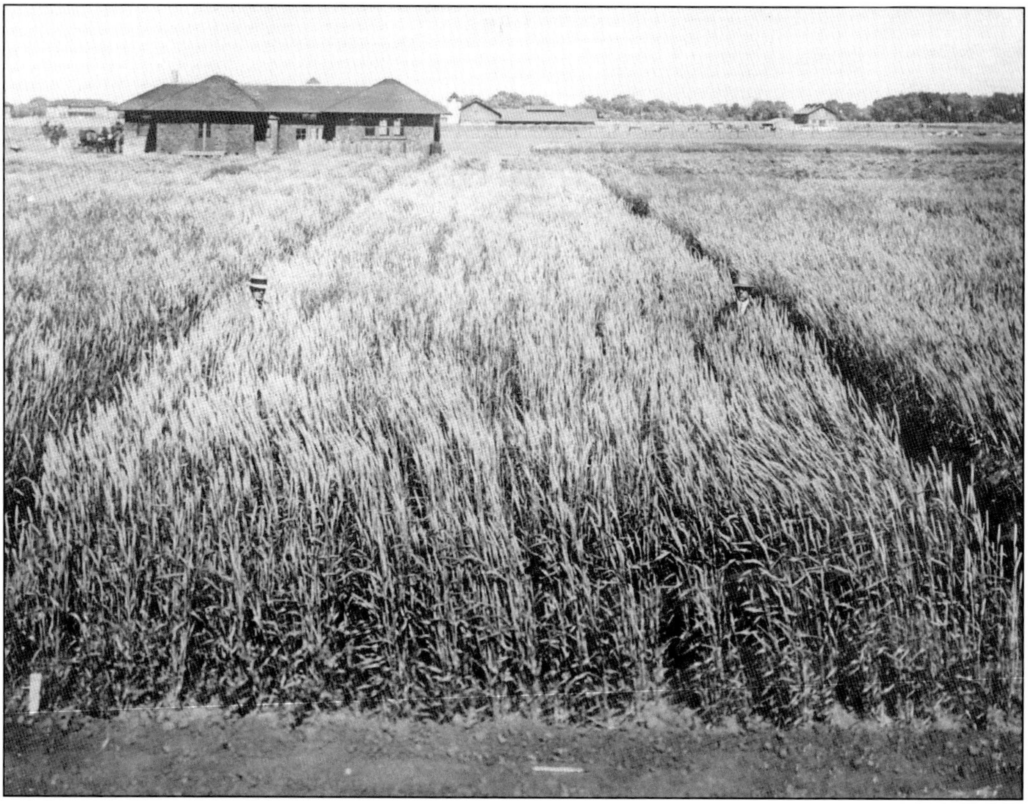

Field crop research at Davis took off strongly under the direction of Ben Madson, chair of the agronomy division in the 1920s and 1930s. With his encouragement, emphasis shifted from crop production to more scientific studies. Some university fields like this one were the envy of visiting farmers. (SCL.)

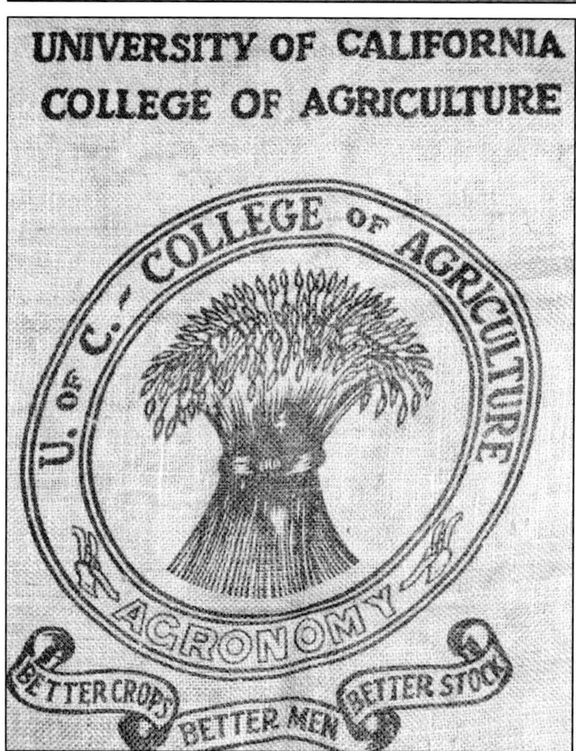

In 1934, Davis agronomists organized the California Approved Seed Plan to ensure a steady supply of pure seed of standard and improved field crops. In cooperation with the State Department of Agriculture and the California Farm Bureau, the university worked with cooperating farmers to produce seed under strict supervision. Distributed in sacks like this, the final product was labeled "Calapproved" to guarantee its freedom from contamination. (HWM.)

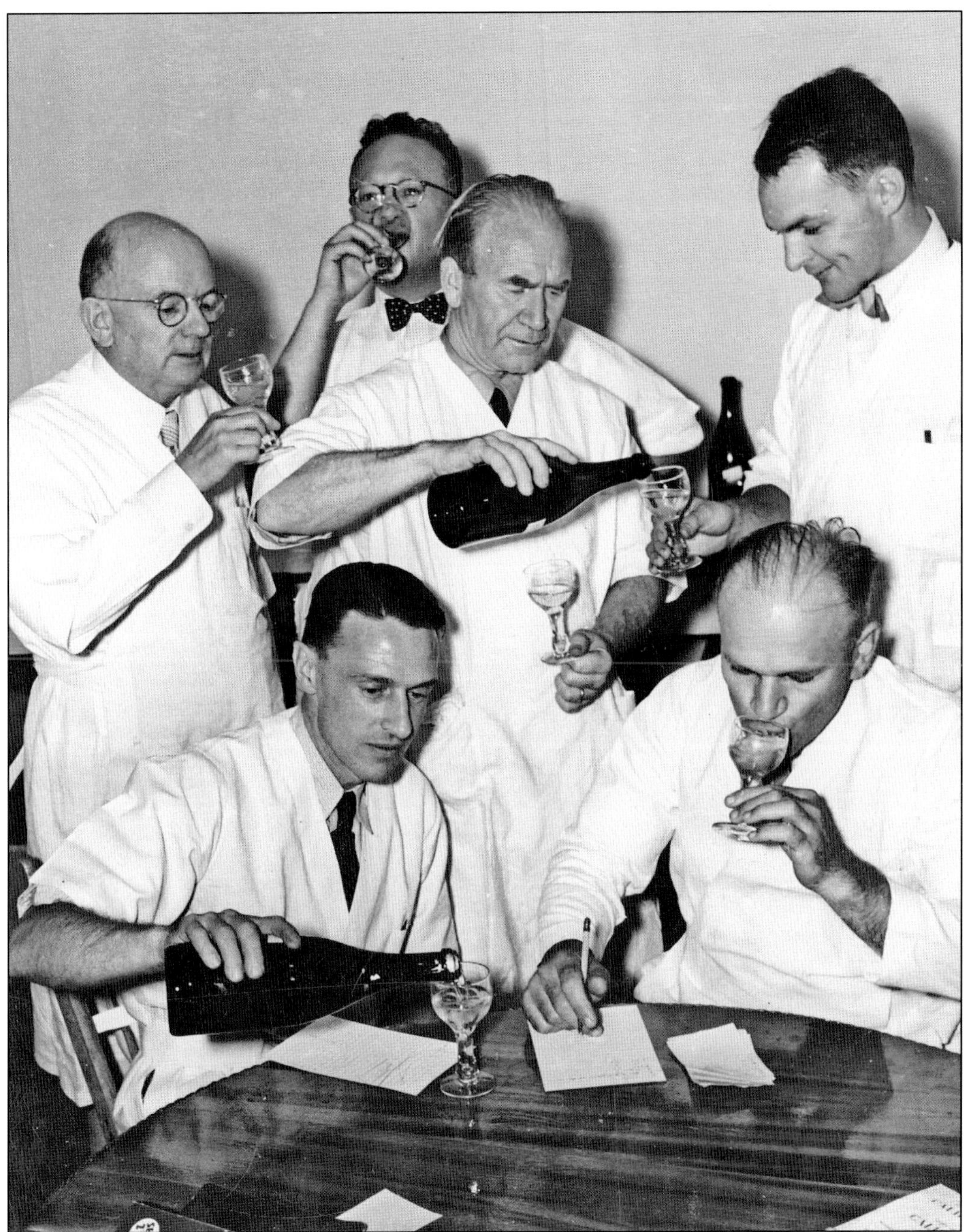

After repeal of Prohibition in 1933, the College of Agriculture actively resumed work in viticulture and enology, which was moved entirely from Berkeley to Davis. By the time of the California State Fair in 1939, the division was sending its experts to help judge the retail wine competition, which was just then beginning to flourish. Three of the giants of the university's winemaking program are shown on the judging panel here: William Vere Cruess, highly respected head of the food technology program, pours a glass for the young Maynard Amerine on the far right. Albert Winkler, lower right, assesses a sample and takes notes. Both Amerine and Winkler enjoyed long and productive careers at Davis. (SCL.)

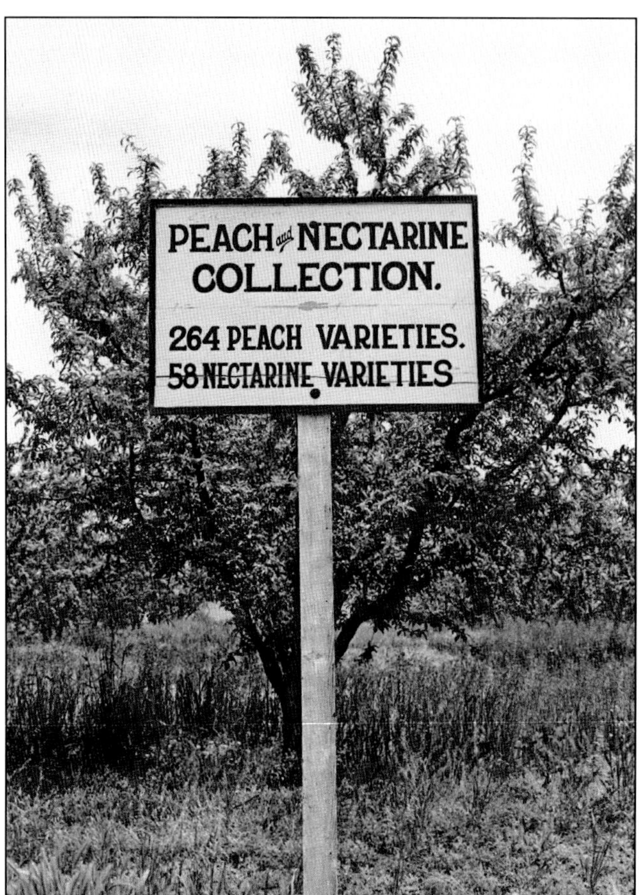

Out in the extensive reaches of the campus, university research pomologists tested literally hundreds of varieties of fruit crops for their suitability for California. This research was quietly but doggedly pursued over the years to track variety, vigor, productivity, flavor, and other characteristics. Ansel Adams liked this sign well enough to photograph it. (SCL.)

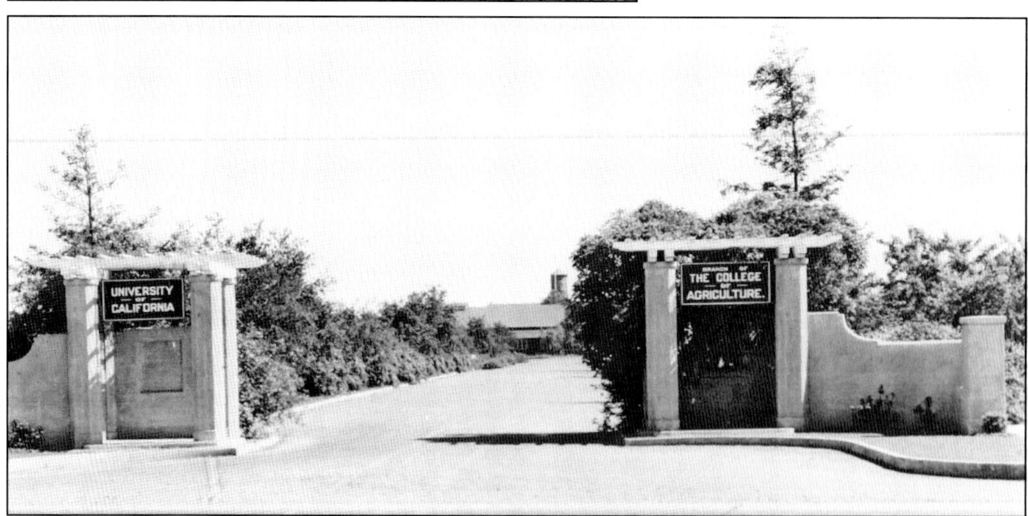

On Labor Day 1928, a volunteer student work crew helped erect this handsome gate for the University Farm, now officially called the College of Agriculture at Davis. The trellises were planted to wisteria vines, which bloomed profusely in spring and presented a welcoming vista into the campus from Russell Boulevard, or what was then Highway 40, just outside the gate. (SCL.)

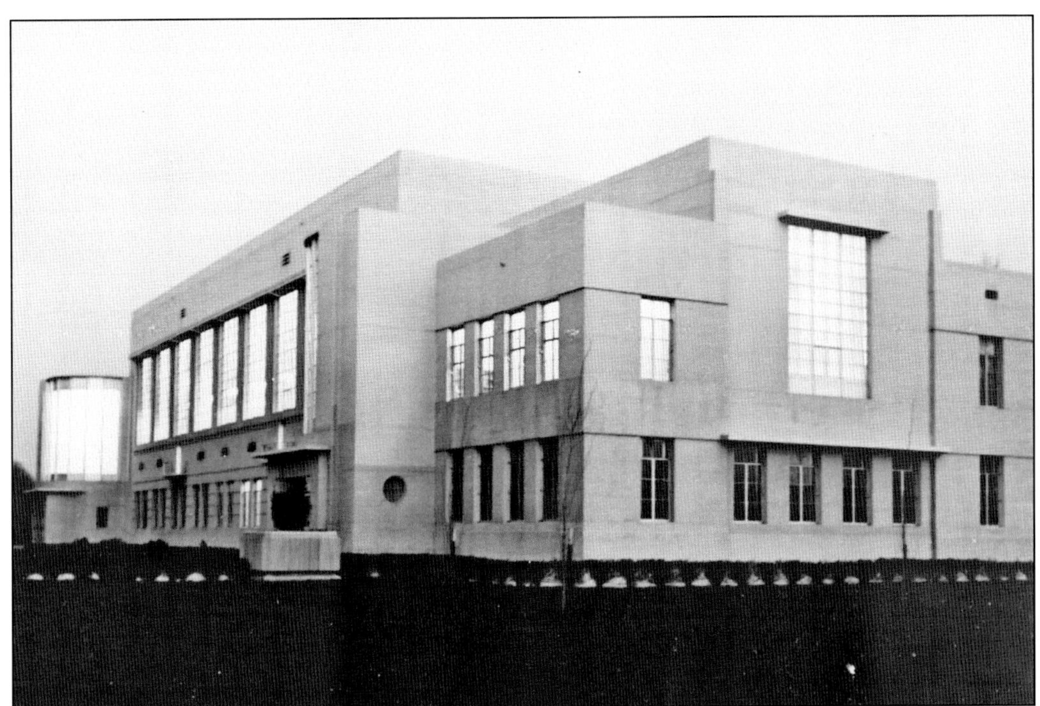

The original classroom-library building next to the original creamery proved to have structural deficiencies and was torn down in the late 1930s. Federal funding from the Works Progress Administration underwrote the construction of a new library, which opened in 1940. Art Deco in style and providing a handsome anchor to the south side of the quad, the new structure allowed the library to expand its collections significantly, leapfrogging the campus ahead in its academic resources. (SCL.)

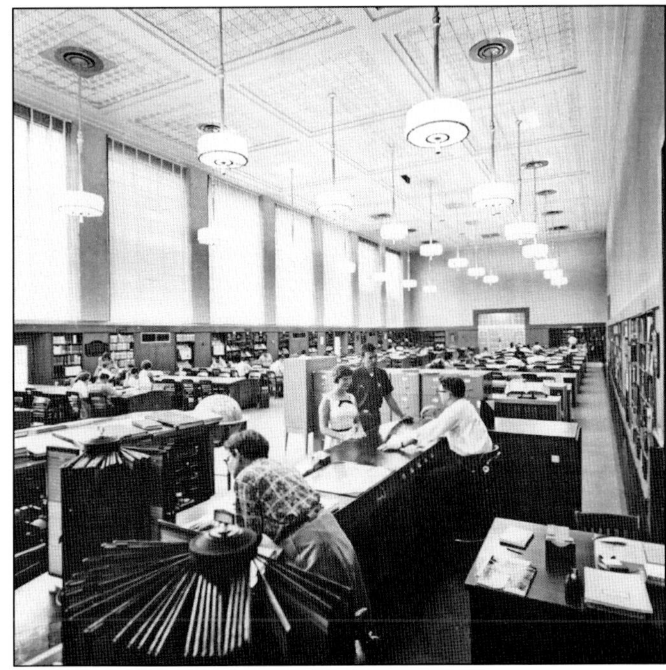

The main reading room was a well-lit and welcoming place, much favored by students for quiet study time. During the wartime closure of campus when the US Army Signal Corps conducted training at Davis, soldiers used the library reading room as well. (SCL.)

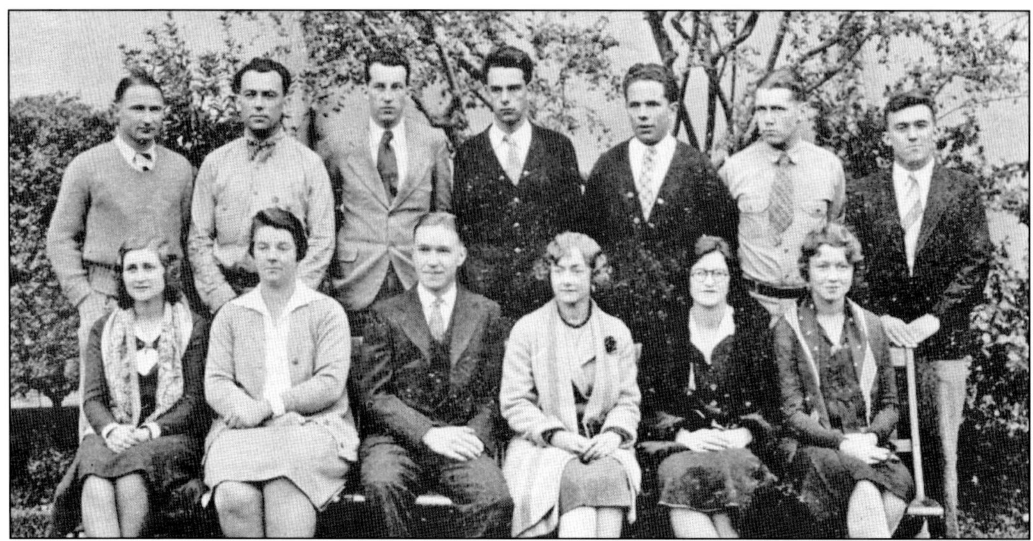

In 1928, Celeste Turner, the first full-time female faculty member and first doctor of philosophy in the humanities at Davis, came from Berkeley to head the English instructional program and supervise dramatic productions. Pictured here, she is seen seated fourth from the left in the front row. Not much older than her students at the time, she spent the next 50 years dedicated to the Davis campus. She married a student, becoming Celeste Turner Wright, and was a mentor to many others. (YB, JL.)

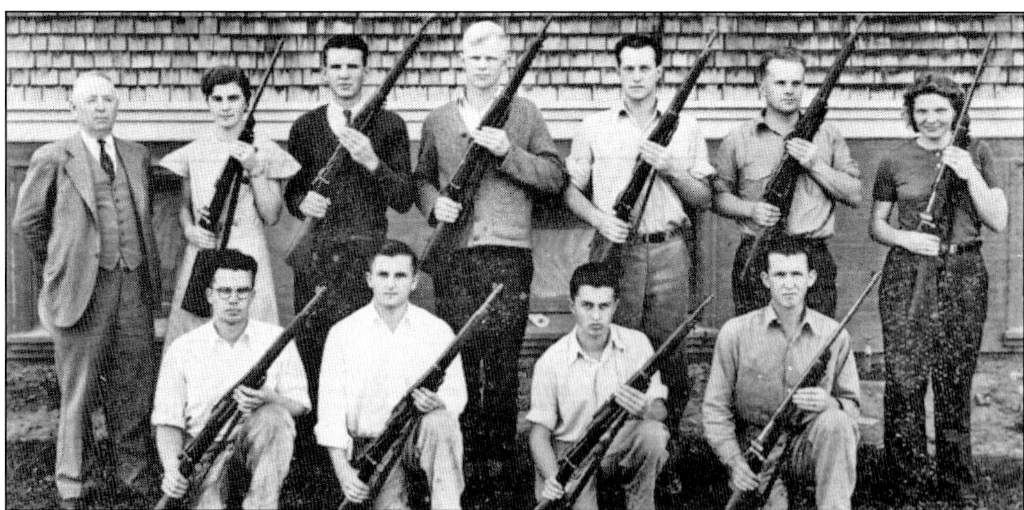

In 1934, the student yearbook published this picture of an ROTC rifle team. Military science—required at all land-grant institutions—was first offered at Davis in 1923 with an instructor commuting from Berkeley twice weekly. In 1929, the Davis campus formed its own ROTC unit. During the 1920s and 1930s, women students were also trained as sharpshooters under the supervision of military personnel. Several yearbooks show women obviously comfortable with rifles. (YB, JL.)

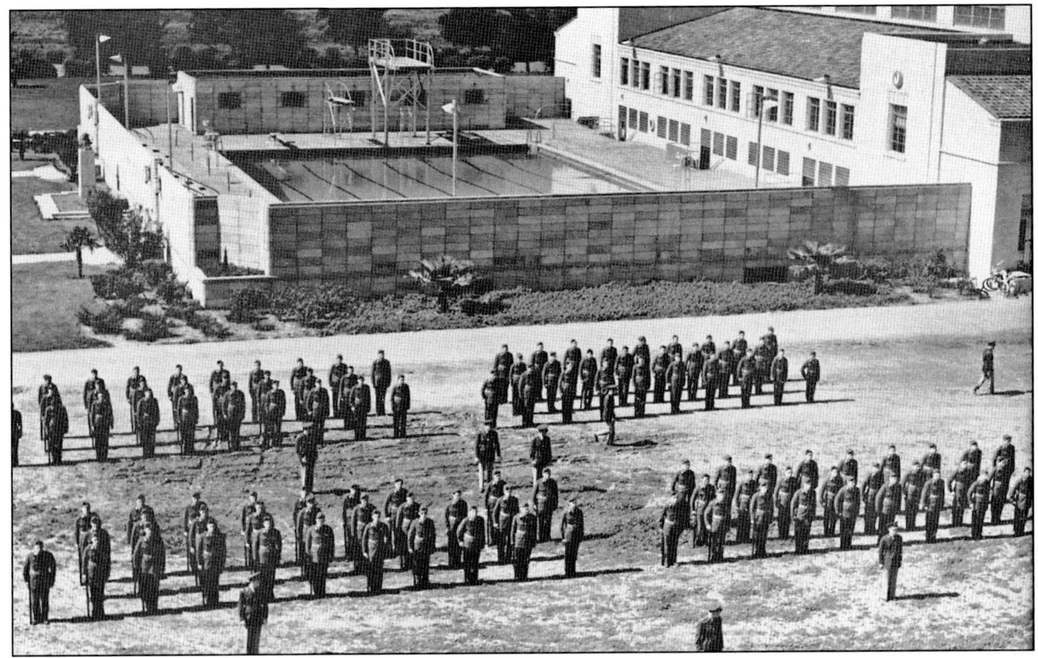

A new gymnasium and the campus's first swimming pool were constructed with WPA funding in 1939 to the enthusiastic response of both the student body and townspeople. Three years later, with the entry of the United States into World War II, the campus was converted into a military training school for the US Army Signal Corps. The soldiers used the gym facility for exercise and did some of their drilling in the adjacent field. (YB, PKO.)

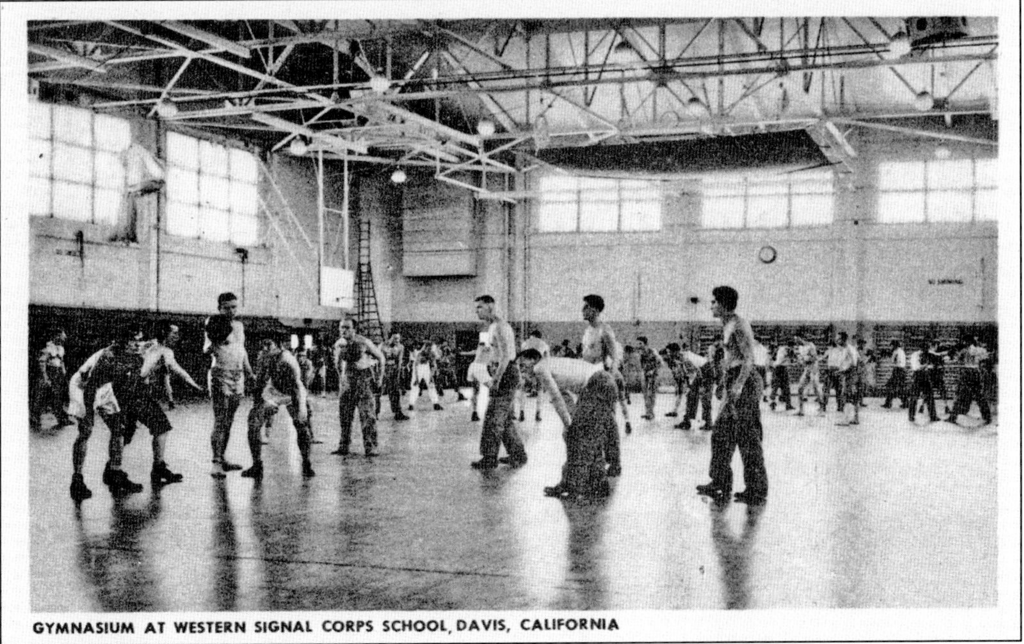

GYMNASIUM AT WESTERN SIGNAL CORPS SCHOOL, DAVIS, CALIFORNIA

In a brand-new gym and a perfect facility for physical fitness, soldiers preparing to go to war could still enjoy some of the less-demanding competition of organized sports like basketball. All three courts of the big gym are in use. (PKO.)

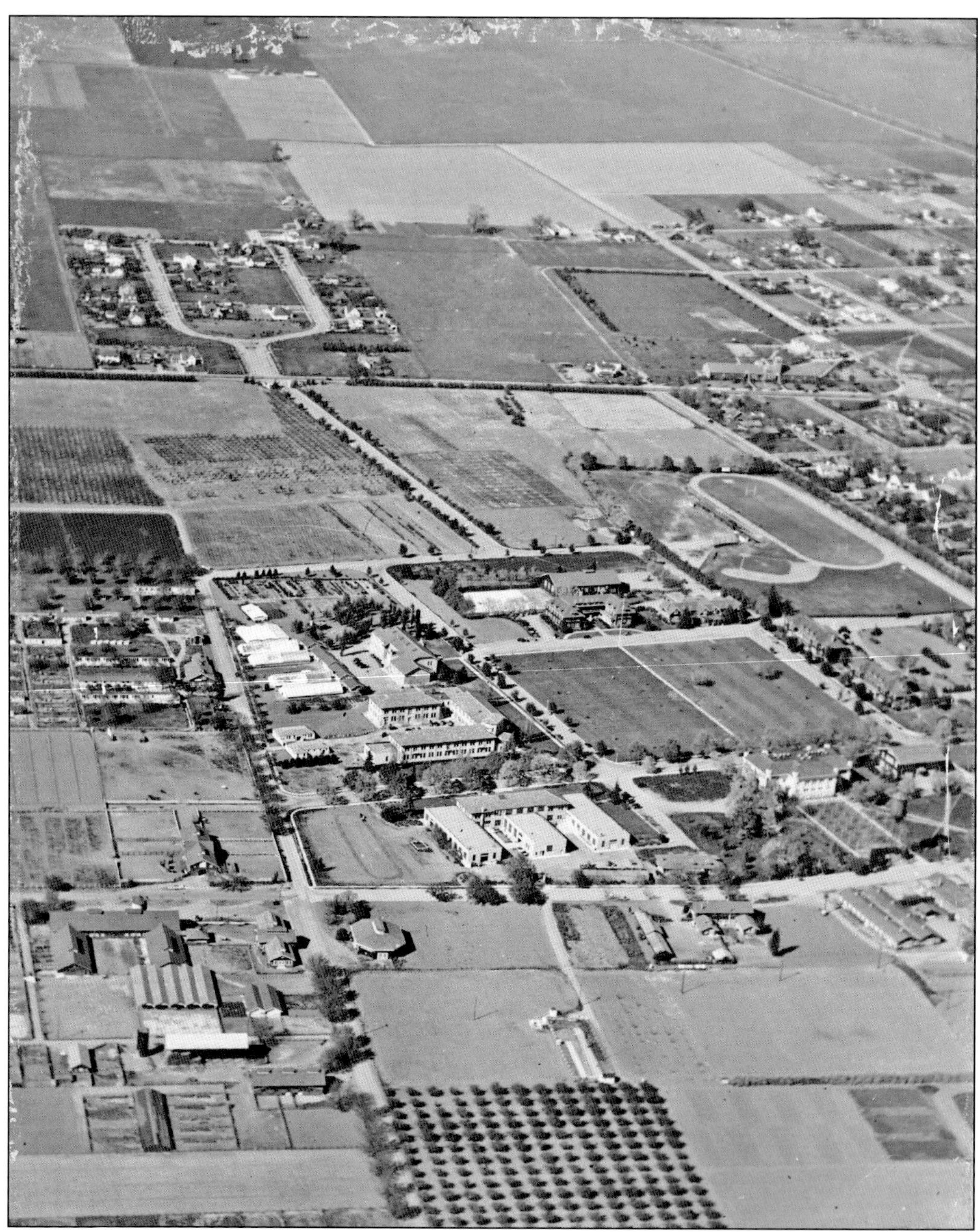

This aerial view of the campus shows the quad, its surrounding buildings, and playing fields as they appeared just before World War II. Outside the campus, the town of Davis is still very small, but directly to the north, the horseshoe-shaped streets of College Park can be seen. This was a residential area, developed by the College Park Association, formed in 1924 to develop a 20-acre field for mostly faculty homes. (SCL.)

Three

CAMPUS GROWTH

1946–1958

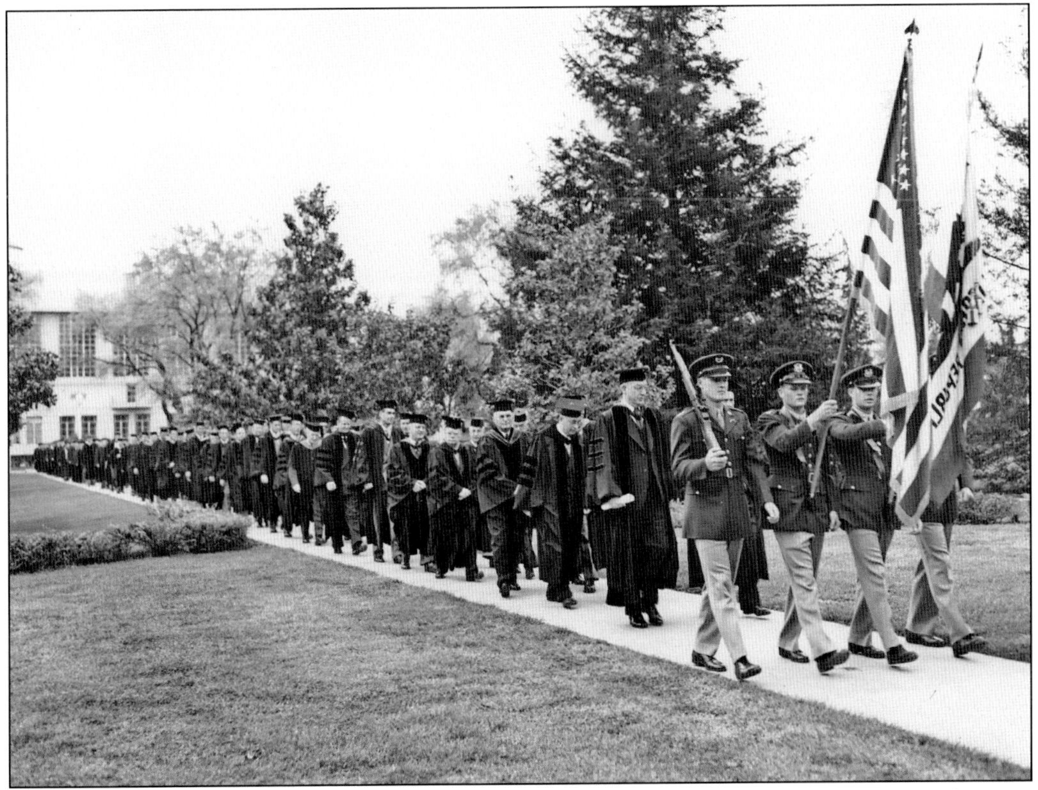

Until 1948, all students in the four-year program at Davis received their degrees in graduation ceremonies at Berkeley. That year, the regents agreed to decentralize graduations, and the Davis campus had its own independent commencement for the first time. The academic procession, led by an honor guard, moved across the quad from the student union to the library, where the ceremony took place in the open air of the tree-shaded sunken garden behind the building. Receiving their diplomas from university president Robert Sproul, members of the class of 1948 were awarded 101 bachelor of science degrees in agriculture and 195 certificates from the two-year curricula. Very soon, there were even more big changes in store for Davis. (SCL.)

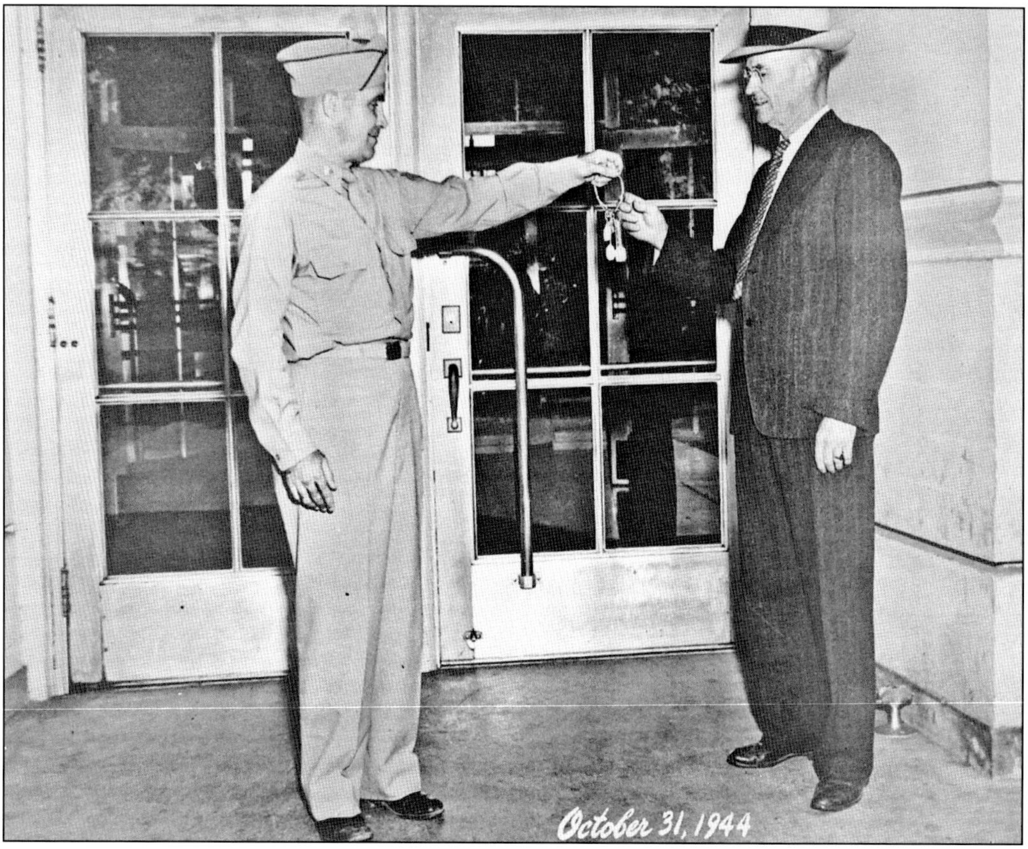

The US Army Signal Corps School ended its training activities at Davis in late 1944. A military representative here ceremonially presents the keys to the campus to Ira Smith, chief acting university officer at the time, signifying the Army's departure and the reopening of the campus to university use. (SCL.)

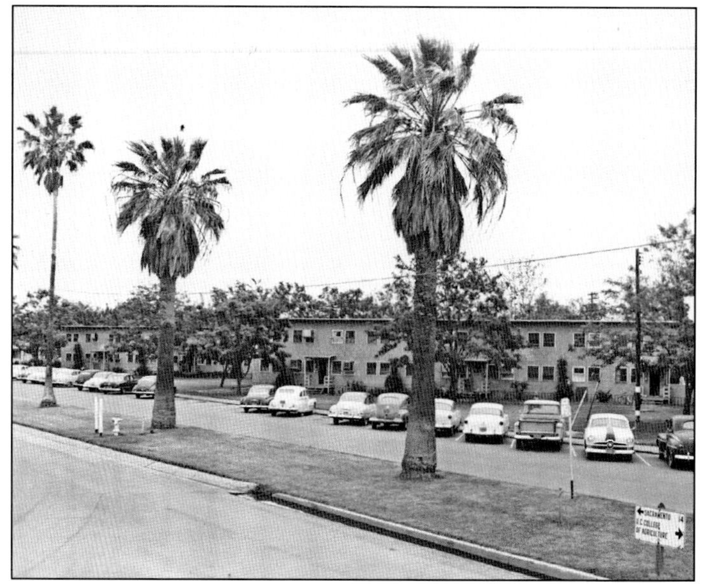

The Aggie Villa complex consisted of surplus Army barracks transported from the Bay Area in the late 1940s for temporary student housing for the scores of military veterans enrolling at Davis on the GI Bill after World War II. The barracks were plain but serviceable, situated in a convenient location between campus and town, and were used for years. Their residents sometimes remembered them with real nostalgia. (SCL.)

The veterans who flooded into college after the war were eager to get back into civilian life, get on with their education, start their families, and find peacetime jobs. Some of the Aggie Villa barracks reserved for young couples rang with childish laughter, and friends made here could last a lifetime. (YB, JL.)

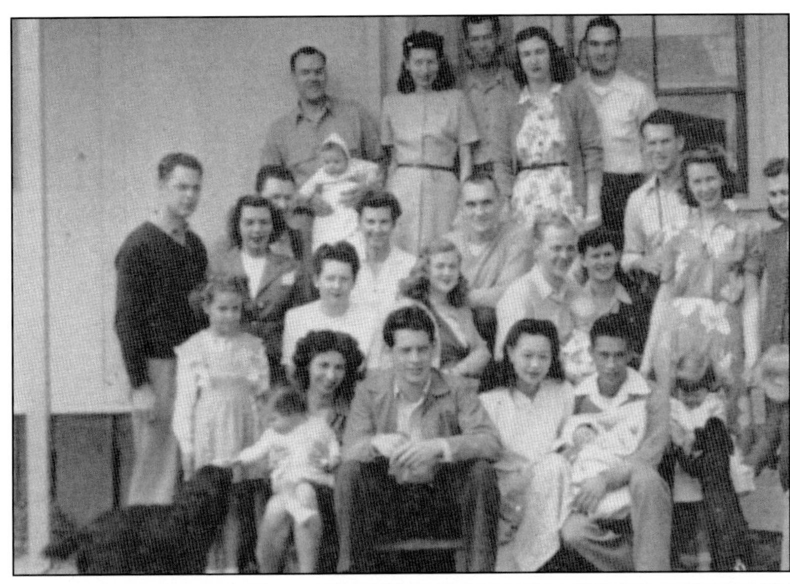

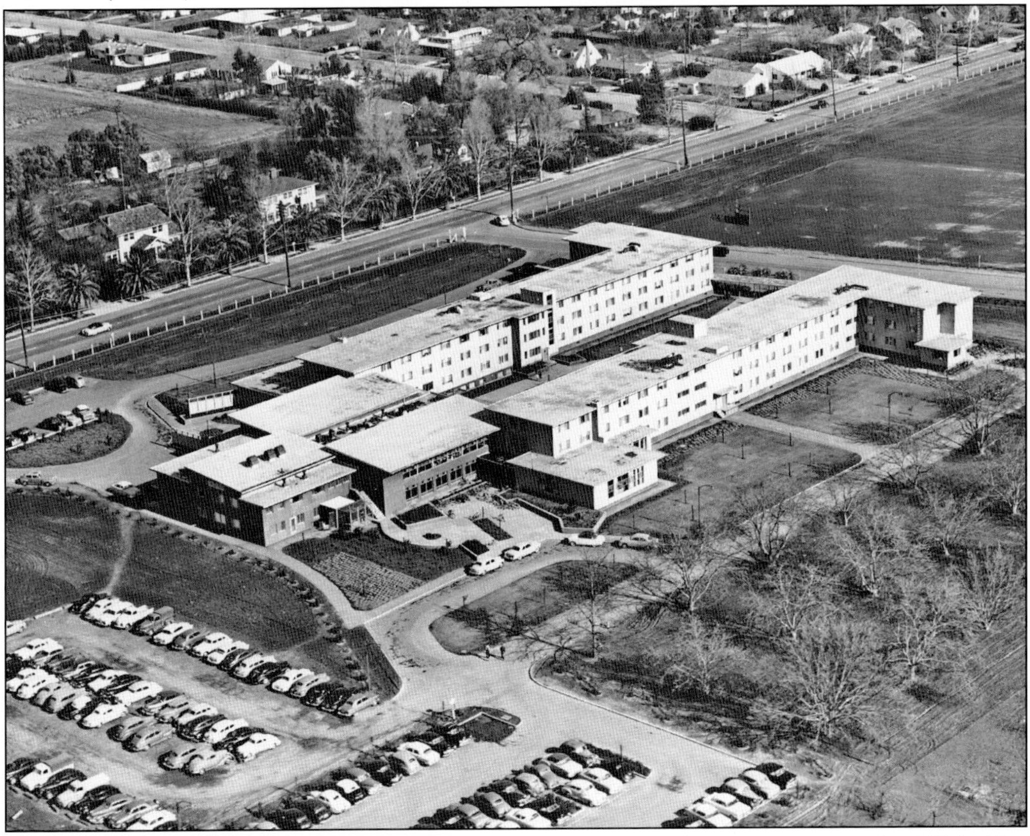

Greatly needed, new, undergraduate dormitory buildings began going up in 1951. The Primero complex along Russell Boulevard consisted of Beckett and Hughes Halls and later expanded with Struve and Titus Halls. They were positioned a bike's ride away from the center of campus and located near the new Cowell Student Health Center, completed in 1952. (SCL.)

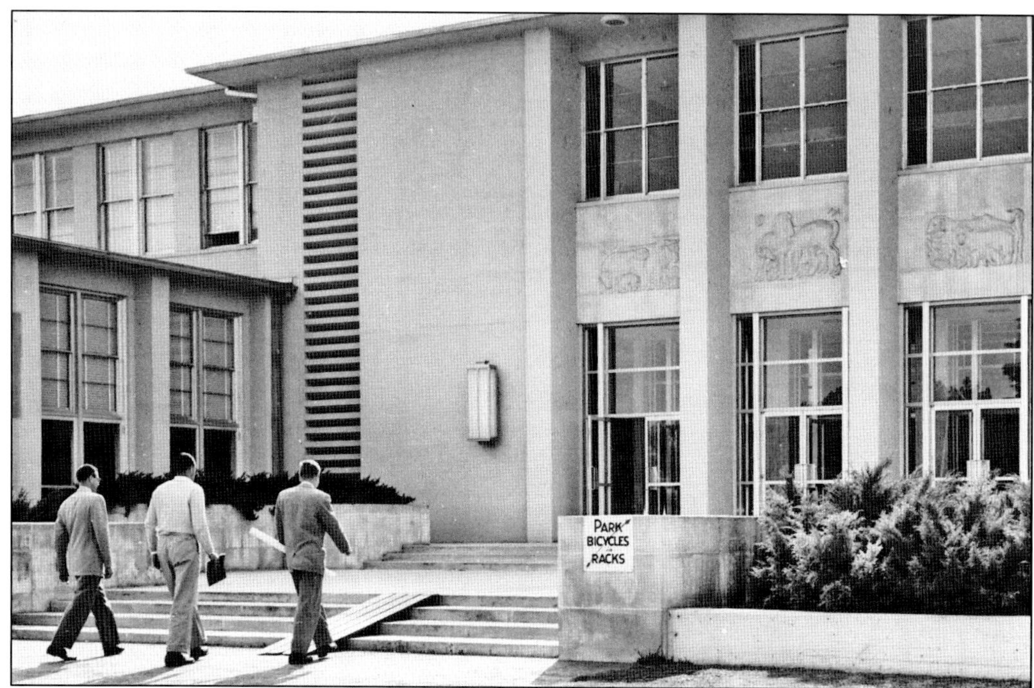

A School of Veterinary Medicine was approved by the California Legislature in 1941, but the search for an appropriate site coincided with World War II. Plans for the school had to be put on hold. After the war, making up for time lost, the Davis campus was chosen for the school, and in 1948, the first students began classes in temporary quarters. Built at a cost of $5 million, this building was completed two years later. (SCL.)

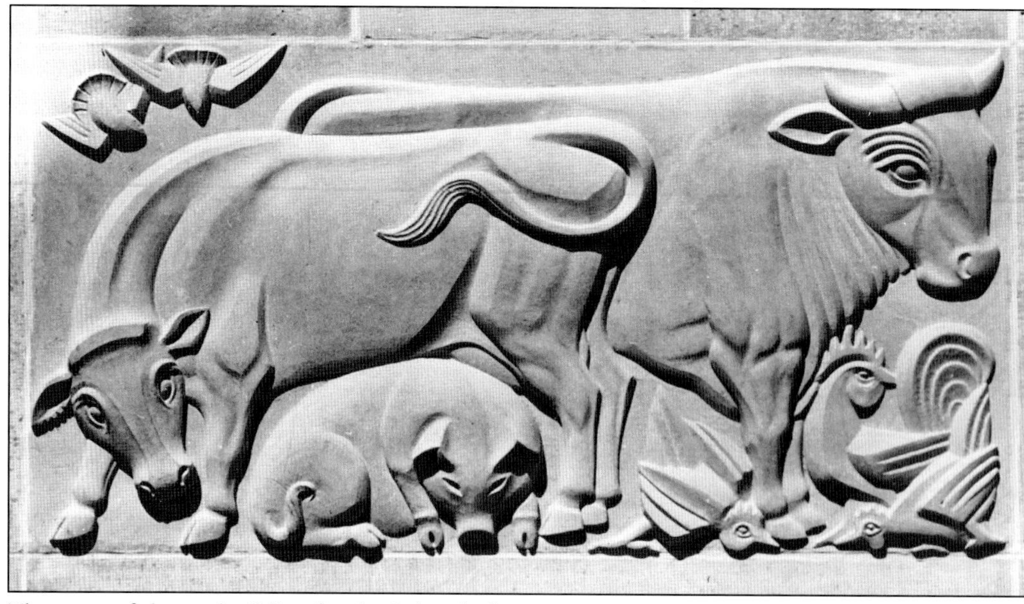

The state-of-the-art building for the School of Veterinary Medicine included skillfully executed decorative concrete friezes of domestic animals, such as these cattle, pigs, and poultry. At the end of Peter Shields Avenue, the structure was then the largest on campus. It is now known as Haring Hall, after the first dean of the school. (SCL.)

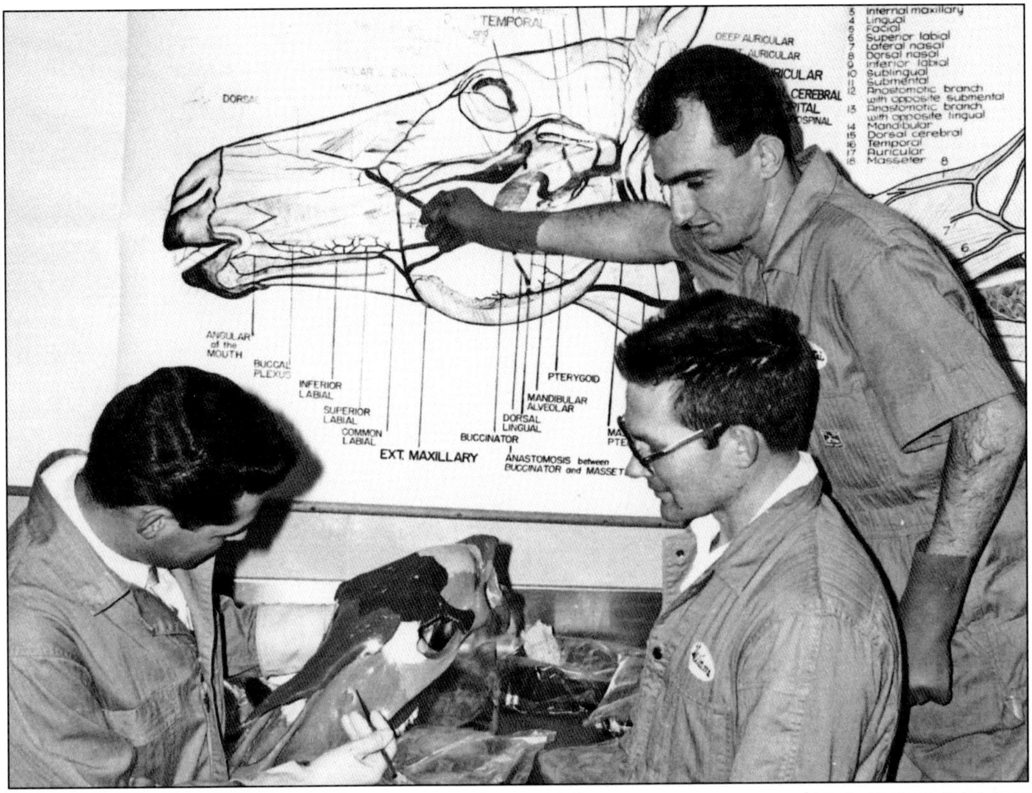

Students in veterinary medicine take rigorous instruction in anatomy before moving into clinical work. Pictorial wall displays are supplemented here with hands-on models. (SCL.)

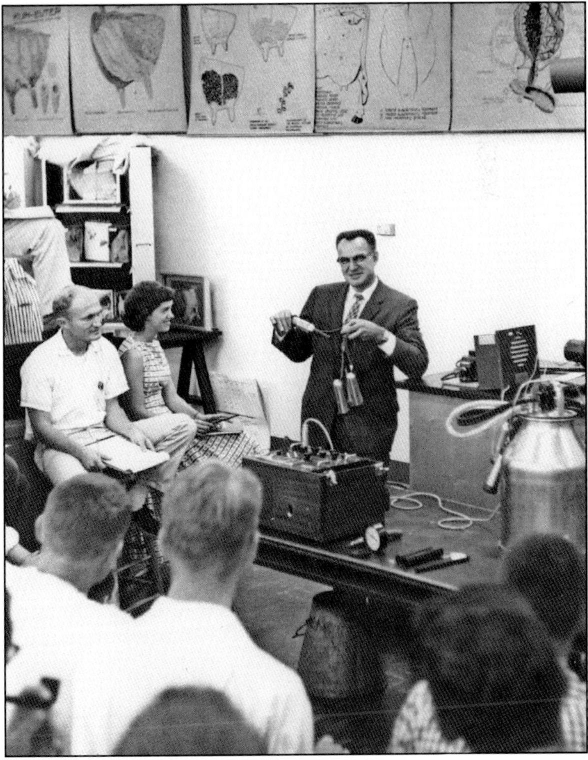

Oscar Schalm, one of the founding faculty members of the School of Veterinary Medicine, was an eminent specialist in bovine mastitis, diagnostic hematology, and clinical pathology. One of his notable accomplishments was the development of the California Mastitis Test, a standard for diagnosis of milk quality throughout the world. In this photograph, he demonstrates use of a mechanical milking device. (SCL.)

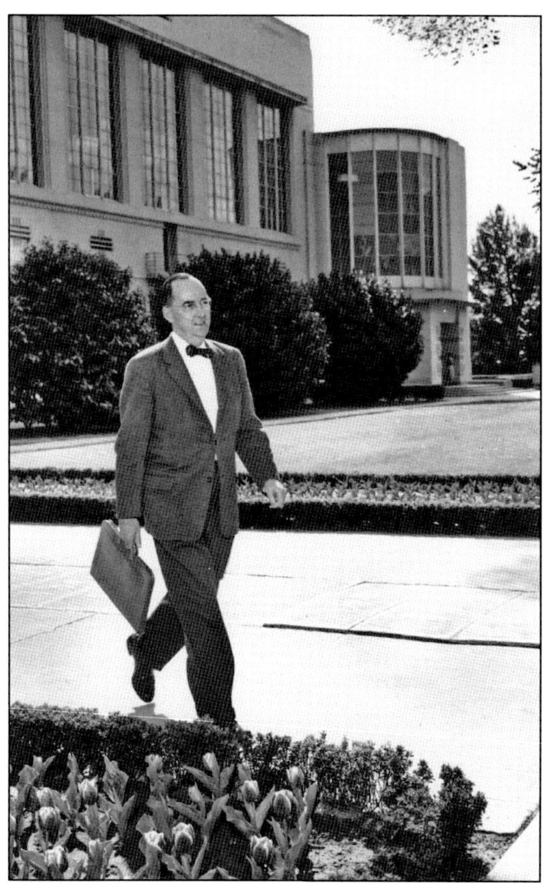

Stanley Freeborn began his academic career as an entomologist at Berkeley and became known for his research on malarial mosquitoes. He was appointed the first provost of the Davis campus in 1952. Here, he strides in front of the library-administration building, no doubt on his way to a meeting. In 1958, as the campus passed another milestone, he became its first chancellor, serving for a year until he retired. (SCL.)

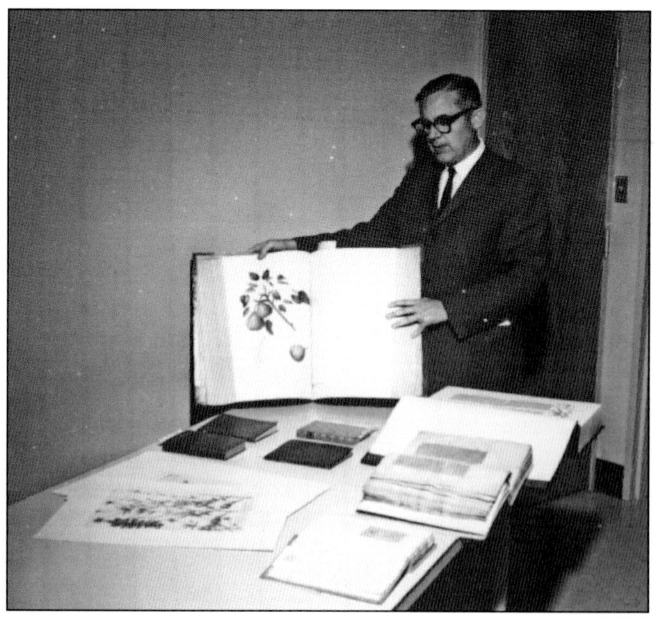

J. Richard Blanchard arrived at Davis in 1951, appointed university librarian after service at the Library of Congress and the US Department of Agriculture (USDA) Library in Washington, DC. Possessed of a broad perspective and twinkling humor, Blanchard worked hard at expanding the UC Davis collections. These are only a few of the important rare books and botanical manuscripts he gathered over the years. Another prized item was a fine Second Folio of Shakespeare's works. The total library collection grew from 80,000 books in 1951 to more than 1,000,000 in 1974. (SCL.)

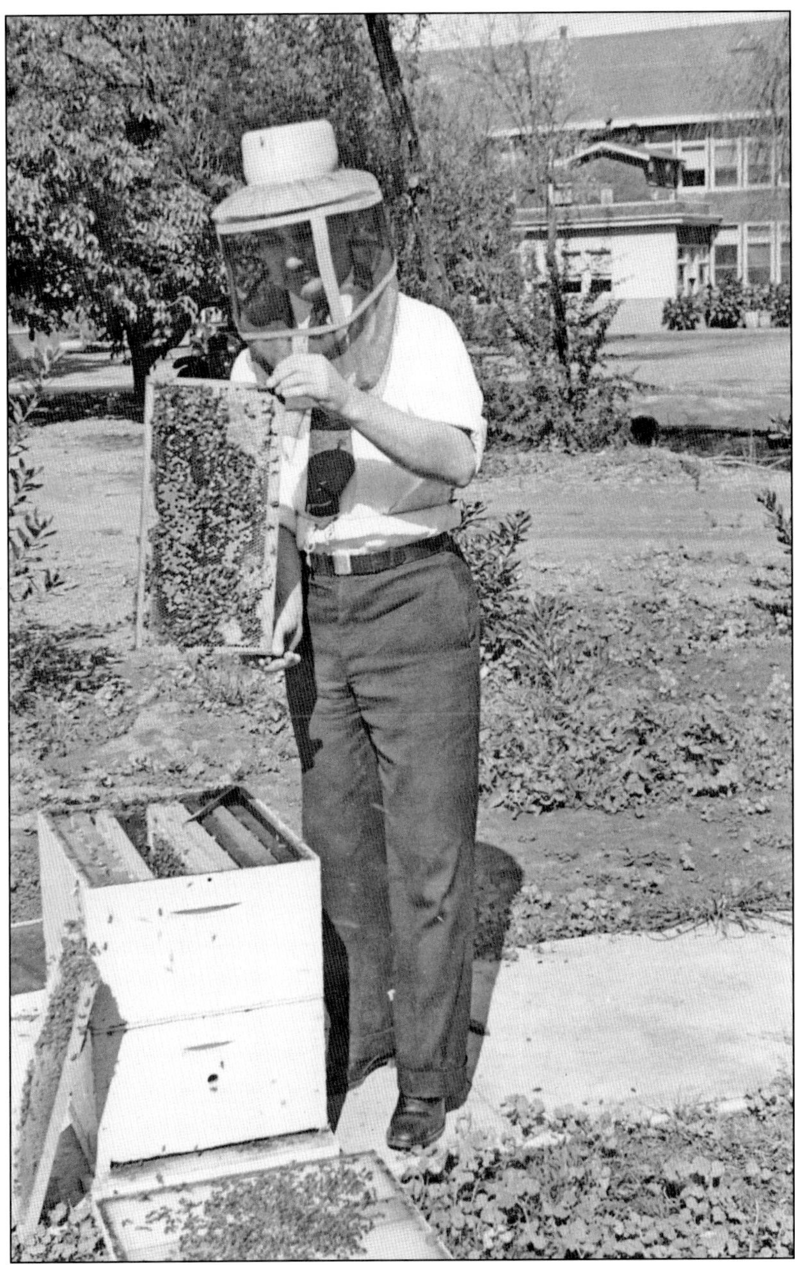

The study of entomology has a long history at Davis, starting with the first short courses offered at the University Farm and classes at the Farm School. Agricultural pests have long been a focus of research by many specialists. The honeybee has been another rich subject for long-term practical and theoretical study. As vital to many crops as sunlight, water, and fertilizer, bees have been the specialty of campus apiculturalists since the 1930s. Bee biologists have studied reproduction, nutrition, bee behavior, and toxicology in what has become the largest and most comprehensive apiculture facility in North America. With the assistance of these specialists, California has developed the largest bee-breeding industry on the continent, marketing queens and packaged bees to stock new hives each spring in many northern regions. (SCL.)

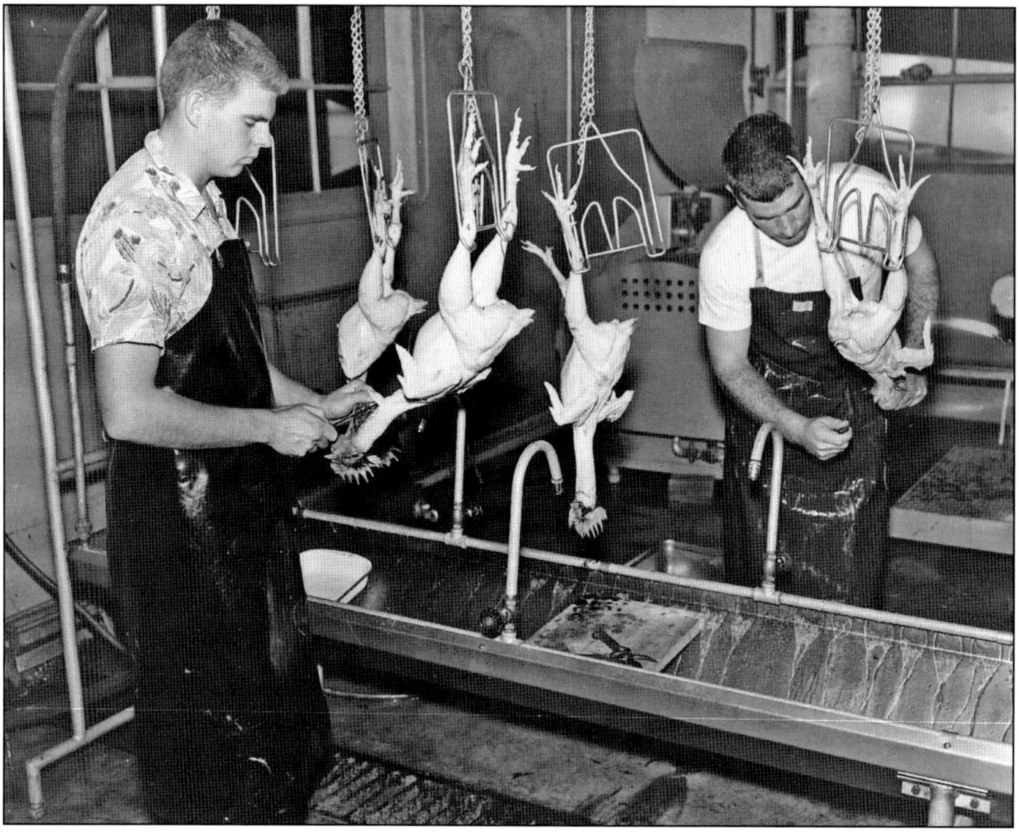

In 1951, the Department of Poultry Husbandry moved from Berkeley into a new building at Davis later named for Vigfus Asmundson. The agricultural experiment station and other government agency funds underwrote many breeding, nutrition, and management studies. Davis graduate students in the program soon outnumbered undergraduates. Classroom work was always supplemented with hands-on work, indispensable for learning to understand poultry problems. (SCL.)

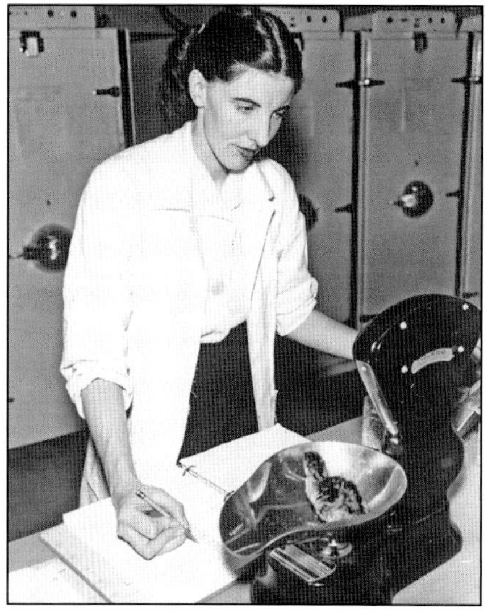

Ursula Abbott earned her doctorate at Berkeley and joined the Davis faculty in poultry husbandry in 1957, eventually becoming chair of the department. Her research in developmental genetics enriched her teaching, and she was often consulted by commercial poultry breeders and government agencies. Over the course of her career, she lectured around the world and was awarded numerous honors. Pictured here as a young researcher, she weighs a chick and takes notes. (SCL.)

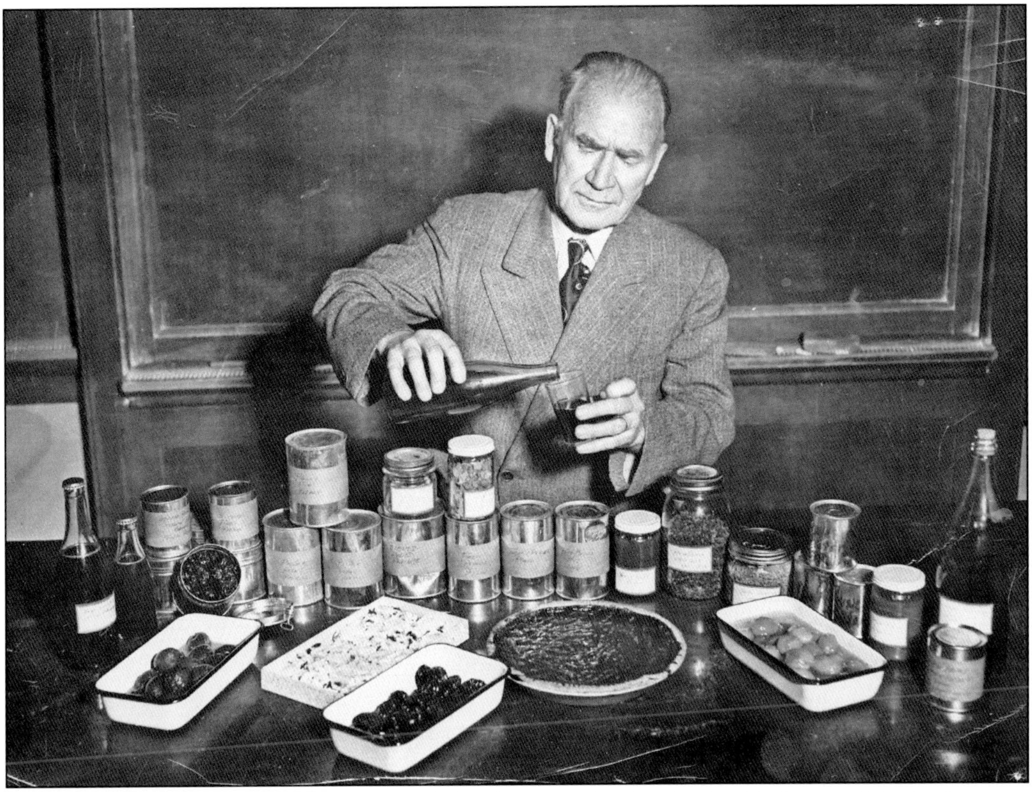

William Vere Cruess was a renowned food technologist in the College of Agriculture at Berkeley. He established the technology of fruit dehydration, introduced olive processing, worked on canning and freezing techniques, and even wrote the first post-Prohibition winemaking textbook. Although he remained in Berkeley, he encouraged the Department of Food Technology in its move to Davis in the 1950s. His student Emil Mrak was a faculty member there before he became the campus chancellor in 1959. (SCL.)

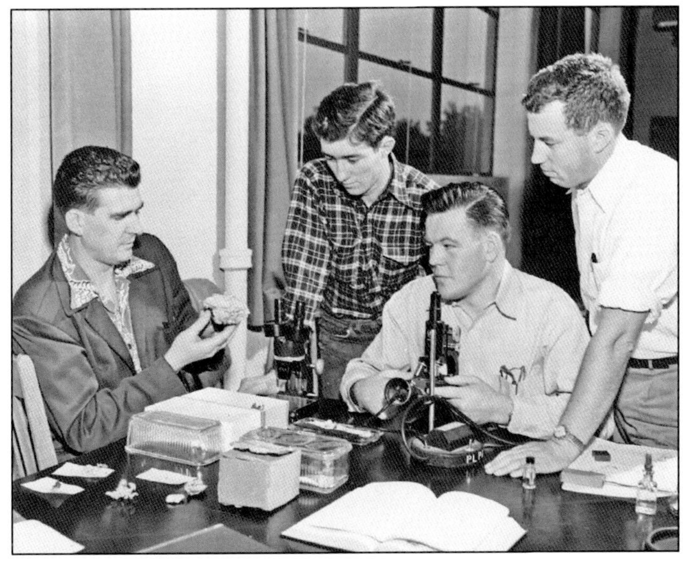

The first class in plant pathology, the study of plant diseases, was offered at Davis in 1913, but by 1949, the campus was able to grant graduate degrees in the field. George Nyland, assistant professor in the 1950s, shows a portion of a common tree mushroom to three students in a class on mycology, the study of fungi. Microscopes are used to examine the spore formation. (SCL.)

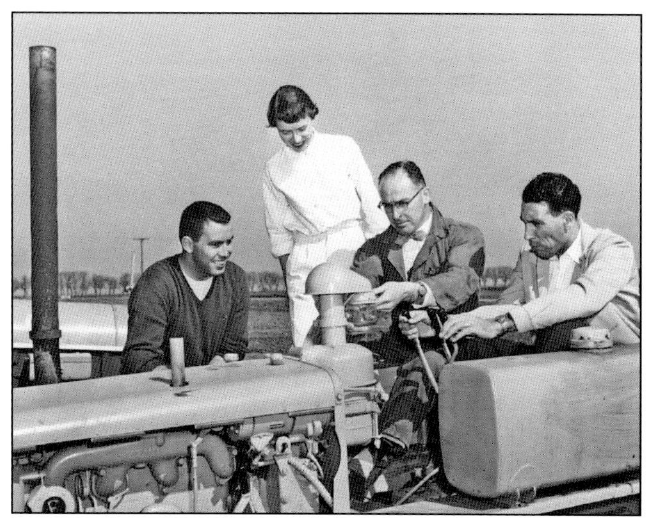

In what appears to be a publicity photograph, Harry B. Walker demonstrates tractor driving to three students, including a coed and probably a foreign visitor. For many years, agriculture students were required to prove their competence in farm skills by passing "Examination A," but after the war, tractor driving became an elective popular with non-agriculture students as well. Walker was actually far too busy as an engineer and administrator to teach this kind of course. (SCL.)

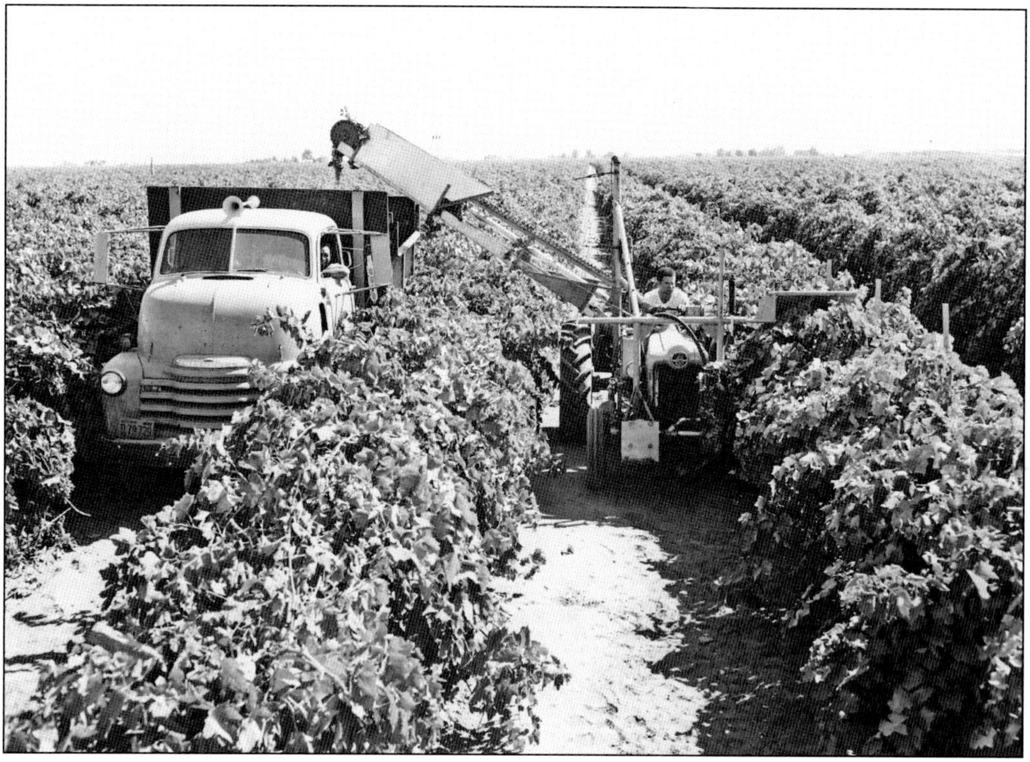

Davis agricultural engineers worked on many mechanical harvester projects after the war. This image shows a prototype grape harvester, but the mechanical tomato harvester attracted most public attention. Designing mechanical harvesting equipment was no small challenge because harvesting entails multiple functions, including cutting and lifting the vines, separating the fruit, and conveying the product to a wagon. Early engineering designs went through multiple iterations. (SCL.)

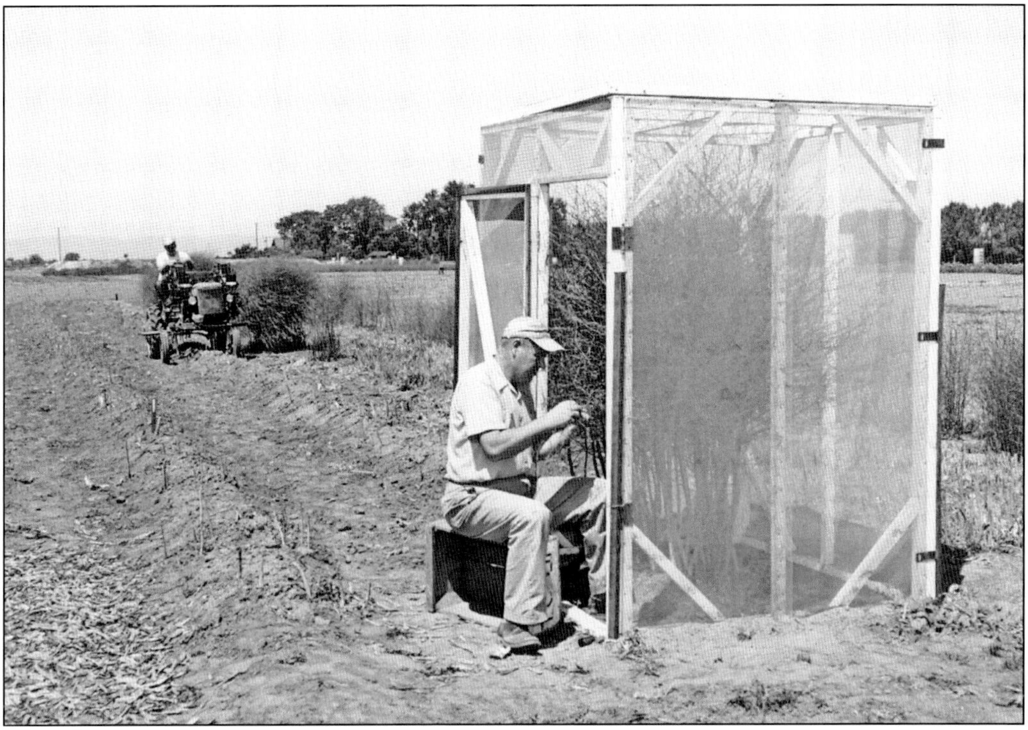

Gordie "Jack" Hanna was a dedicated plant breeder who helped revolutionize the tomato-processing industry by developing a tomato suitable for mechanical harvesting. Early mechanical tomato harvesters often crushed the ripe tomatoes until, over a period of years, Hanna produced a firmer, blockier variety that could withstand mechanical handling. By the late 1950s, his years of effort paid off when he teamed up with Coby Lorenzen, a designer of the experimental harvester. (SCL.)

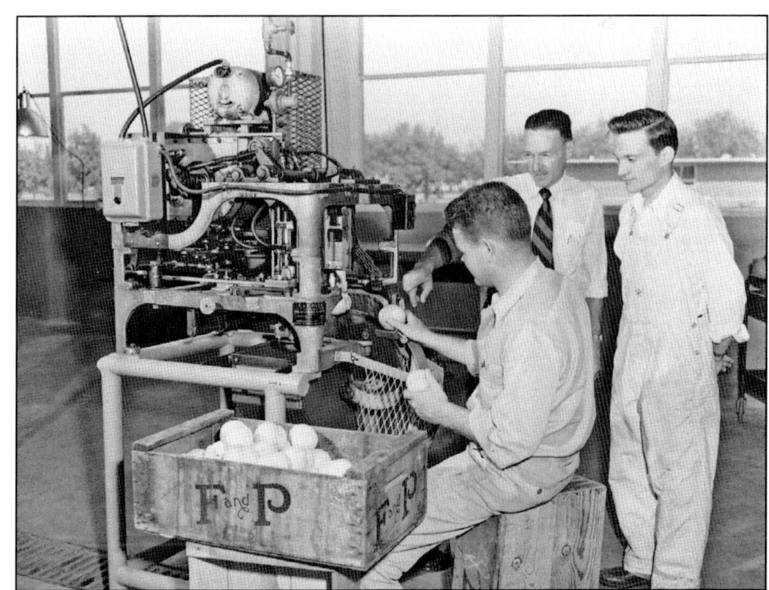

This elaborate contraption seems to be a fruit-pitting machine. Agricultural engineers were always seeking ways to make processing more efficient, and food technology experts sought quality control as well. These peaches may be destined for canning. (SCL.)

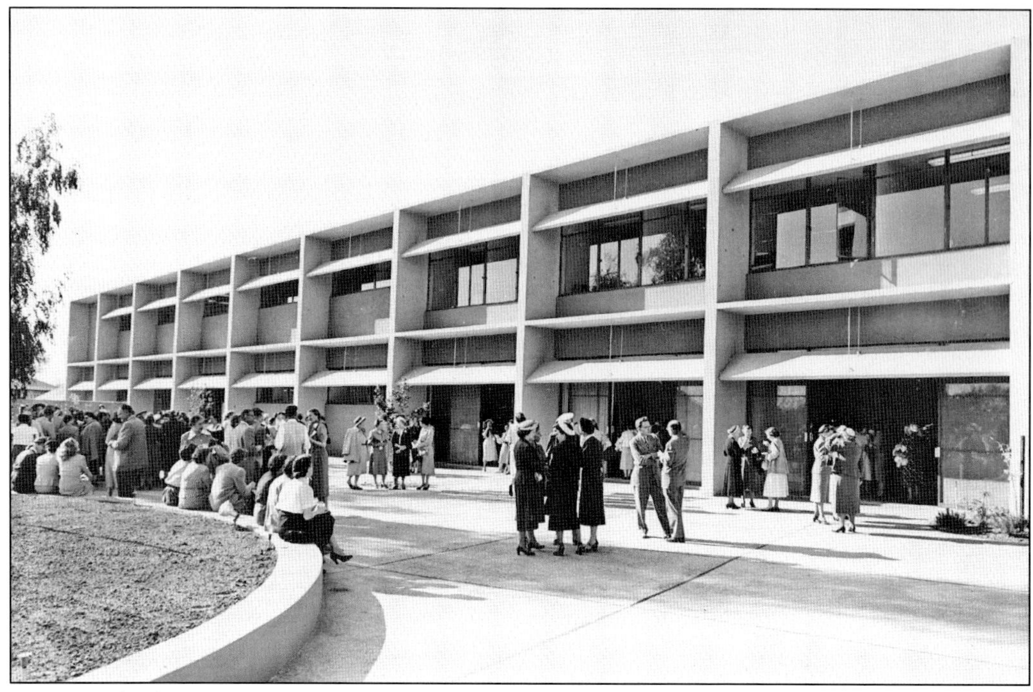

In 1951, the home economics program at Berkeley was phased out and transferred to the Davis campus. Guests and staff seen here celebrate the opening of a modern home economics building in 1952, situated on Hutchison Drive across from the agricultural engineering building and close to the library. Now called Everson Hall after Gladys Everson, a noted biochemist and nutrition expert, the building contains not only classrooms and laboratories but also a comfortable lounge with a fireplace. (SCL.)

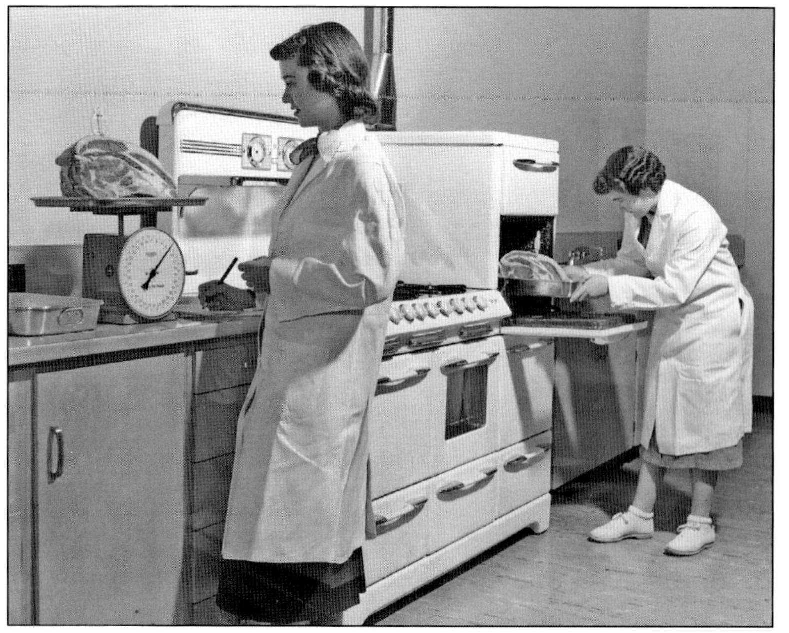

Up-to-date kitchen equipment helps student cooks prepare what looks like a spectacular meal, but much of the emphasis in the kitchen and the classroom was on good nutrition and the preparation of wholesome diets. (SCL.)

The expanded program at Davis also specialized in textiles and clothing. This 1950s display focuses on textile design, a program popular with students, but faculty research also centered on textile science in the areas of comfort and safety (such as flame resistance) and the chemistry of natural and synthetic fibers. (SCL.)

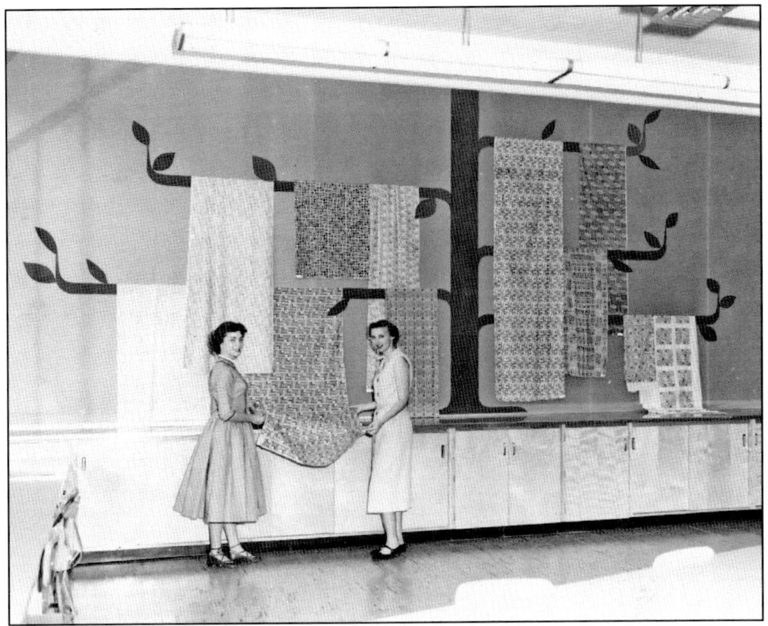

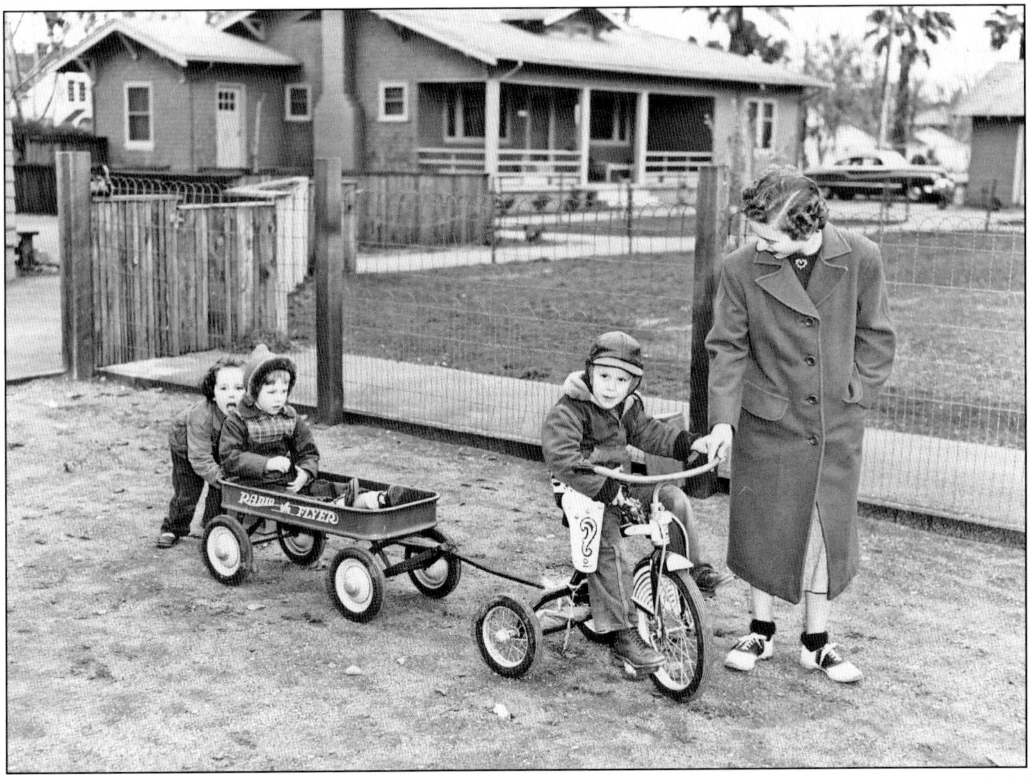

The early years in a child's life are a time of profound development and growth. Child development studies, initially part of the home economics program, have continued to be important on the Davis campus. This picture was taken at the Center for Child Studies near Aggie Villa, a center that still exists. (SCL.)

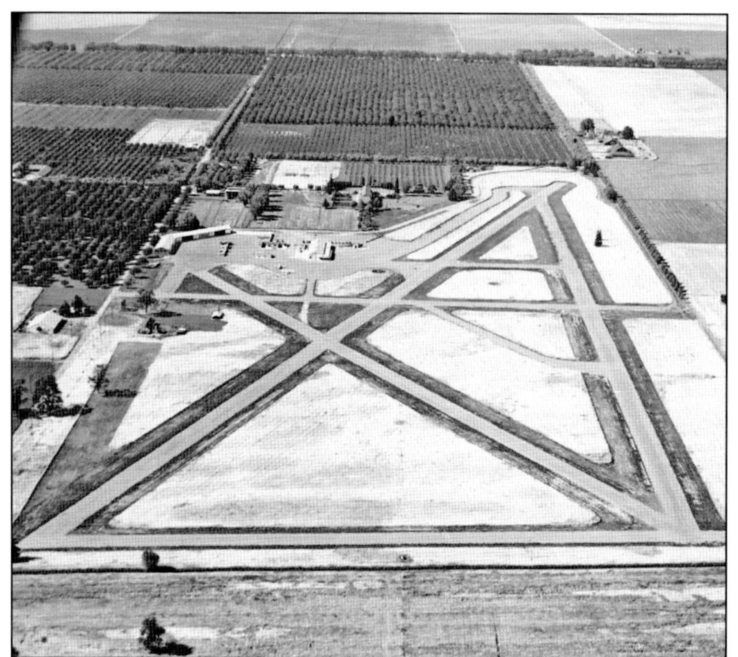

In 1949, the university purchased the Straloch Farm about a mile west of the Davis campus, which included a first-class private airport built in 1946 by its owner, Harry Hopkins. Thus, UC Davis acquired what was then the first university airfield in the nation and is still the only one in the UC system. Over the years, it has served many research staff members, university officials, and visitors. (SCL.)

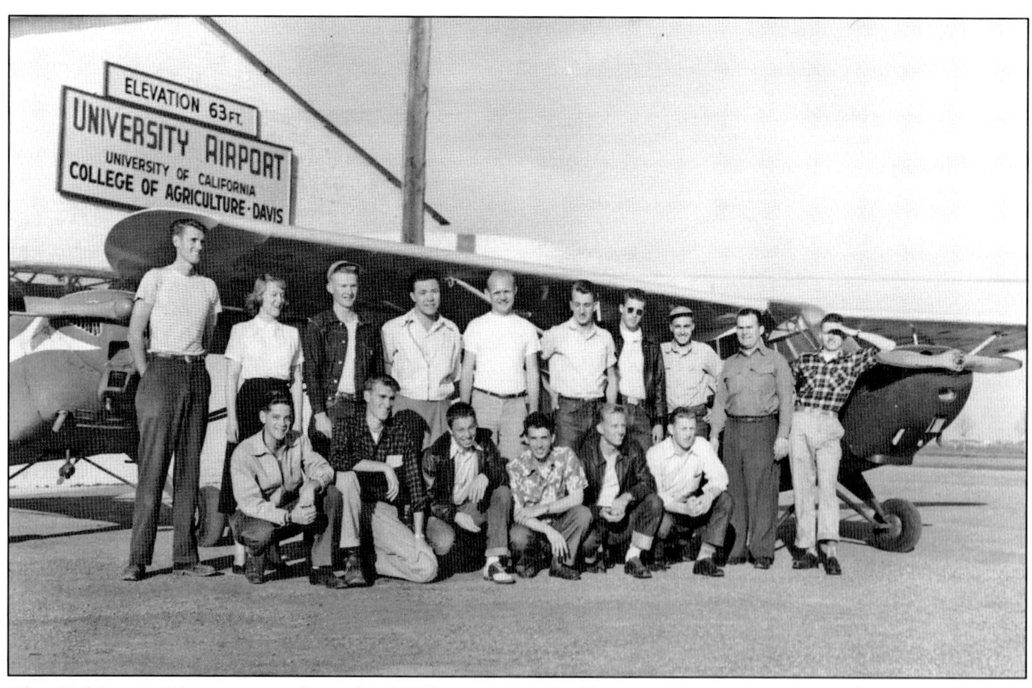

The Cal Aggie Flyers, seen here in 1950, consisted of more than a dozen students, including one coed. Some of them may have been veterans who learned to fly during the war. Hundreds of students also welcomed the chance to fly with their professors, observing the resources and diversity of the state in a way impossible from the ground. (SCL.)

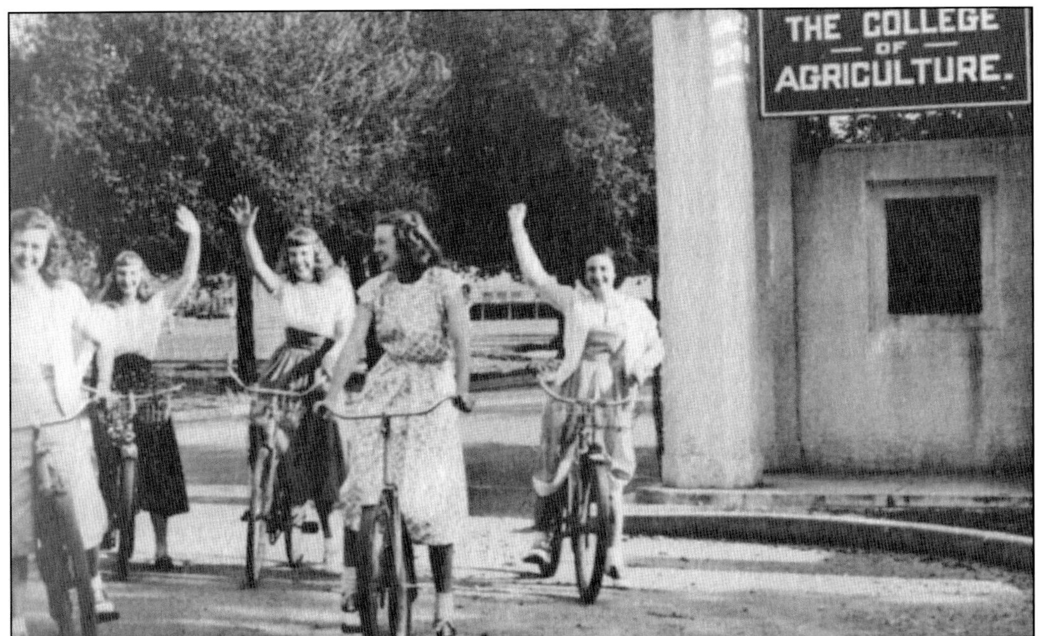

Postwar coeds wave happily on their bikes for this yearbook snapshot from 1947. Despite the strains of postwar adjustments, the campus thrived, and the future looked bright. With new buildings on the way and a widening circle of activities, bicycles became the modus operandi for student and staff movement across the grounds. (YB, JL.)

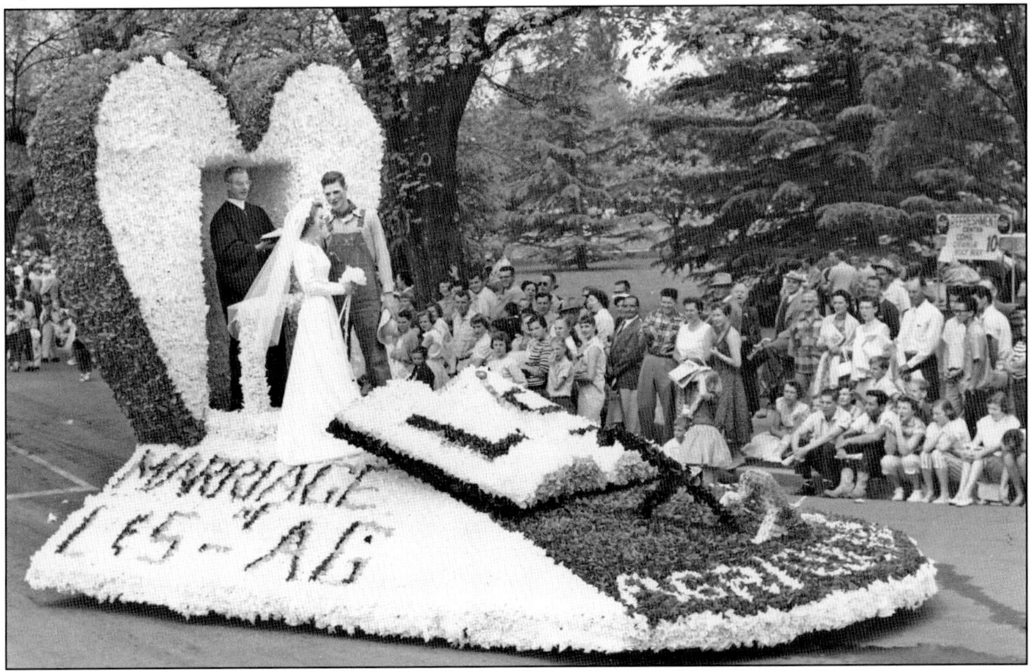

This Picnic Day 1955 parade float celebrated the "Marriage of L&S and AG" with a connubial scene representing the joining of the College of Agriculture by the College of Letters and Science three years earlier. Picnic Day parades remained hugely popular, and floats were often very elaborate. (SCL.)

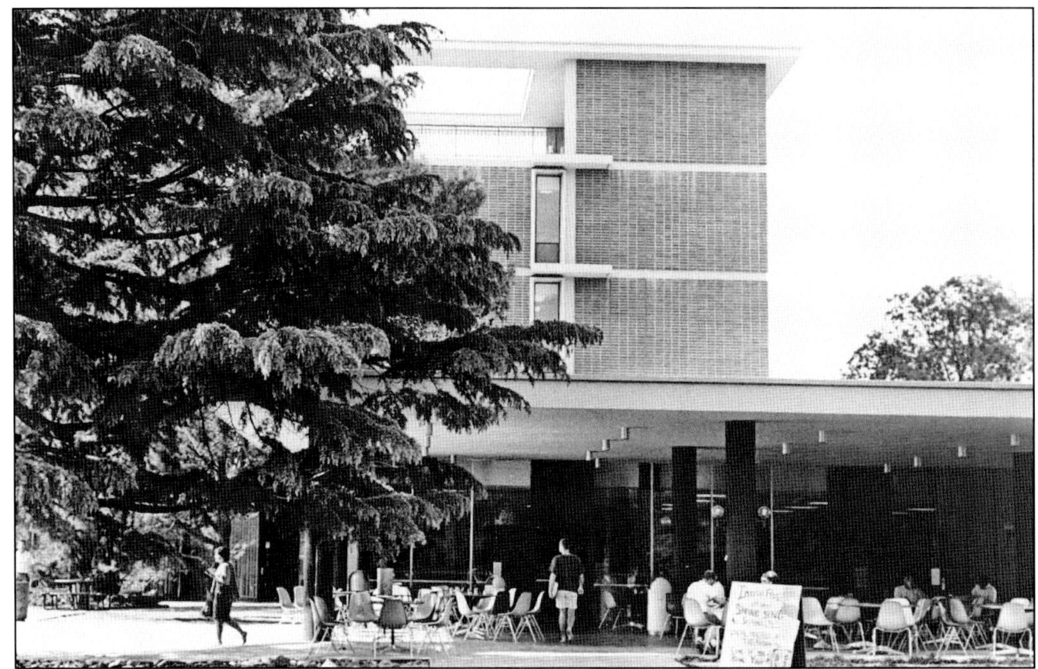

After a long fundraising campaign, the Memorial Union for student activities was completed in 1955. Replacing both the decrepit old Recreation Hall and West Hall, the new building was dedicated to the 128 Davis students lost in military service over the years. The union, holding a coffeehouse, conference room, bookstore, and various offices, was designed for later expansion and has been remodeled several times. (SCL.)

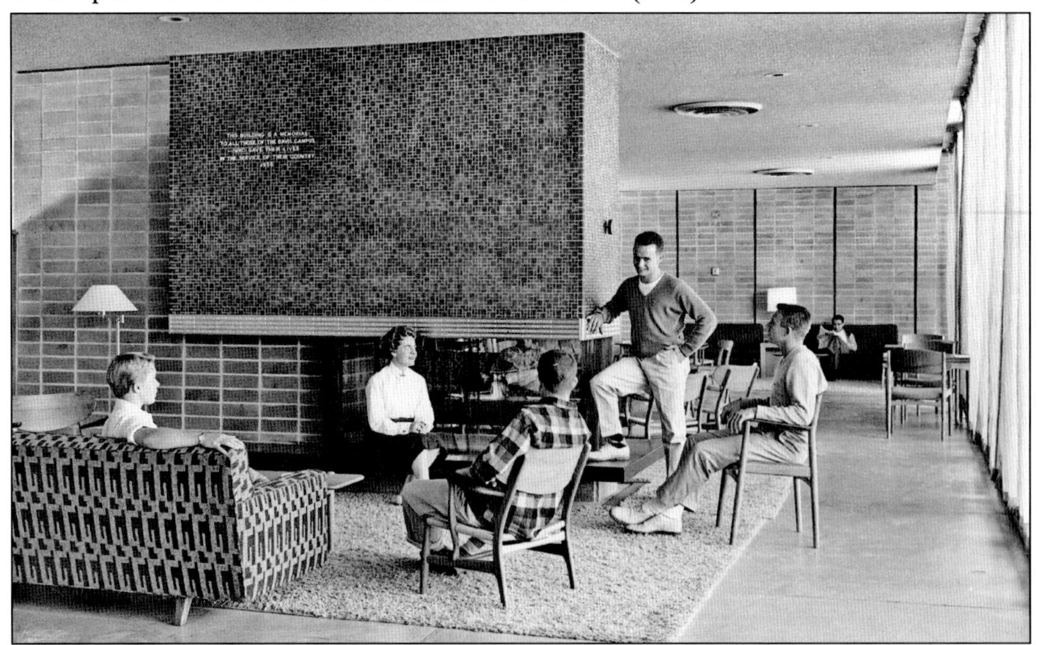

The lounge of the new student union holds a collection of typical 1950s modern furniture arranged for easy student socializing. It also holds a Golden Book recording the names of the memorialized UC Davis students. (SCL.)

Four

A Full University 1959–Present

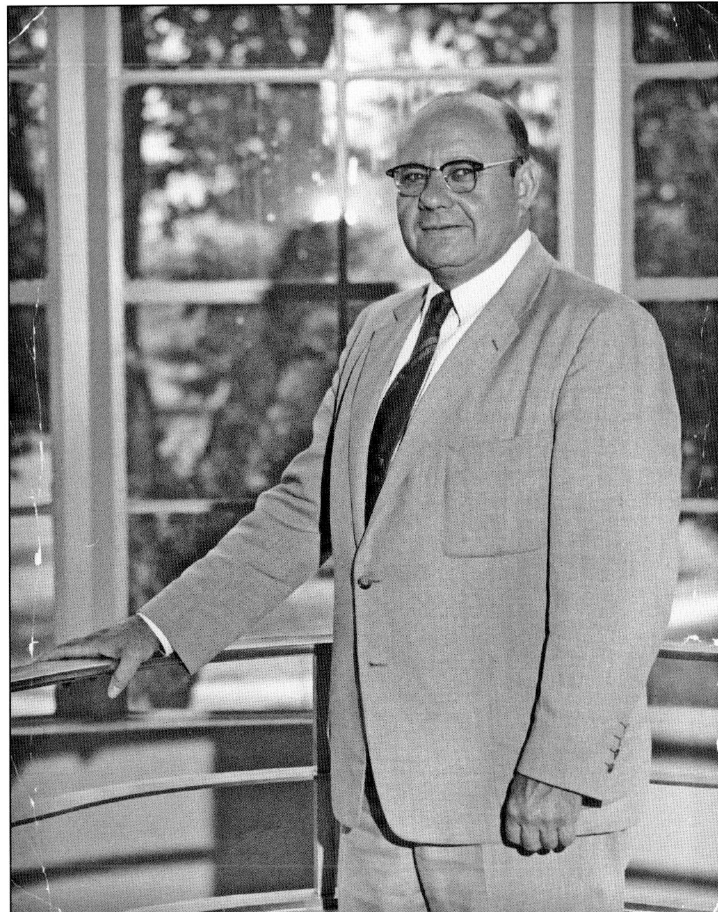

In the 27 years after 1959, two chancellors oversaw great diversification in campus programs. Both were longtime Davis faculty with agricultural and scientific backgrounds. Both had charismatic personalities and set a tone of friendliness and accessibility yet had high expectations. This formal portrait of Chancellor Emil Mrak shows him in his official capacity as the public face of UC Davis. Mrak, an expert in yeasts and professor of food science, served 10 years in the chancellor's office from 1959 until 1969. Having grown up in an orchard in the Santa Clara Valley and remembering his childhood bike riding, he strove to make the Davis campus a bike-friendly place. (SCL.)

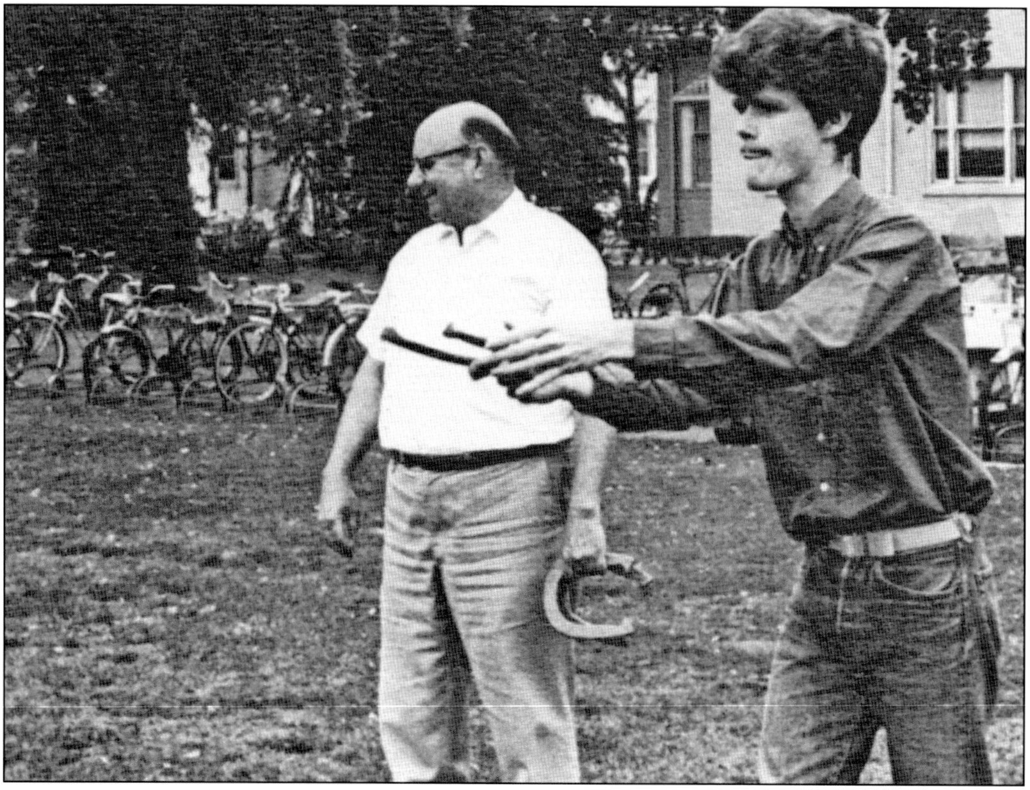

It was often said that Chancellors Mrak and Meyer kept the Davis campus calm during the turbulent 1960s and 1970s by being accessible to students. Mrak's gregarious personality is seen here in 1967 at a game of horseshoes with student government president Bob Black. Like Mrak, Black was a creative force for launching and encouraging new activities and programs, many of which were led and ran by students. (YB, JL.)

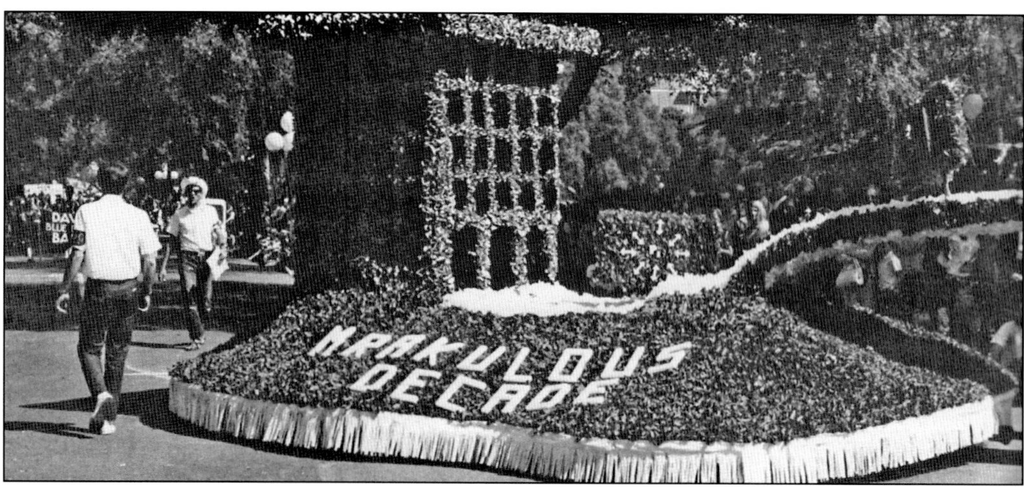

This Picnic Day parade entry from the spring of 1969 celebrates the retiring chancellor's "Mrakulous Decade." That year saw the renaming of the three-year-old, large, prominently situated administration building as Mrak Hall. (YB, JL.)

Chancellor from 1969 to 1987, James H. Meyer was an Idaho farm boy who attended the University of Idaho and the University of Wisconsin before joining the Davis faculty in animal science. Winner of the Picnic Day cow-milking contest for 13 years, he never lost his common touch and was known for his inclusive managerial style. His tenure included years of slow growth on campus during which UC Davis achieved a top-20 national research ranking. In 1987, Meyer Hall opened to house food and agricultural sciences. (SCL.)

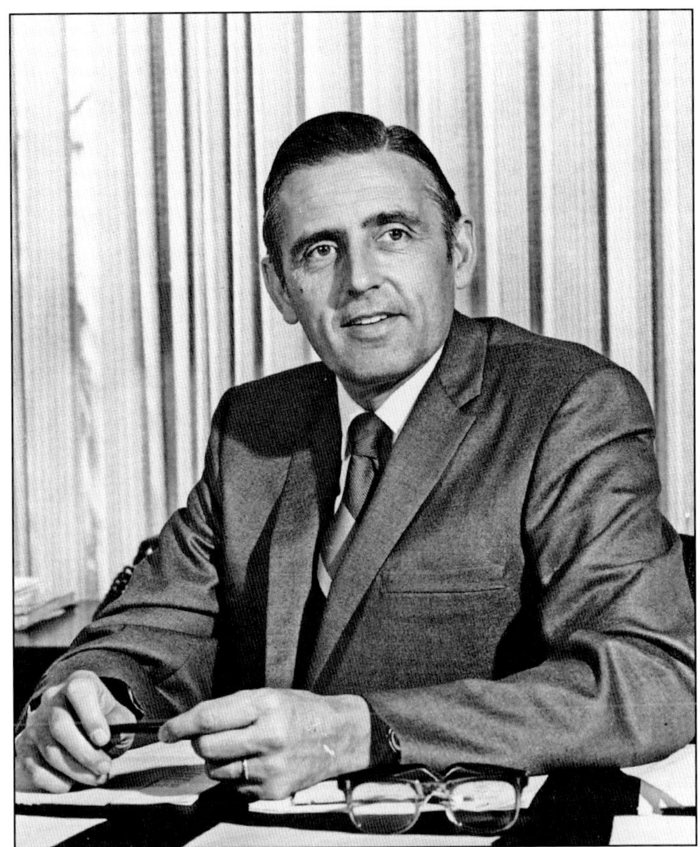

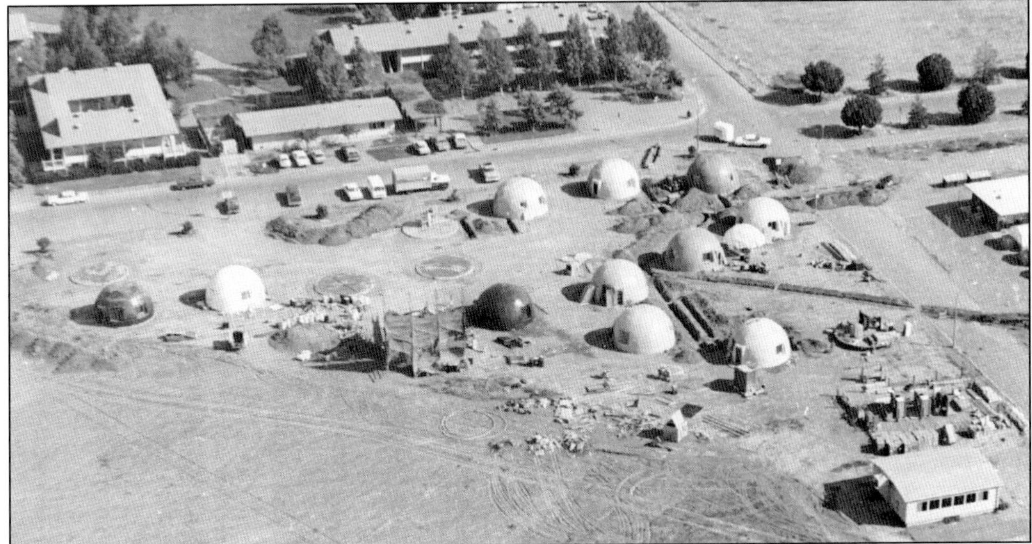

An explosion of environmentalist initiatives in the 1960s and 1970s received the chancellors' overt or, at least, passive support. Near the student farm center and garden plots is a baker's dozen of housing units with distinctive dome shapes. A combination of students, faculty advisors, and astute campus housing officials funded and built these innovative units in 1972. (SCL.)

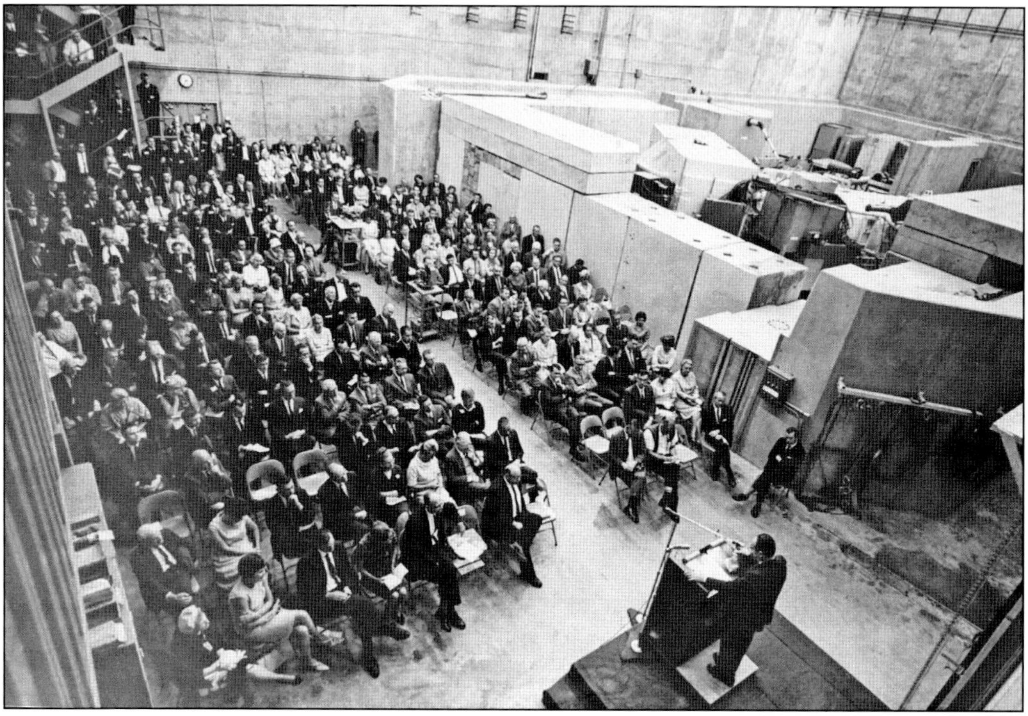

The physics department's expanding nuclear program added the 60-inch cyclotron shown here at a 1965 ceremonial occasion. Housed in the new Crocker Nuclear Laboratory building, it was near the engineering complex, but also for the next three decades it was incongruously adjacent to the still-used hog barn. Recently, it was named in honor of longtime physics professor John Jungerman. Innovative uses of the machine include air-pollution particle tracking and the dating of a Gutenberg Bible and the Vineland Map. (SCL.)

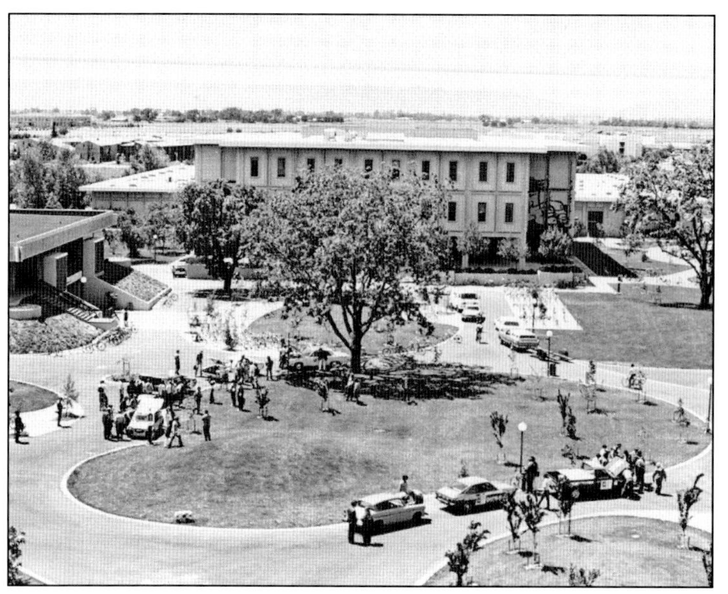

Bainer Hall, epicenter of engineering programs since 1966, anchors a cluster of physical sciences buildings around a subsidiary quad west of the original one. The new College of Engineering created in 1962 was greatly diversified from the original agricultural engineering program. The landscaping is a major break with the old right-angled regularity in its curving sidewalks and irregular greenery. (SCL.)

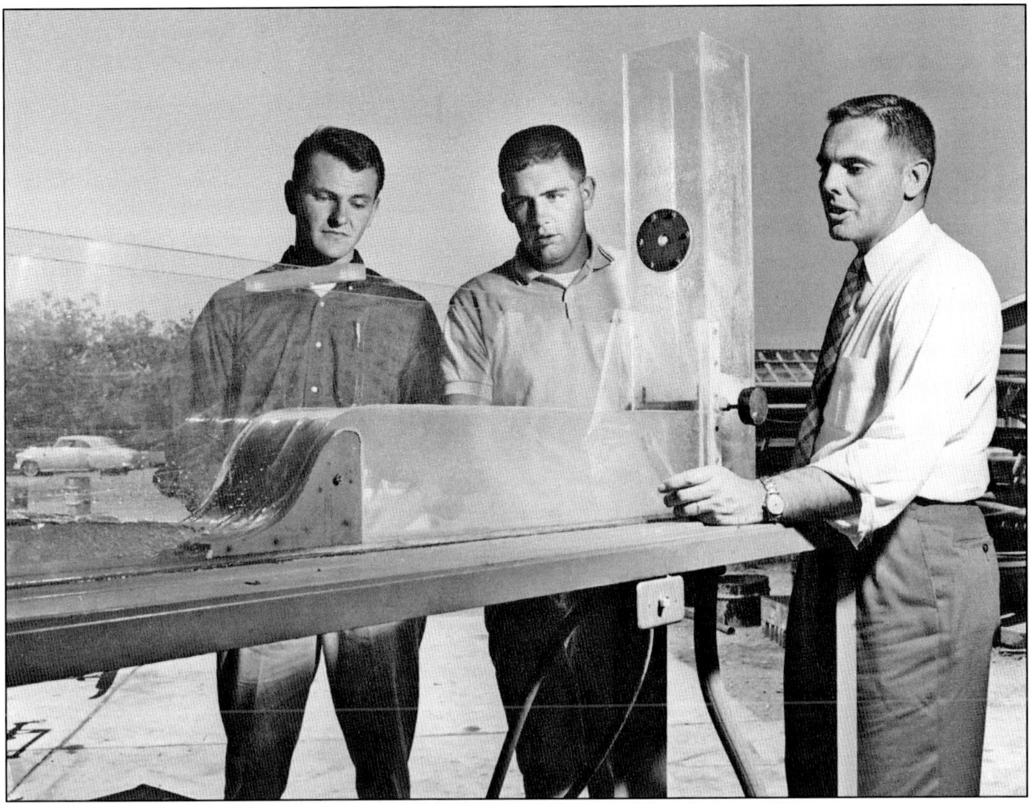

Verne H. Scott, professor of land, air, and water resources, is shown here with a model for simulating water flows in irrigation systems. Work such as his continued one of the earliest and strongest academic specializations at Davis. (SCL.)

Chancellor Mrak, fourth from left, stands with the founding faculty of the new UC Davis School of Medicine. C. John Tupper, fourth from right, effectively guided the new school as dean from 1966 to 1979. The school was at first housed in rudimentary temporary buildings, but its failure to get funding for an on-campus teaching hospital brought about an even better alternative. The School of Medicine purchased the Sacramento County Hospital, located 25 miles away, and began its long drive toward excellence. (SCL.)

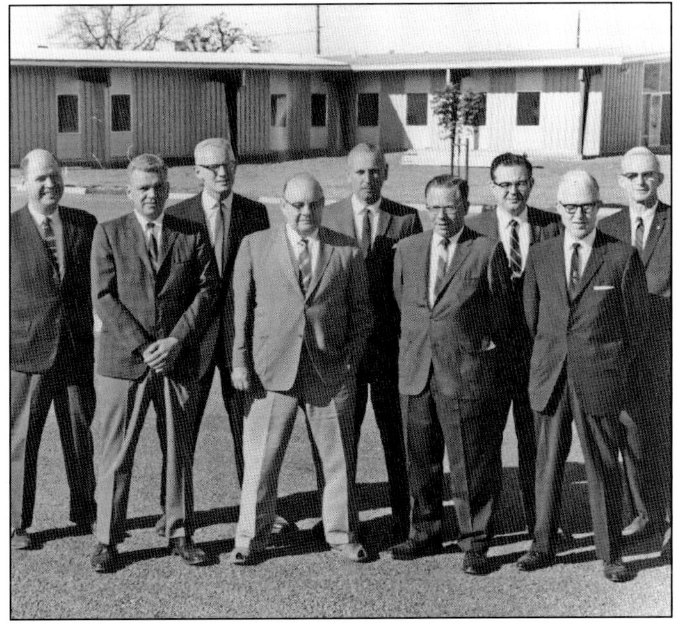

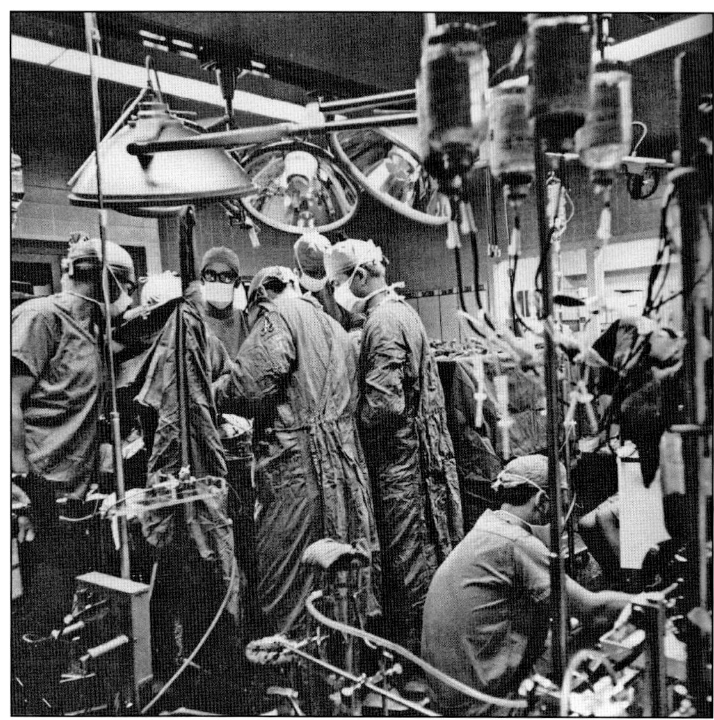

This scene from 1971 illustrates the complexity and teamwork of major surgery. The School of Medicine admitted 48 students in its first class in the fall of 1968; by the fall of 1971, one hundred future doctors were admitted. While classroom instruction in the early years was on the campus in temporary buildings, surgery took place at the Sacramento hospital. Only in 1978 did the name for the renovated Sacramento campus become the University of California, Davis Medical Center. (YB, JL.)

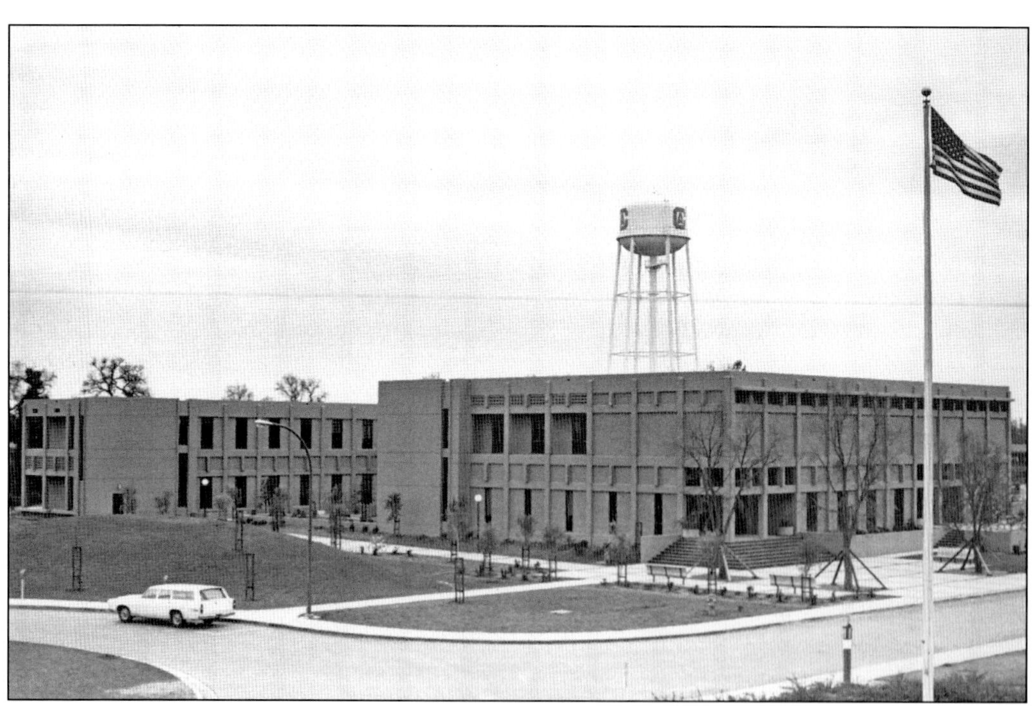

School of Law classes met in temporary buildings from 1965 until moving to this permanent building in 1968. Students of the new school led the effort to have it named in 1969 for slain civil rights leader Martin Luther King Jr. Located near Putah Creek, the school is on a quiet corner of campus. It has been nationally recognized for its high quality of student life. (SCL.)

The carefully chosen law library has helped to ensure the school's rapid accreditation and high national ranking. Its first librarian was Mortimer D. Schwartz, seen unpacking an early shipment of books. The library's physical facilities were well designed to become the intellectual and social center for faculty and students. Law students sponsored many activities, including an infant care co-op conveniently located to the library. (SCL.)

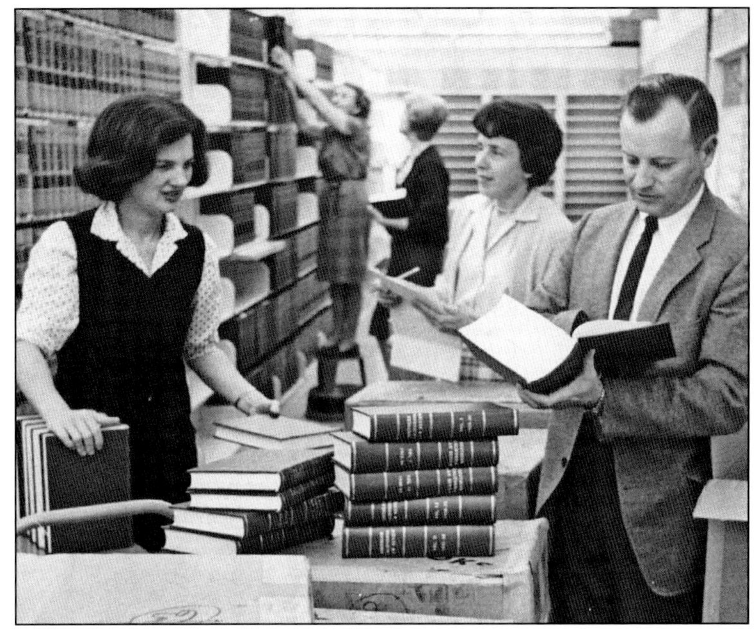

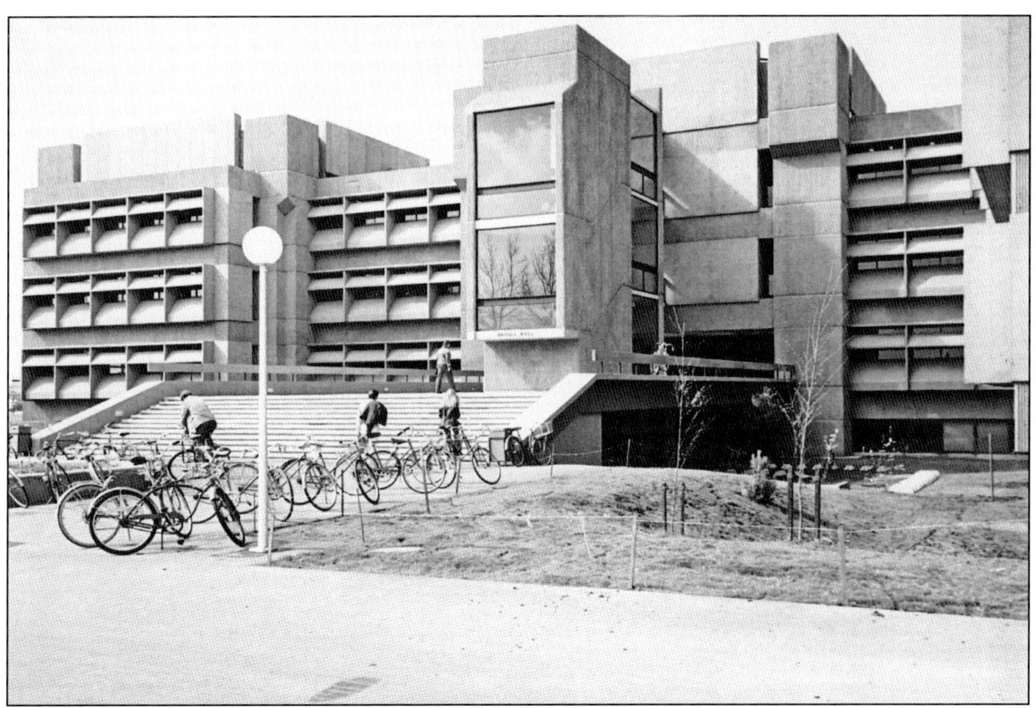

Briggs Hall, named in 1971, anchors the west end of the life sciences mall. Kleiber, Storer, Hutchison, and Haring Halls, all named for notable scientists, adjoin the walkway. The harsh aesthetics of the architecture here seems a mismatch for the beloved agronomy professor Fred Briggs, who quipped, "Work very hard, but be careful not to appear to be working hard." (SCL.)

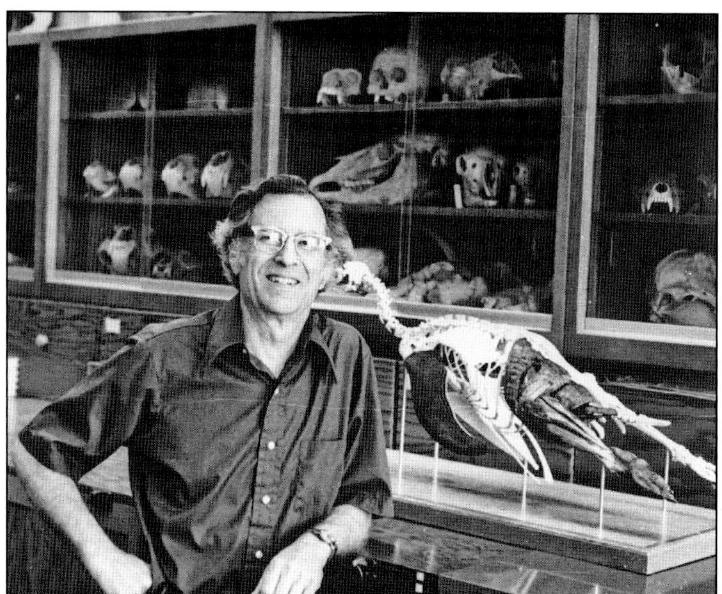

Professor of zoology Milton Hildebrand both advocated and practiced good teaching. He cochaired a high-profile committee that defined the attributes of good college teaching. He also taught a rigorous course on human sexuality to annual enrollments of 1,700 when few other accomplished scientists would touch the subject. He is shown here in characteristic good humor. (SCL.)

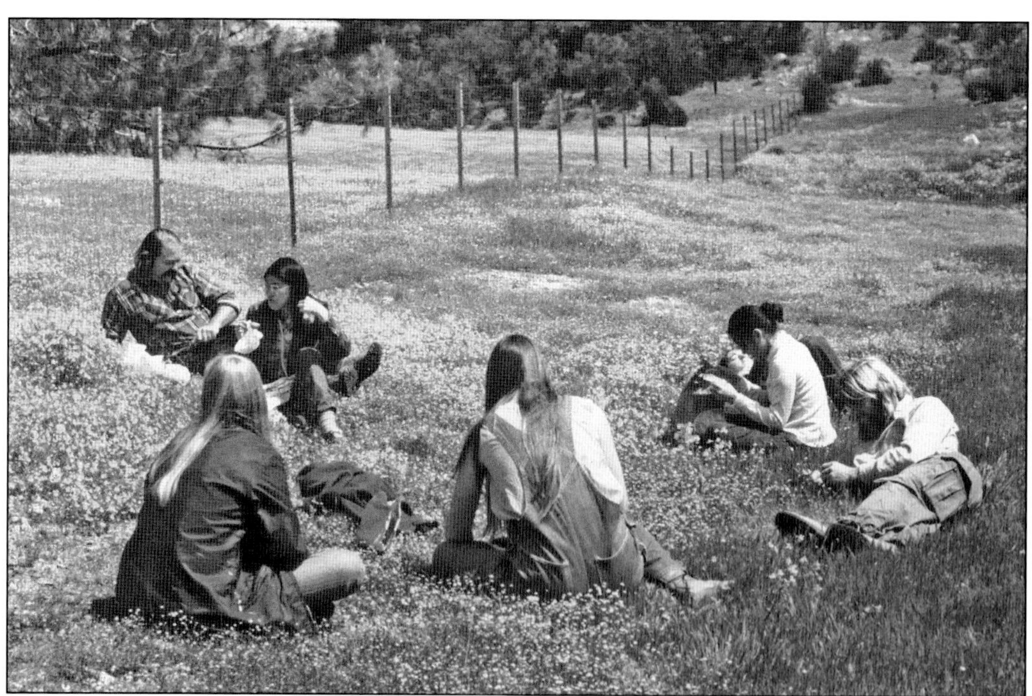

These students are on a botany field trip to the foothills of the Sierra Nevada in Amador County. Such ventures to diverse environments within a day's journey of campus continue to be a hallmark of the graduate student experience. The class called California Floristics required three weekend field trips. (PSH.)

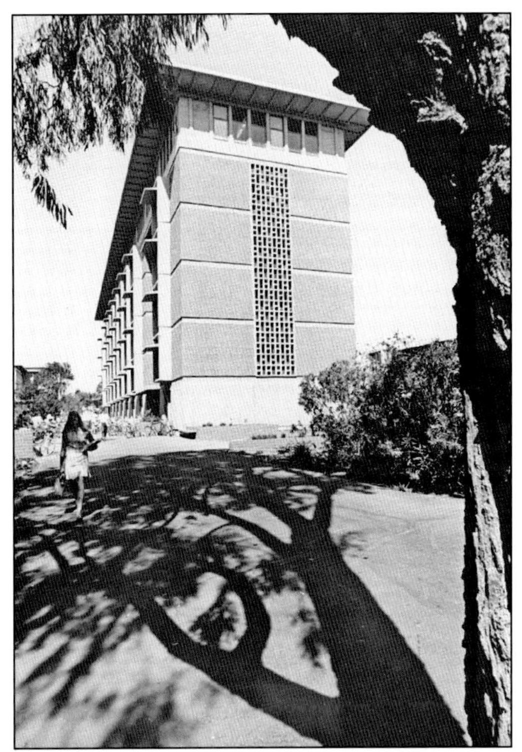

Kerr Hall, along with neighboring Wellman Hall, replaced the old horticulture building in 1969. Its six-story height was predicted to become the norm, but it still stands as the second-tallest structure in the core campus. Named for university president Clark Kerr, it has housed various sciences and social sciences departments. (SCL.)

Robert Gordon Sproul, president of the University of California for 28 years, was the namesake for this 1963 high-rise concrete slab building. Erected in just a few weeks, Sproul Hall was, at the time, the tallest precast, prestressed concrete building on the West Coast. Programs in the humanities have been major tenants, and a "Sproul owl" that took up residence near the top was a famous resident during the 1980s. Nearby are other buildings devoted to the arts and social sciences. (SCL.)

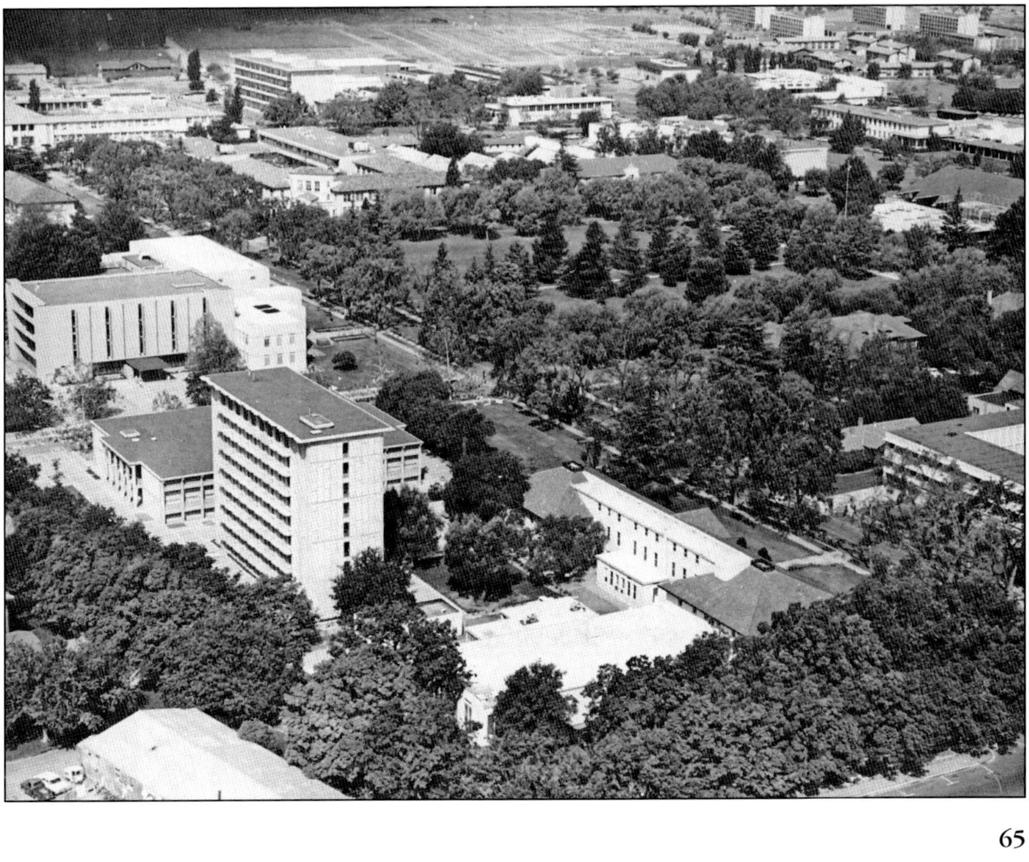

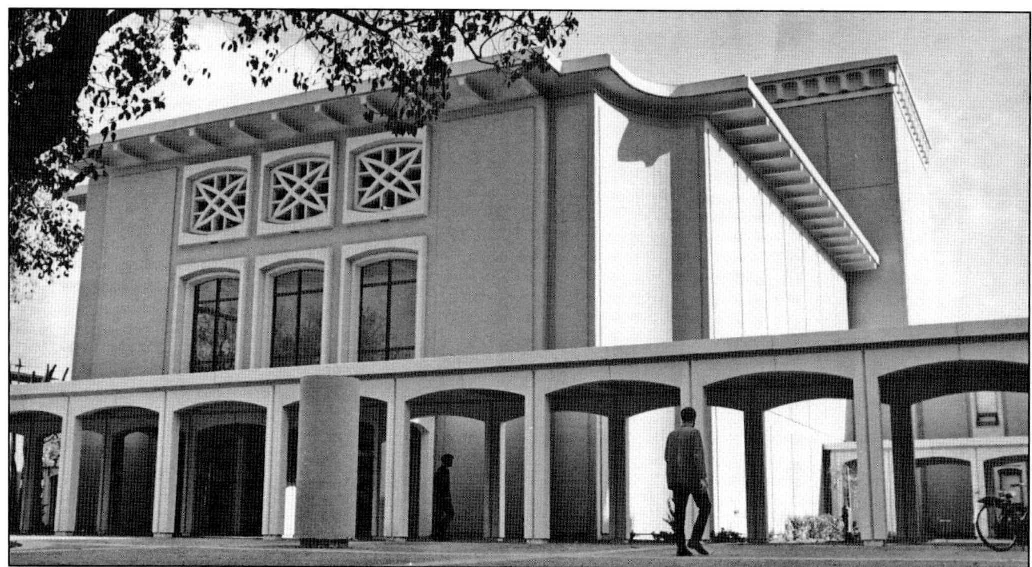

The dramatic art building opened in 1966 adjacent to similar structures for art and music. Three decades later, it was named for Celeste Turner Wright, who began her 51-year career at Davis in 1928. She taught English and classics and directed plays for a student body that initially had only eight female students (out of 350 total). A distinguished scholar and award-winning poet, she was also a respected administrator and a powerful faculty voice. (SCL.)

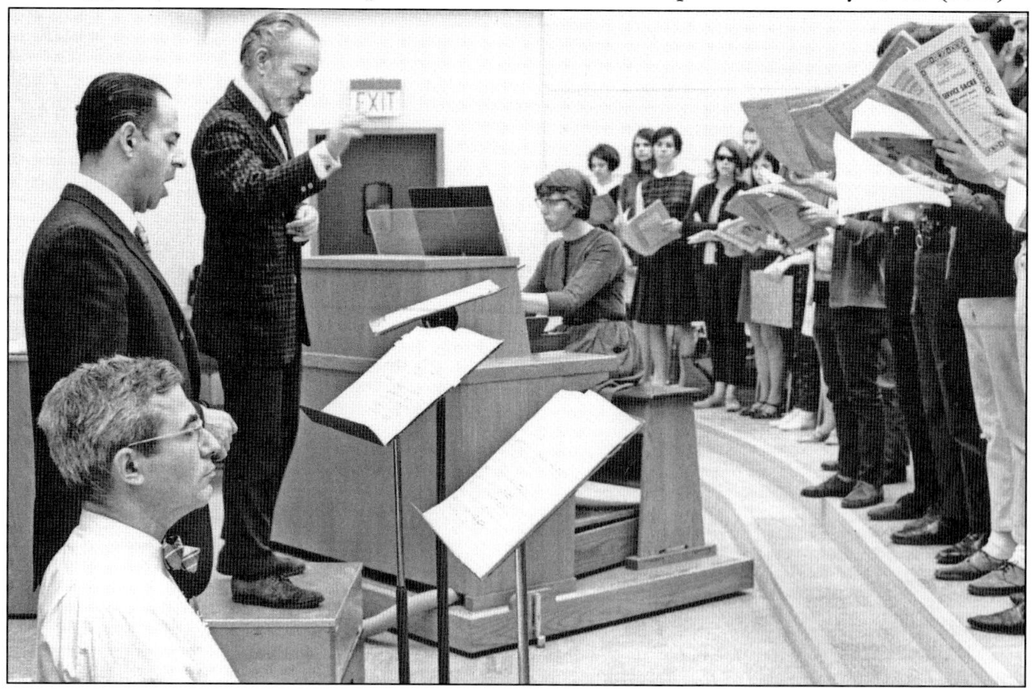

The founding professor in 1952 of what became the Department of Music, Jerome Rosen is seen here conducting a choral ensemble in the department's recital room, where he occasionally played clarinet during Thursday noon concerts. Rosen and his fellow faculty musicians went on to win dozens of major prizes and awards for their compositions, performances, and publications. (SCL.)

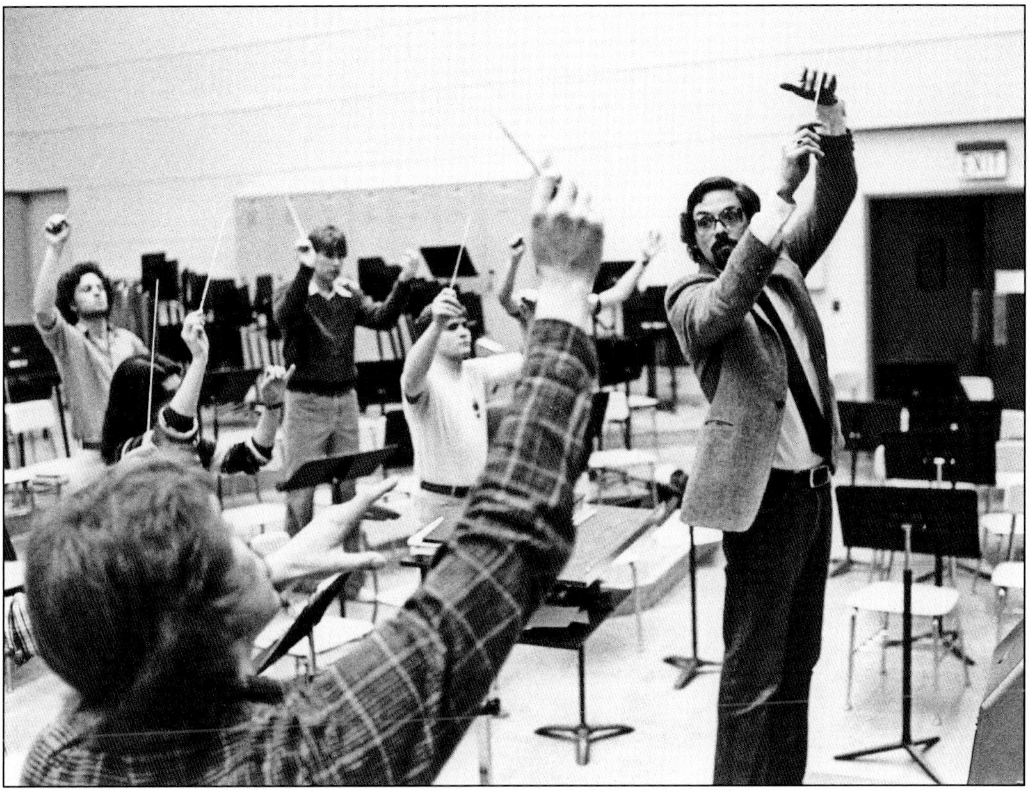

Kern Holoman, professor of music and conductor-with-a-flair of the university's orchestra, is pictured teaching his dramatic techniques, most likely to students in Music 113 (Introduction to Conducting). Ten years as department chair were wedged into Holoman's busy schedule of performances great and small (including most graduations) and his scholarship, which culminated in a major work on Berlioz. (SCL.)

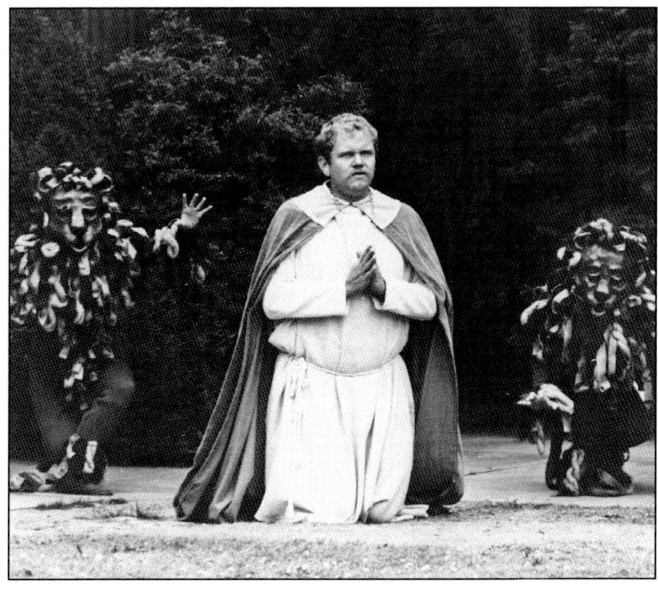

Warren Roberts, shown here in a 1976 dramatic production of the 13th-century *Play of Daniel* is a well-known campus personality. With a fine voice and stage demeanor, music could well have been his profession. Instead, his interest in botany led him to become the superintendent of the UC Davis Arboretum. Known for his arboretum field trips, Roberts has become a walking encyclopedia of plants, ecological relationships, and plant lore. (SCL.)

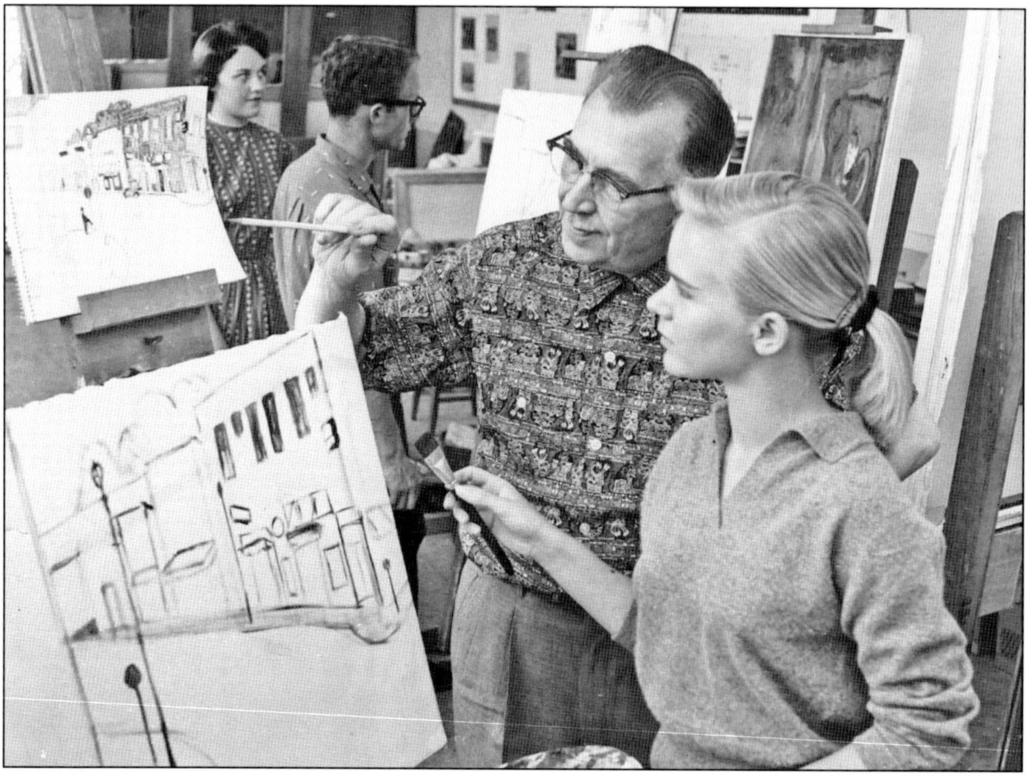

Richard L. Nelson chaired the art department from 1958 to 1966, a time when a several notable artists were recruited and brought eminence to the department. The attraction of Davis for artists was sometimes said to be due to the freshness of its atmosphere and lack of departmental politics. The main campus gallery is named after Nelson, a painter with works in major museums. (SCL.)

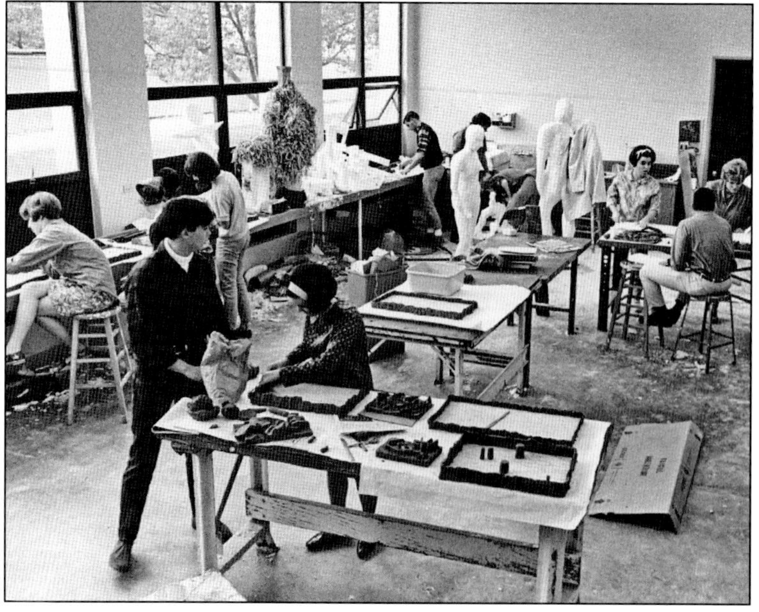

Shown here is instruction in a sculpture studio. The Art Annex near the main art building holds studio spaces like this one, and the more famous Temporary Building 9 (TB-9) is home of the ceramics studio. The creative atmosphere in TB-9 was especially electric when students of Robert Arneson and other new California ceramicists practiced their craft during the 1960s and 1970s. (SCL.)

Professor of viticulture A.J. Winkler is shown demonstrating the proper pruning of grape vines, probably during the 1960s. Students in the Department of Viticulture and Enology have gone on to become managers of some of the best vineyards and wineries in the state, the country, and the world. (SCL.)

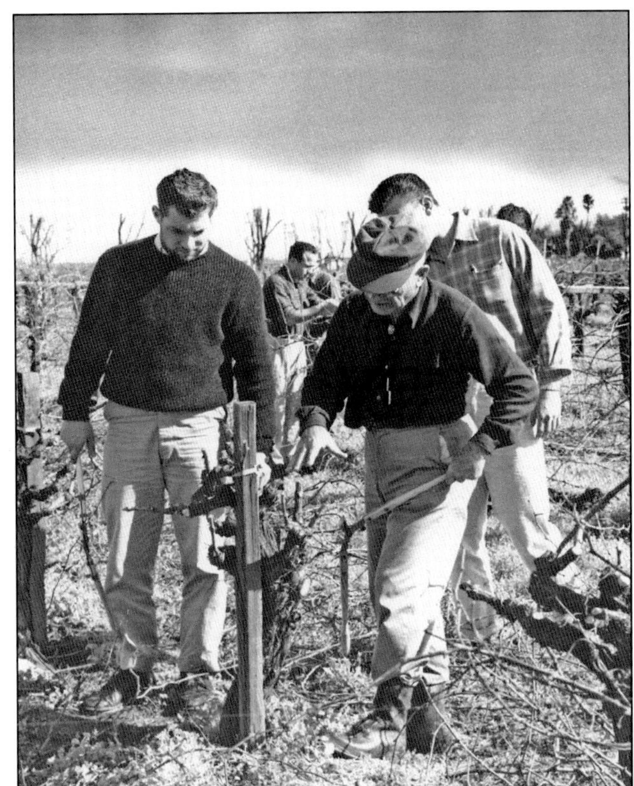

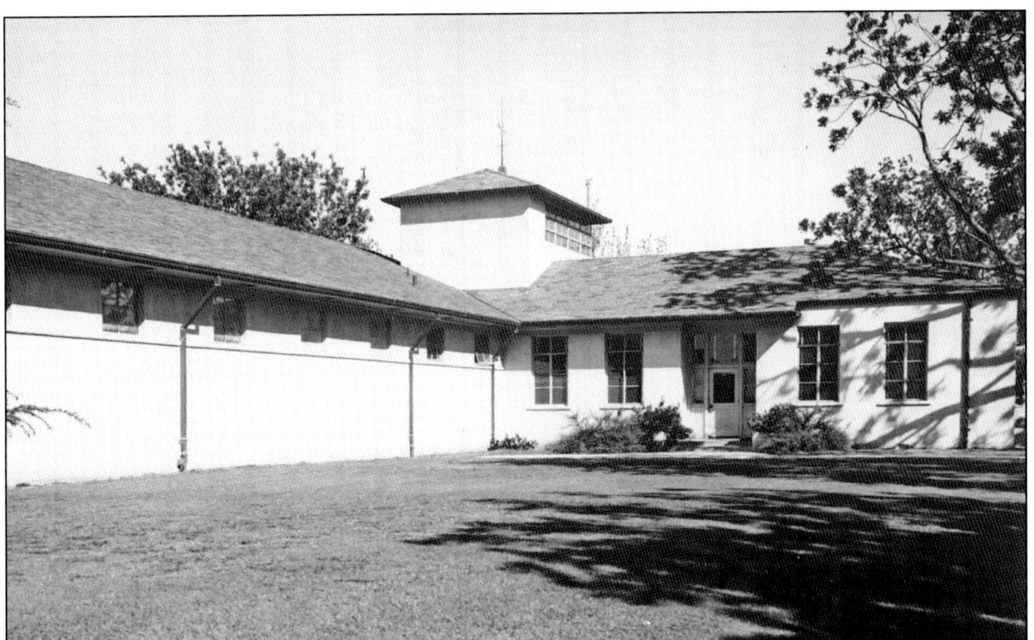

The 14,000-square-foot enology laboratory, built in 1939, featured wine cellar basements, crushing facilities, and a multistory brandy still. Often thought to be an annex to Wickson Hall, the lab actually preceded Wickson by 20 years. For 70 years, this was the center of the campus expertise in winemaking. (SCL.)

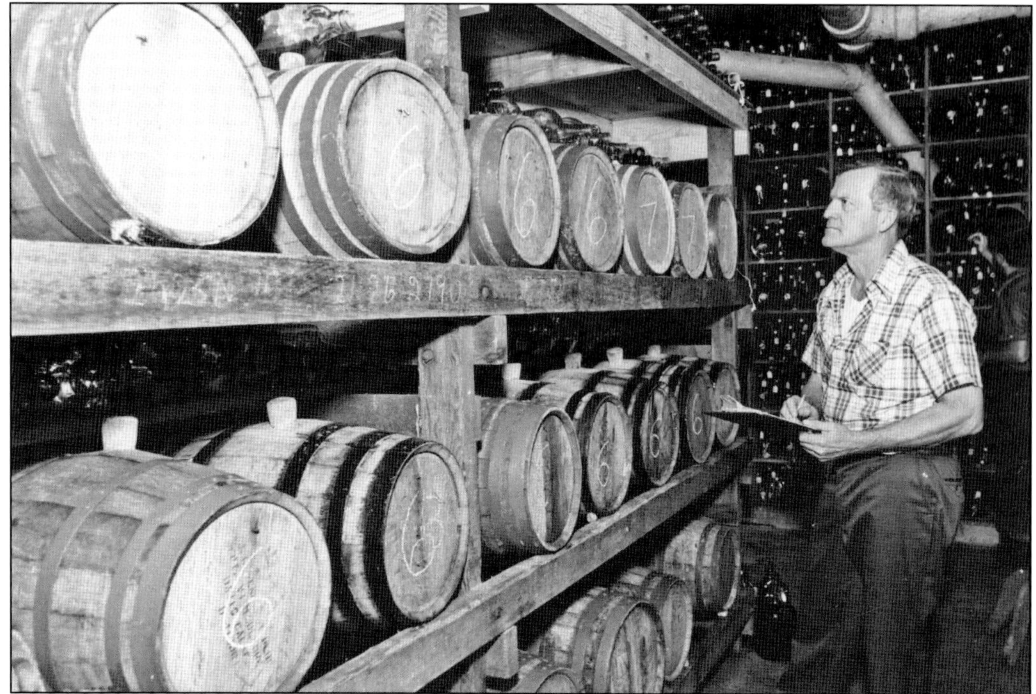

In one of four basement wine cellars, longtime campus winemaker Harry Brenner takes notes. Casks were for sherry or brandy. There was a red wine room, where temperature controls were set differently than in the storage rooms for white wines. Thousands of wine samples from around the state and from decades of vintages were collected here. While this was a research cellar, it was also a resource that savvy chancellors could draw on to impress important visitors. (SCL.)

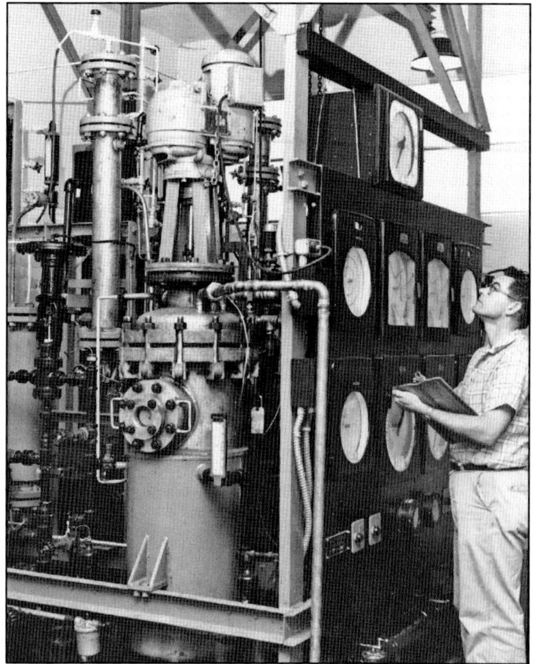

This assemblage of machinery and instrumentation from the early 1950s was used for experiments in winemaking and study of the fermentation process under variable and controlled conditions. Harry Brenner's winemaking career, which spanned 1951 to 1983, began at Davis when he was hired for his aircraft mechanic skills that enabled him to operate this ensemble. Temperature, pressure, and oxygen were some of the variables manipulated and recorded as crushed grapes were stirred and stored on their way to becoming wine. (SCL.)

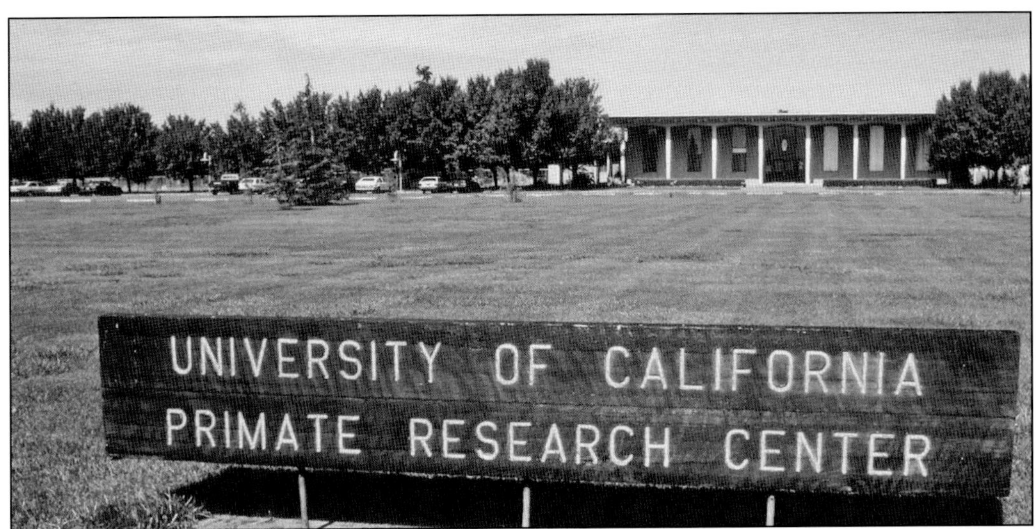

A major addition to UC Davis—300 acres at the far west end of the campus and many millions of dollars per year in research funding—is the Center for Primate Biology, underwritten since 1962 largely by the National Institutes of Health. Designed for the study of the biology and health of primates, this was one of seven complementary centers constituting an integrated national research program. The presence of the veterinarian school on campus and the initiative of Chancellor Mrak are credited with winning this research facility. (CPB.)

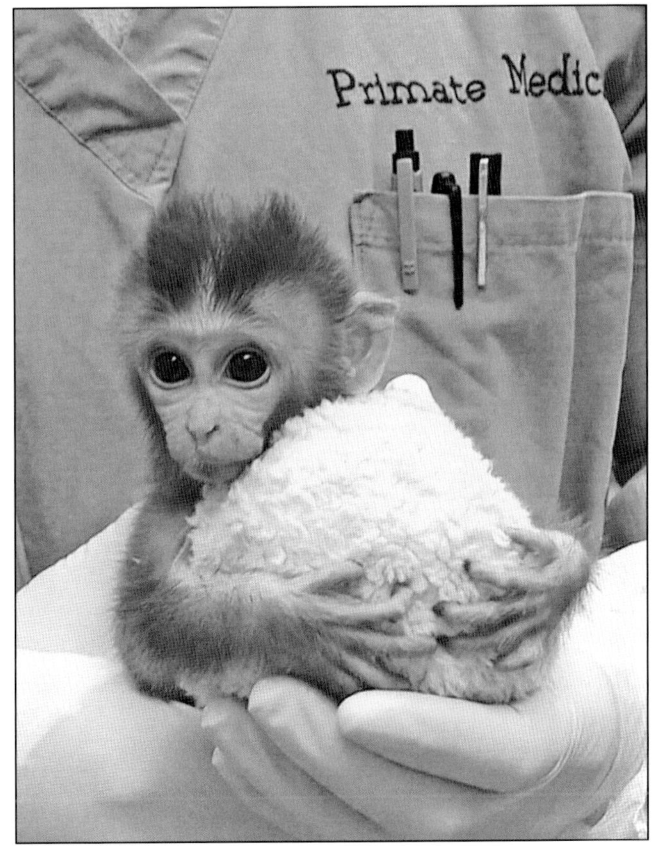

Presently home to around 5,000 monkeys, the Primate Center began studies in primate biology with just 350 monkeys. Research projects have included the effects of air pollution and second-hand smoke on primate lungs. The center was among the first to identify HIV/AIDS. Today's mission is focused on biomedical research pertaining to human health–related problems, to provide necessary information before proceeding to clinical trials in humans for new drugs and therapies. The photograph shows an infant rhesus monkey. (CPB.)

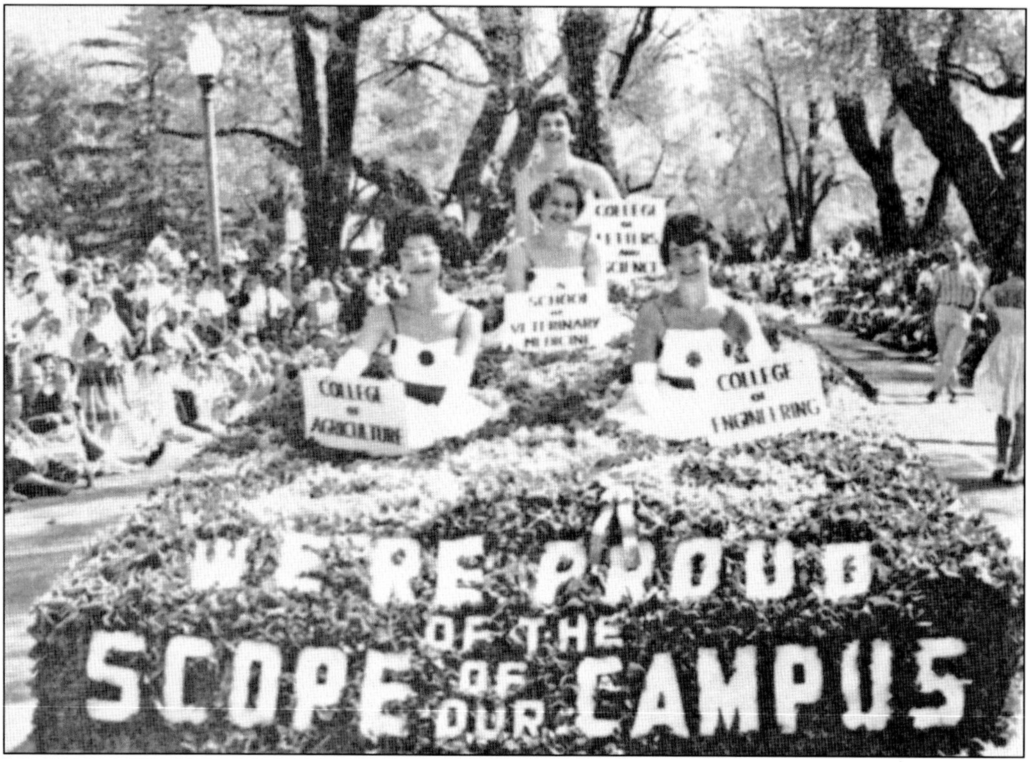

This Picnic Day parade entry in 1962 proclaims that the students of Struve Hall are "proud of the scope of our campus." A float decorated with paper and floral coverings shows three colleges (Agriculture, Engineering, and Letters & Sciences) joined by the School of Veterinary Medicine (depicted on signs held by college women). Before long, a medical school, a law school, a School of Administration, and an array of graduate programs would have to be added to any such float. (YB, JL.)

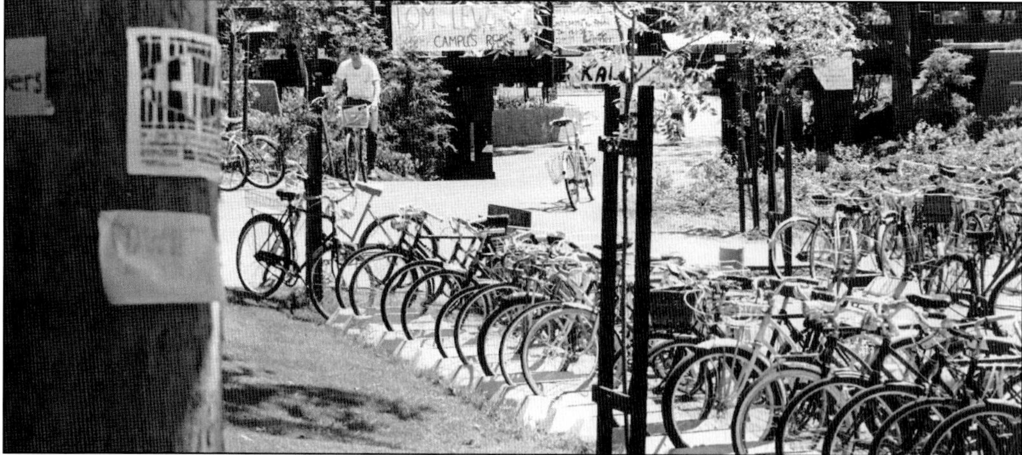

The busiest bike corridor on campus during the late 1960s was this zone between Olson Hall and the library's eastern entrance. Bike facilities added here and elsewhere included bike lanes, traffic circles, and overcrossings and underpasses to separate pedestrians and bikes. Massive bike parking lots and, eventually, bike-locking stands came, and cars were banished from the core campus. (YCA.)

Five

Student Life

Traditions and Activities

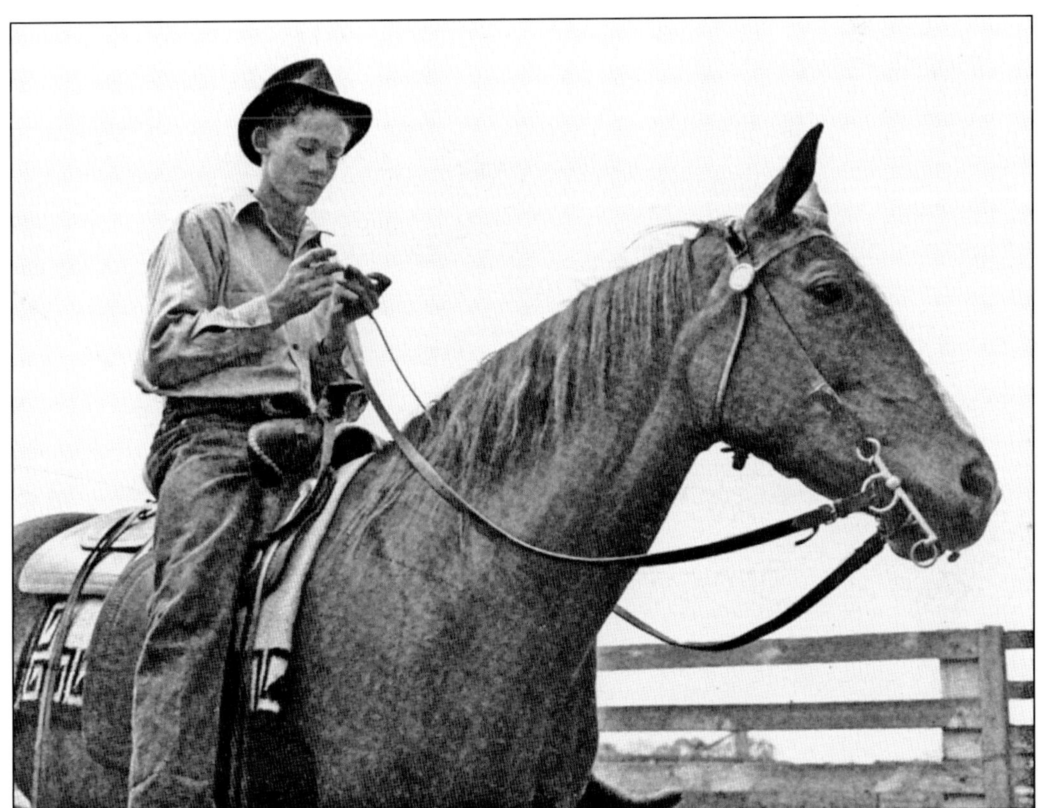

Aggie self-perception linked the campus with ranching and cowboy images. This Ansel Adams photograph from the 1935 booklet *The Farm that Became a College* captures what was once a normal Davis scene. At this school, one can ride a horse. Contrasting images of the farm and the ranch are seen in yearbooks. The peak for horse pictures was in the 1950s, coinciding with Westerns of film and television. (SCL.)

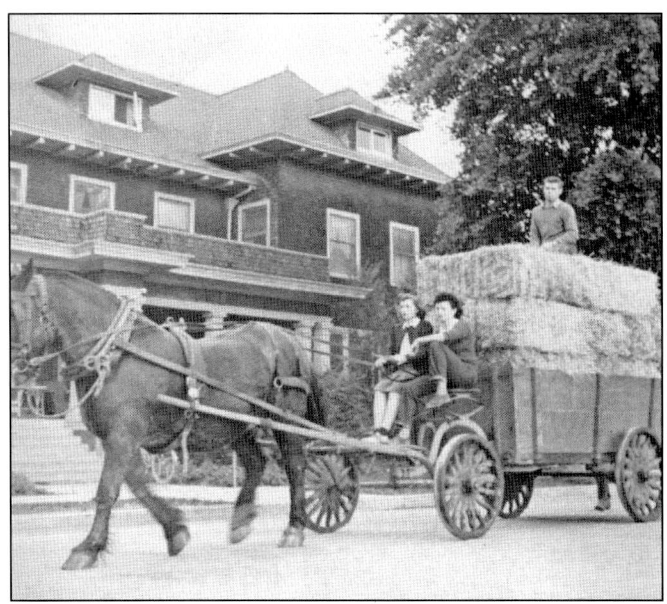

Two coeds are in the driver's seat here in 1941, and 16 bales fill the wagon as it rolls around the quad. Examination A required all students in agriculture to demonstrate their competence in plowing a furrow with a horse, stacking hay, and driving a wagon. At that time, women also took their physical education classes in the form of equestrian training. (YB, JL.)

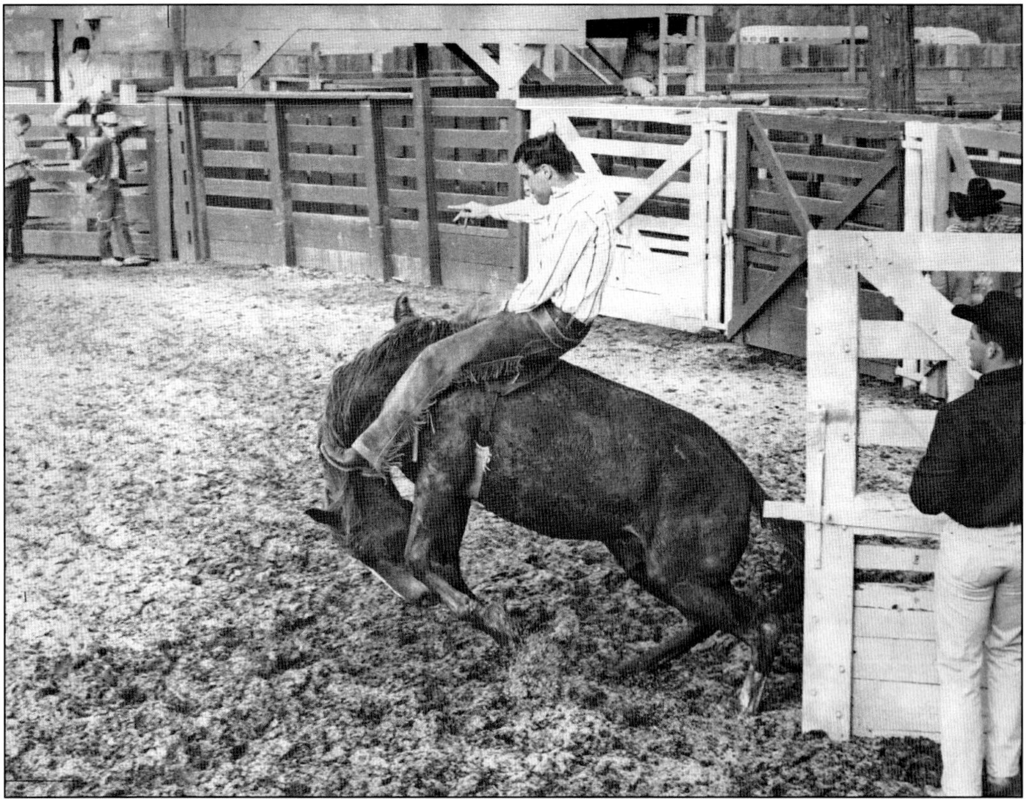

A horse barn, sheds, and arena built in the 1920s cluster near today's Harold Cole Facility for the Study of the Biology of Large Animals. The arena was also once the rodeo grounds. Picnic Day events, stock judging, and even full rodeos went on into the 1960s. The equine side of campus today no longer includes the rough spectacle of bronco riding but with its herd of hundreds of horses, it focuses on teaching and research. (SCL.)

The photograph seen here from the 1941 yearbook is captioned "AGR 'dudes' gather around bunkhouse." The caption suggests a cowboy identity so pervasive that it can be spoofed. Alpha Gamma Rho (AGR), established in 1923, is the longest-lived Greek house among today's fraternities and sororities. Its symbols include a large plow in front of a sprawling ranch house. (YB, JL.)

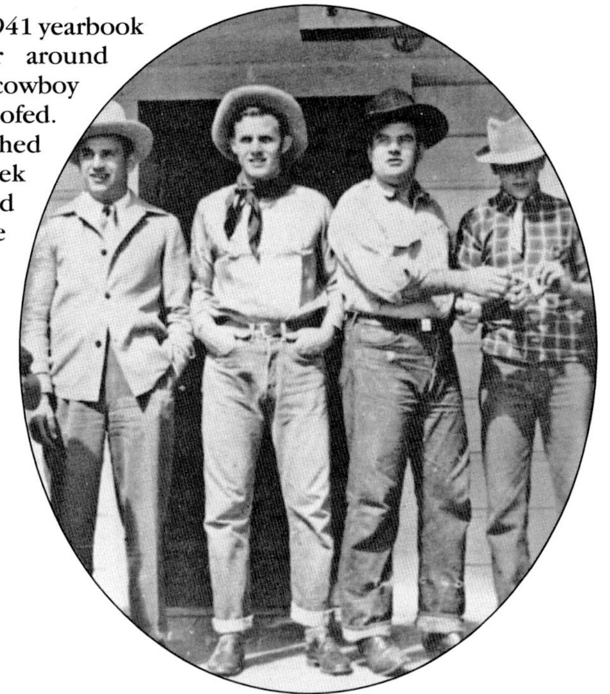

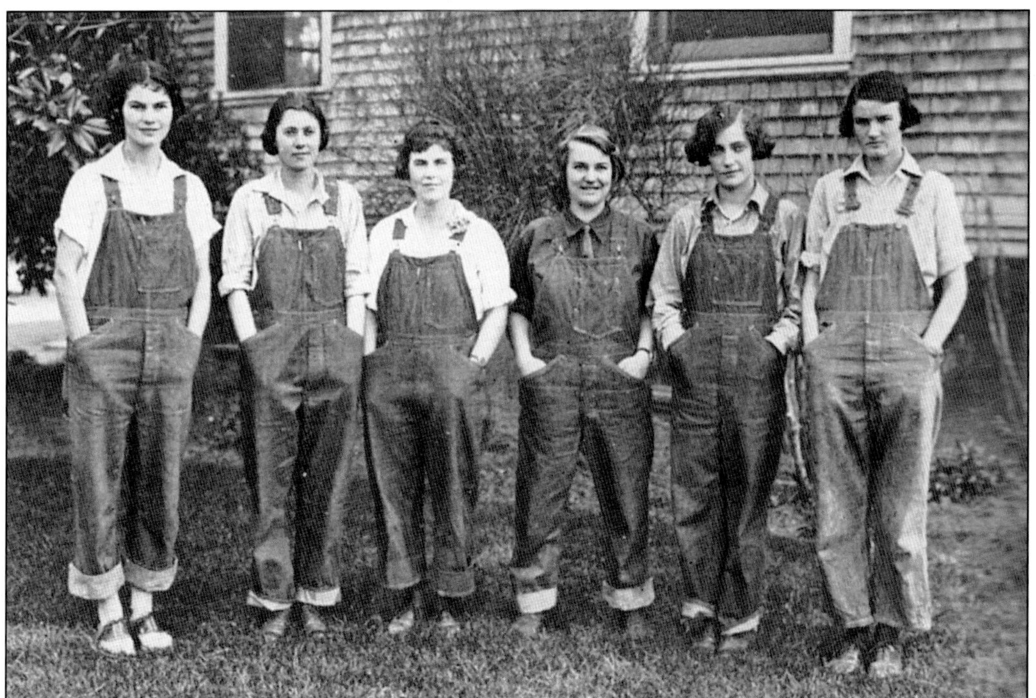

This 1924 photograph is about volunteer work on Labor Day, but few of the small minority of female students actually dressed in bib overalls at other times. Women did participate in winning teams in livestock judging competitions, however, and on a notable day in 1928, Alyce "Williams" Jewett led the Picnic Day parade atop the notoriously spirited stallion Gun Rock. (YB, JL.)

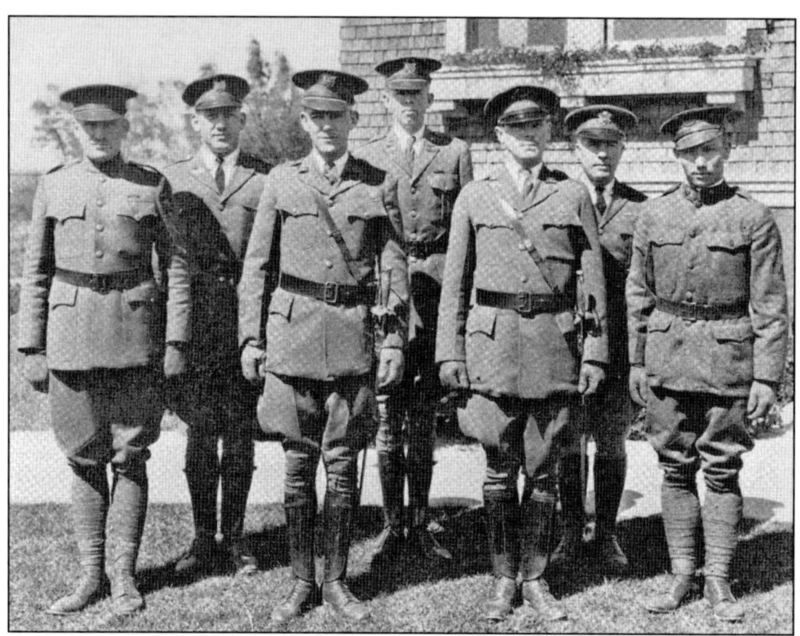

The Reserve Officers Training Corp (ROTC) has been required since the federal Morrill Act of 1862 funded land-grant colleges. Yearbooks suggest a high profile for ROTC at Davis. Here is a 1927 group of trainees. Congruent with military training, Davis has had a strong tradition of competitive rifle shooting teams. (YB, JL.)

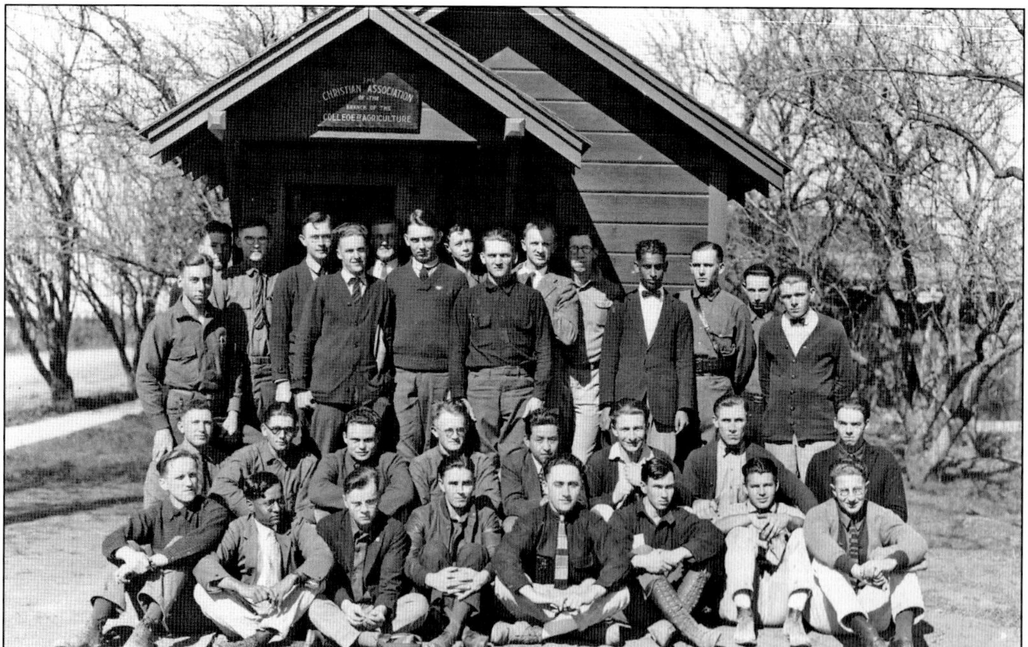

The Christian Association of the Branch of the College of Agriculture is the sign on the door in 1924 when this small building began serving as a chapel. Like most of the state's public college campuses, Davis had no large chapel on campus, though it was common at schools in the East. This structure, more clubhouse in style than chapel, was just off campus at the eastern boundary. (YB, JL.)

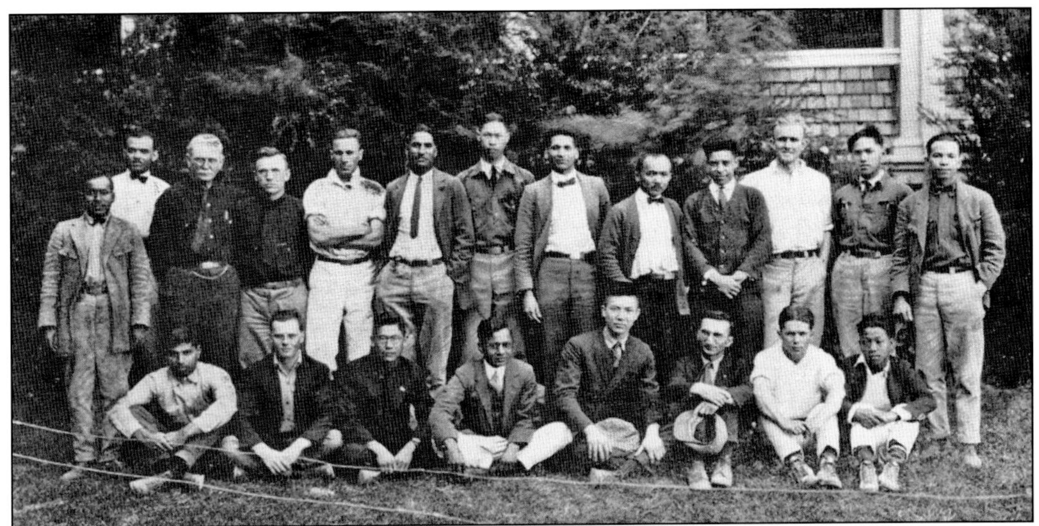

Agronomist John W. Gilmore, who spent years in foreign areas, organized and advised the "Cosmopolitan Club" during most of his nearly 30 years at Davis. Globalist in outlook, club members met in Gilmore's house, joined by Professor Kleiber at times. The club was affiliated with the Carnegie Endowment for International Peace. (YB, JL.)

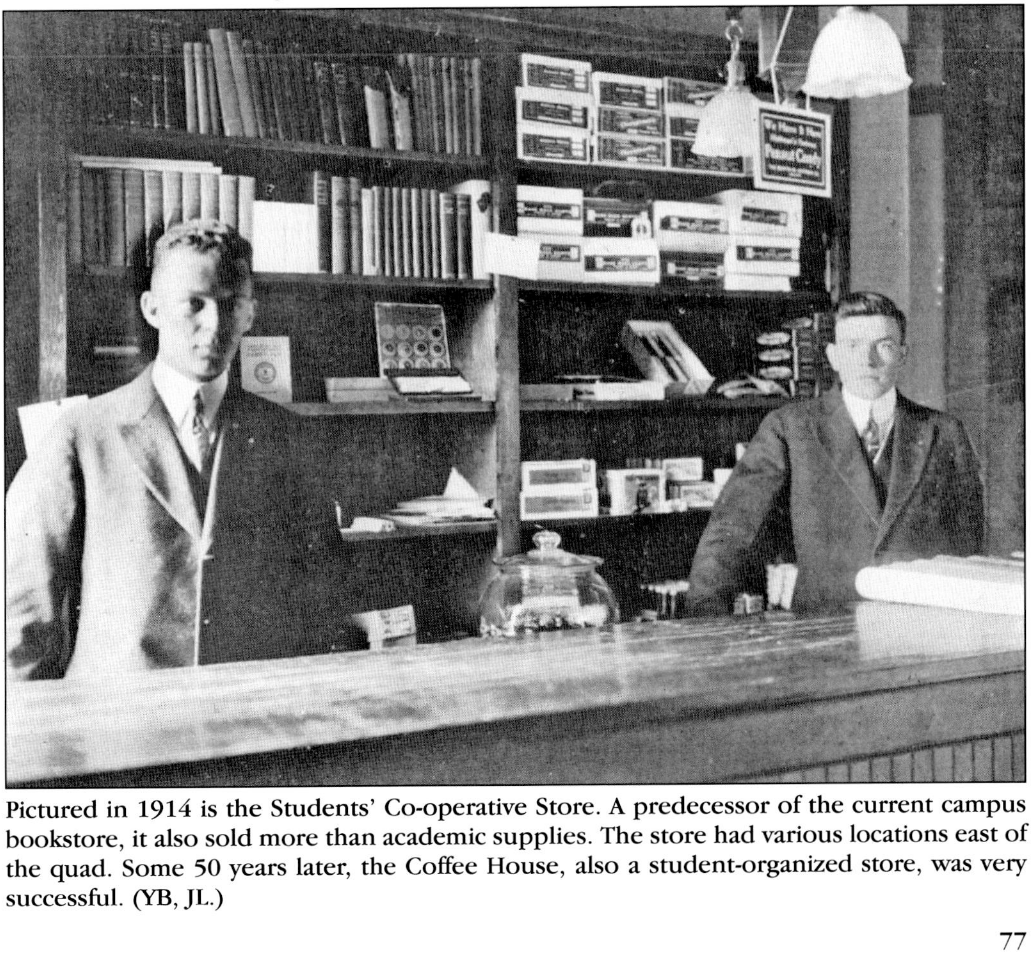

Pictured in 1914 is the Students' Co-operative Store. A predecessor of the current campus bookstore, it also sold more than academic supplies. The store had various locations east of the quad. Some 50 years later, the Coffee House, also a student-organized store, was very successful. (YB, JL.)

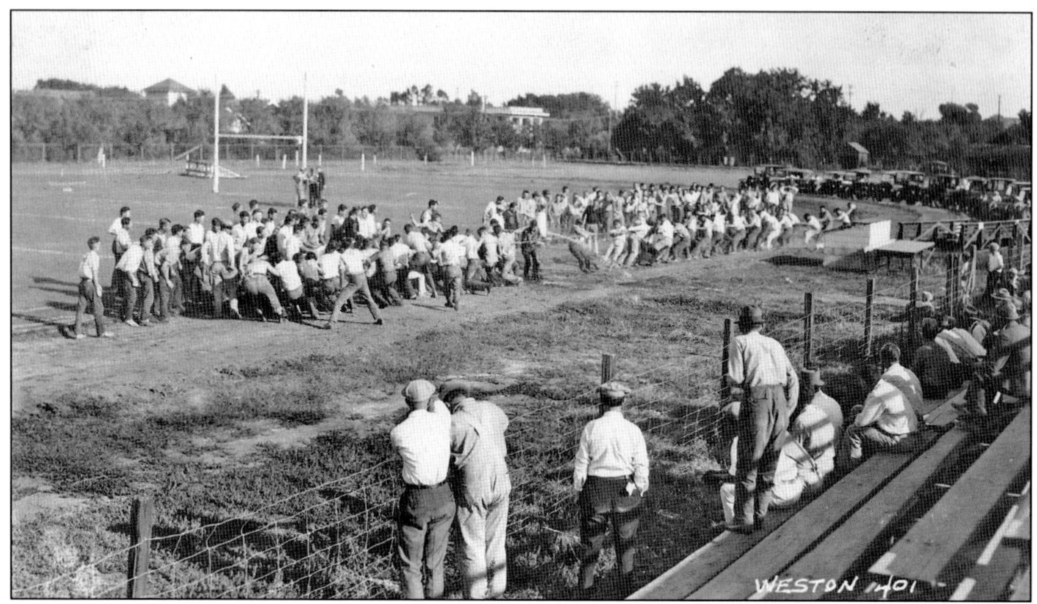

This rare photograph of an early tug of war probably dates from the 1920s. The first-year students competed with upperclassmen in a test of strength and intra-class coordination. The event became part of the frosh-soph brawl, preserved or reenacted into the 1960s. Here, the muddy event takes place in the football stadium. This image also offers a view of houses facing A Street, some of which remain today. (SCL.)

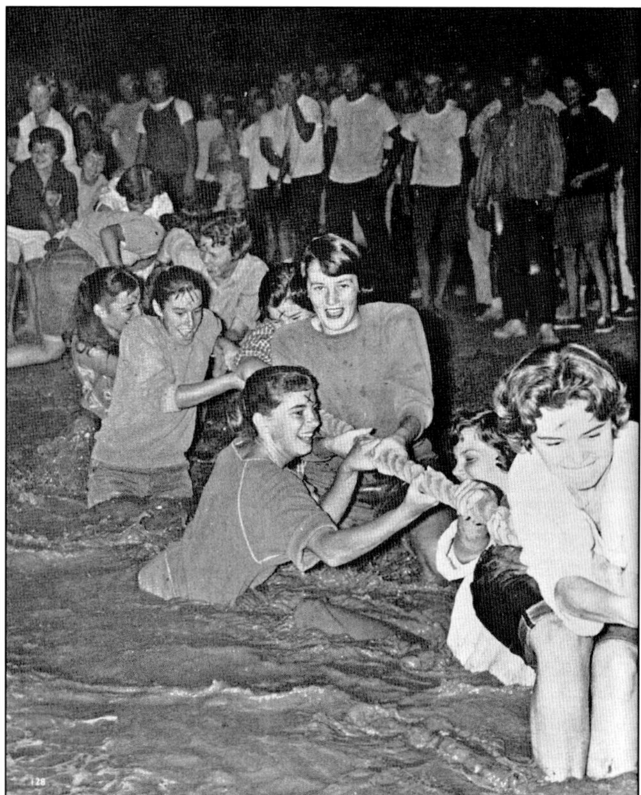

In a traditional competition dating back to the first decade of the University Farm, the frosh-soph brawl ended in a dirty dunk for the losers. In the fall of 1959, the water is deep, and women are doing the tugging. The rewards of winning included permission to stop wearing the freshman "dink" caps. (YB, JL.)

At the conclusion of the fall homecoming Pajamarino event, a bonfire near the football field attracted big crowds. The epic blaze of 1966, one of the last, shot flames 200 feet into the air. One year, the fuel included fruit boxes stacked three stories tall. The night's sequence of events involved a march to the train station to serenade and greet returning alumni. (SCL.)

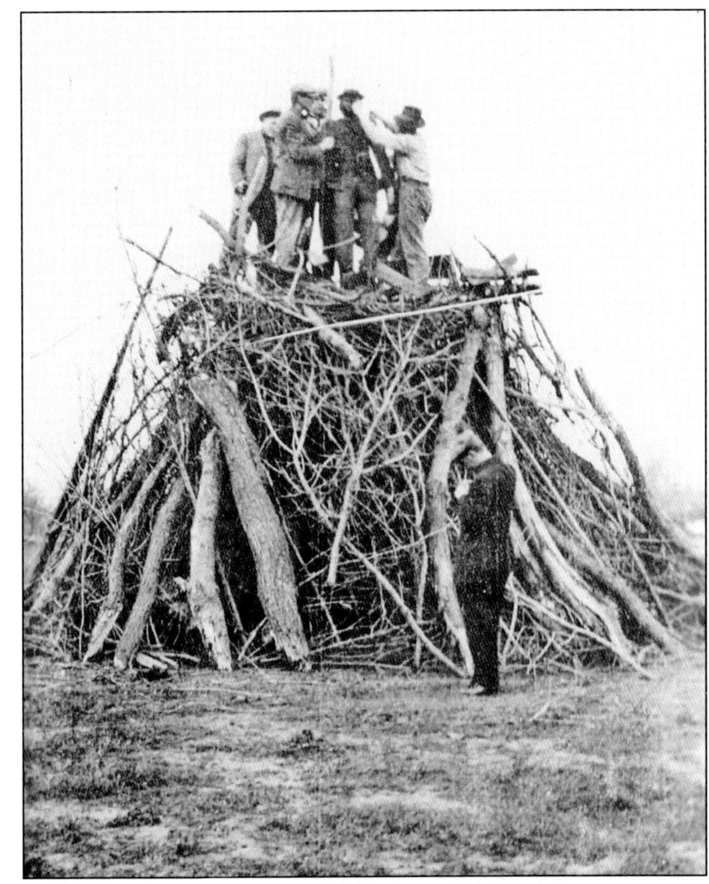

Marching down Second Street from campus to the train station, the Pajamarino of 1959 featured Bill Hollingshead on clarinet, presaging his role with the university orchestra on a European tour 53 years later. Pajama costumes are de rigueur for participants, but a raccoon coat adds wacky diversity. (YB, JL.)

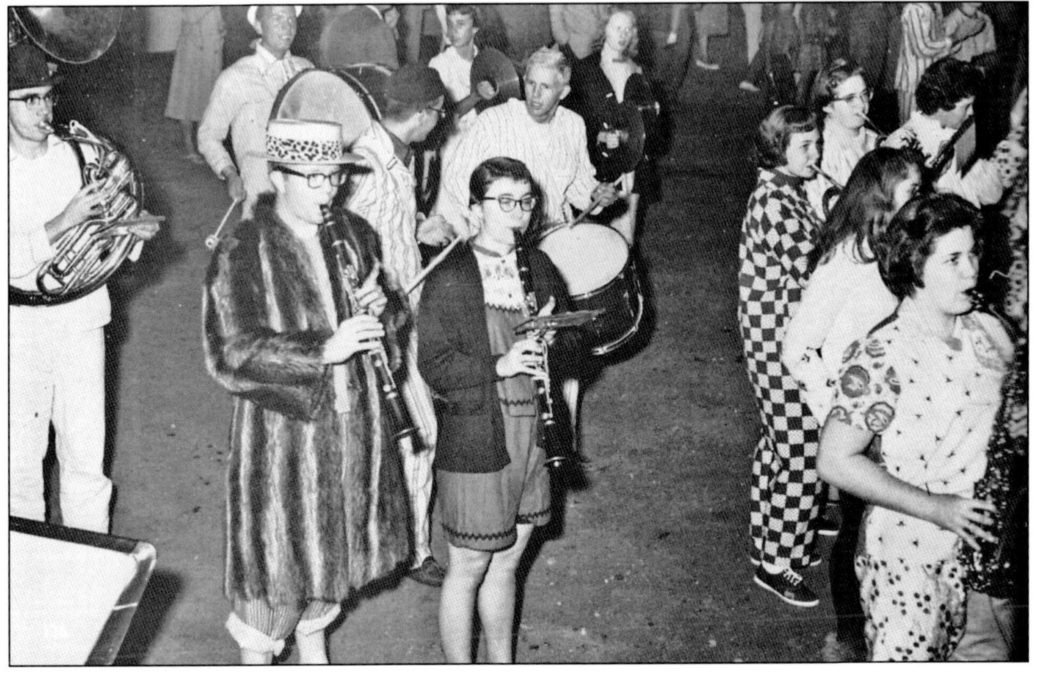

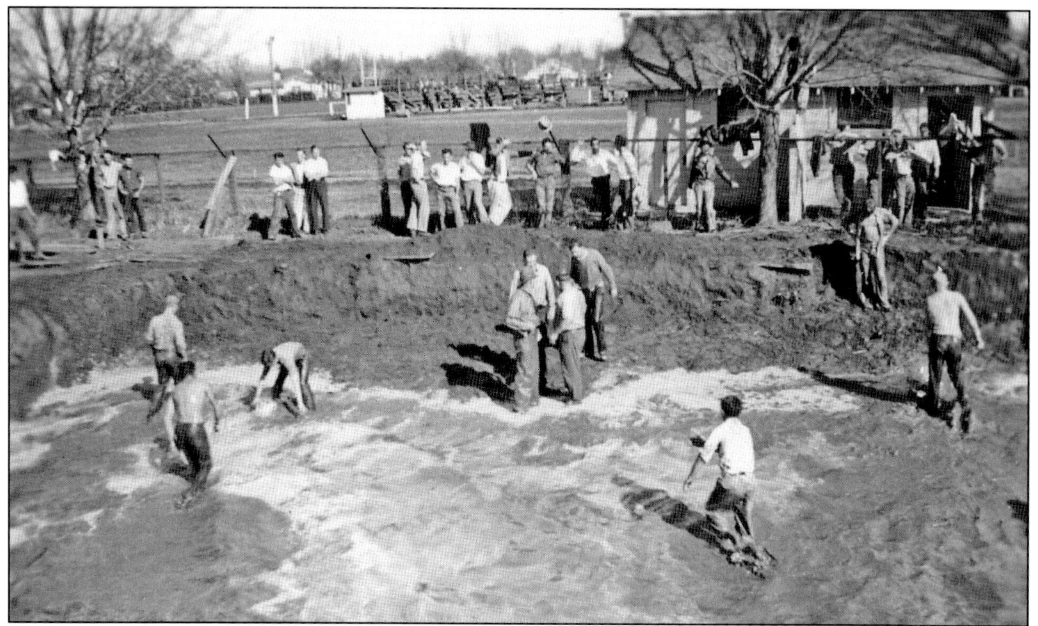

A Labor Day project in 1936 had students digging the hole for what would become the new Recreation Hall (Hickey Gym) swimming pool in 1938. The after-lunch swim in the rapidly filled hole was reported to be a thoroughly muddy experience. Even in later years, the swimming pool, nicknamed the University Plunge, was still a rarity in the county. (SCL.)

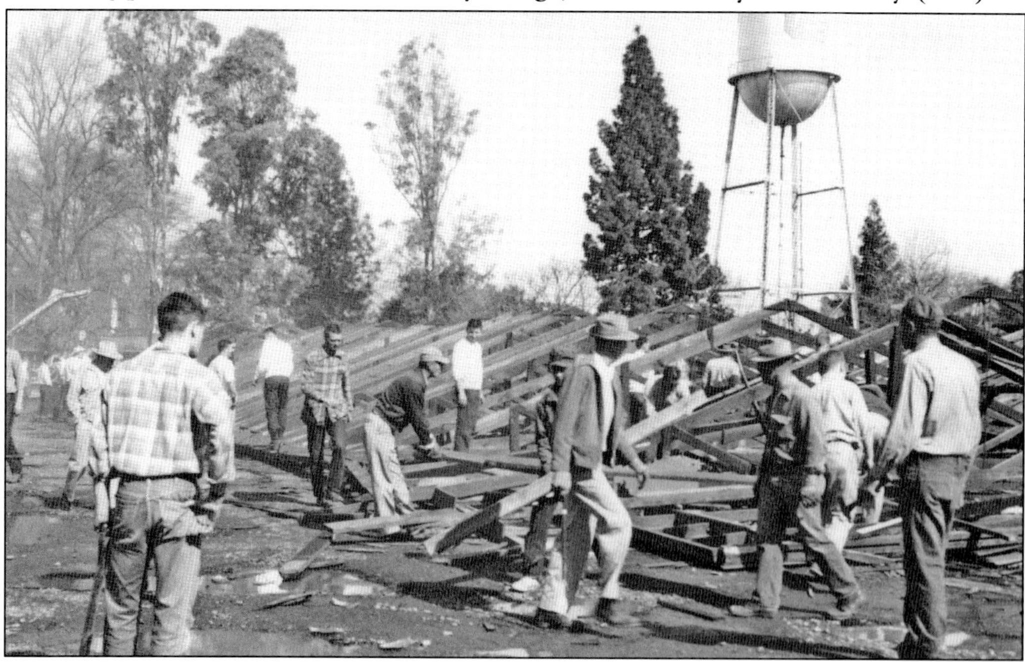

This last sanctioned Labor Day, when students performed volunteer labor on campus improvement projects, was in 1964. During the first Labor Day in 1915, athletic fields, fences, and walks were constructed or repaired. The event was a leap-year tradition for a while. Volunteers seen here are tearing down the old cashier's building. The old-fashioned water tower, a campus icon, is seen in the background shortly before its removal. (SCL.)

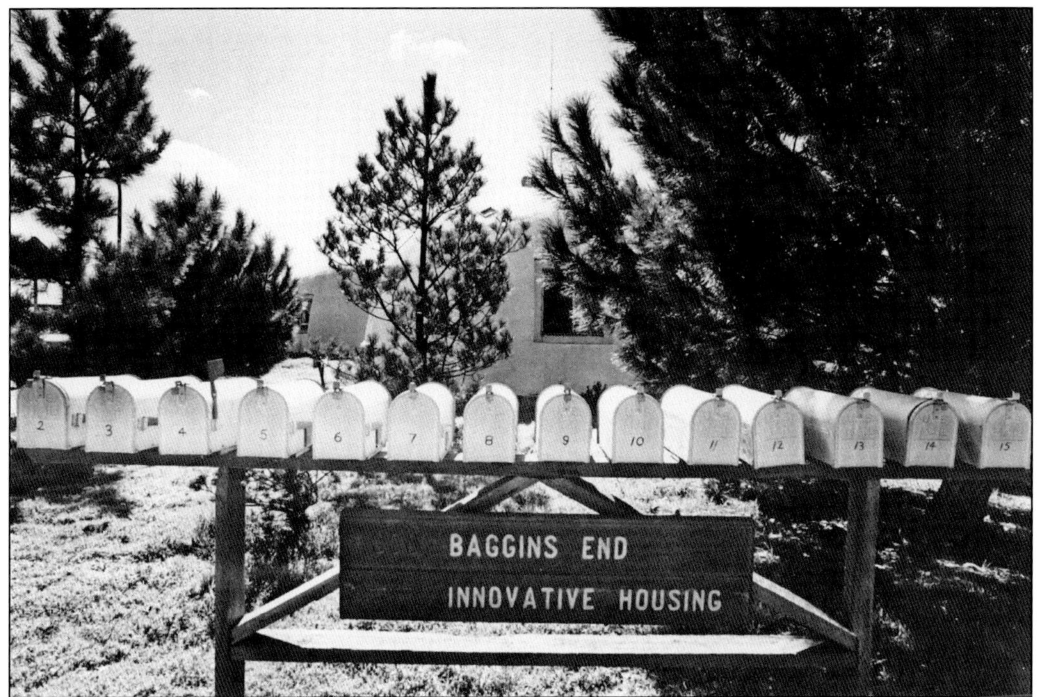

Constructed in late 1972 by professional crews, the Baggins End innovative housing project was a student initiative. Winter and spring that year were spent discussing fiberglass and foam building technologies with engineering faculty and seeking a loan for the dozen dome-shaped student apartments. Adjacent to the Experimental College student gardens, the "foam domes" landscape and lifestyle became a bit of hip heaven. (YB, JL.)

Student-run, free-form radio is shown here in transition from Beckett Dormitory's ad hoc Radio KVD-AM to the permanent KDVS-FM in the Memorial Union. Record librarian Sharron Sekerak is shown withholding an old Rolling Stones album from producer Mike Hutchinson in this 1966 yearbook photograph. Popular shows, presented by university staff as well as by student DJs, included "Waltzing Across Genres," hosted by a veterinary school staff DJ known as "the wonderfully soulful Bones." (YB, JL.)

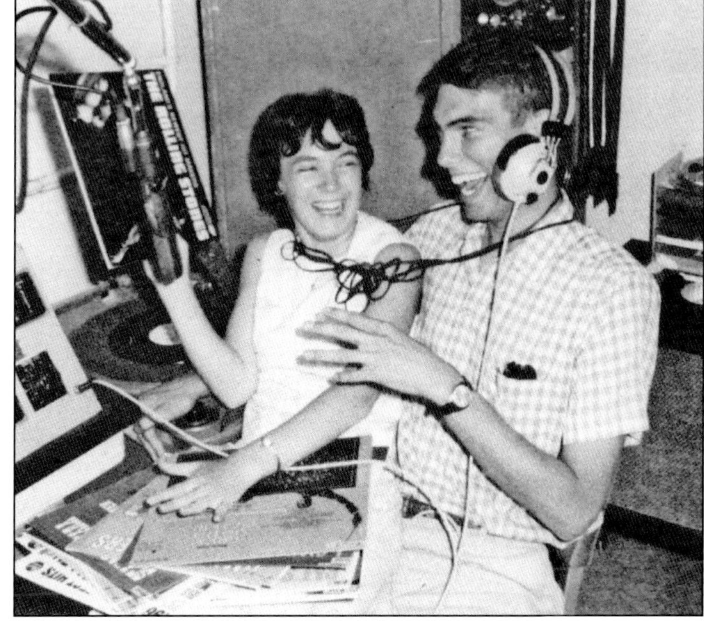

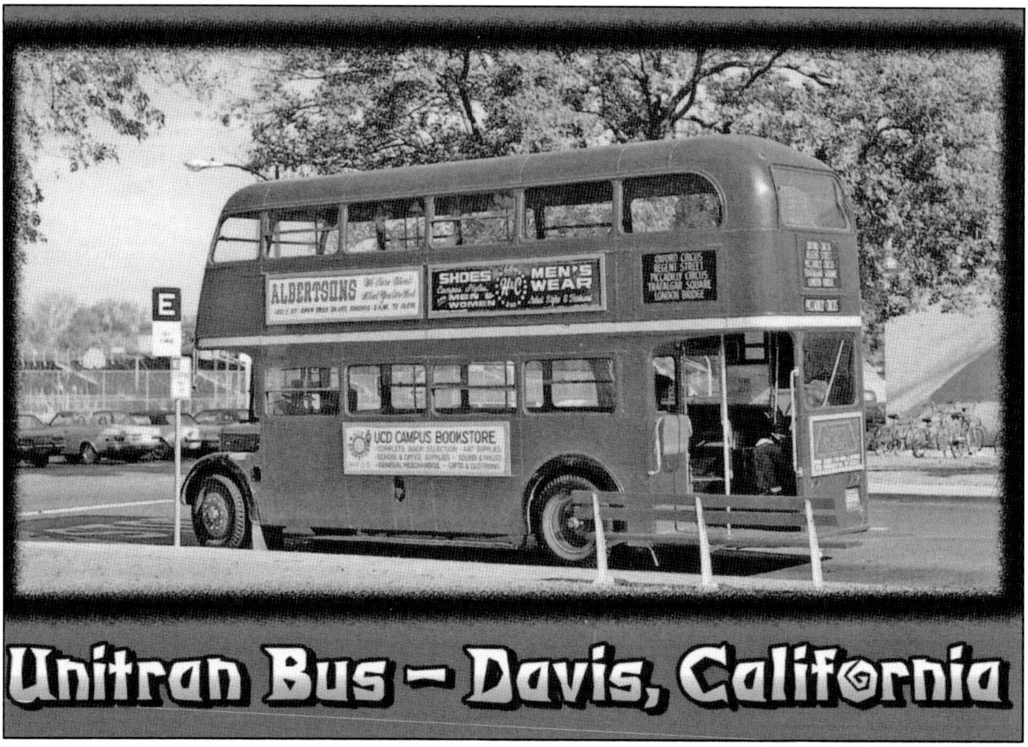

Unitran Bus – Davis, California

When Bob Black was elected president of Associated Students, University of Calfornia, Davis (ASUCD) in 1966, he had a mandate to expand student government beyond social affairs. Public transit was a goal that was achieved in the form of Unitrans, with financial support from both the campus and city. What seemed a wild idea—buying used London buses—proved possible. The buses became the symbol of the largely student-run service. (JL.)

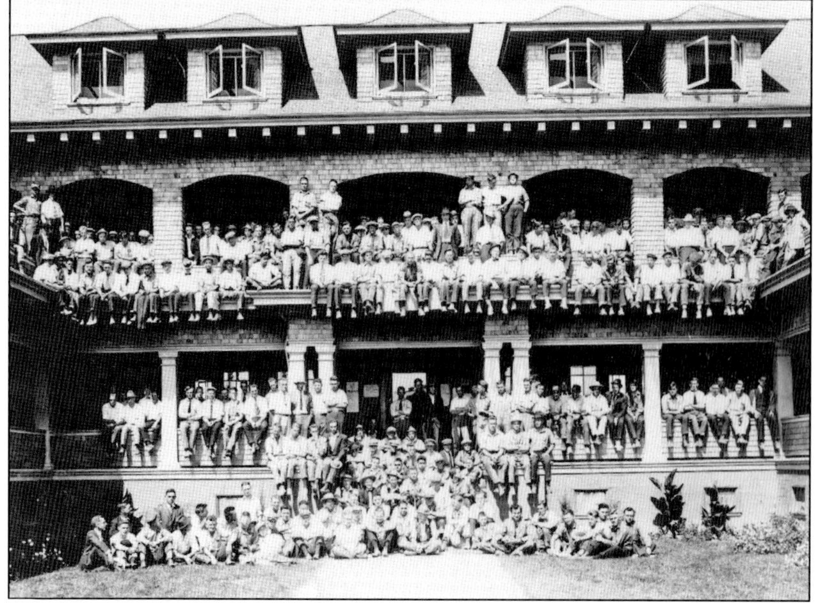

In 1916, the residents of West Hall gather for a traditional picture that became well known. When the old building was torn down in 1953 to be replaced by the new Memorial Union, West Hall exterior wall shingles were prepared as souvenirs to be distributed to alumni. (SCL.)

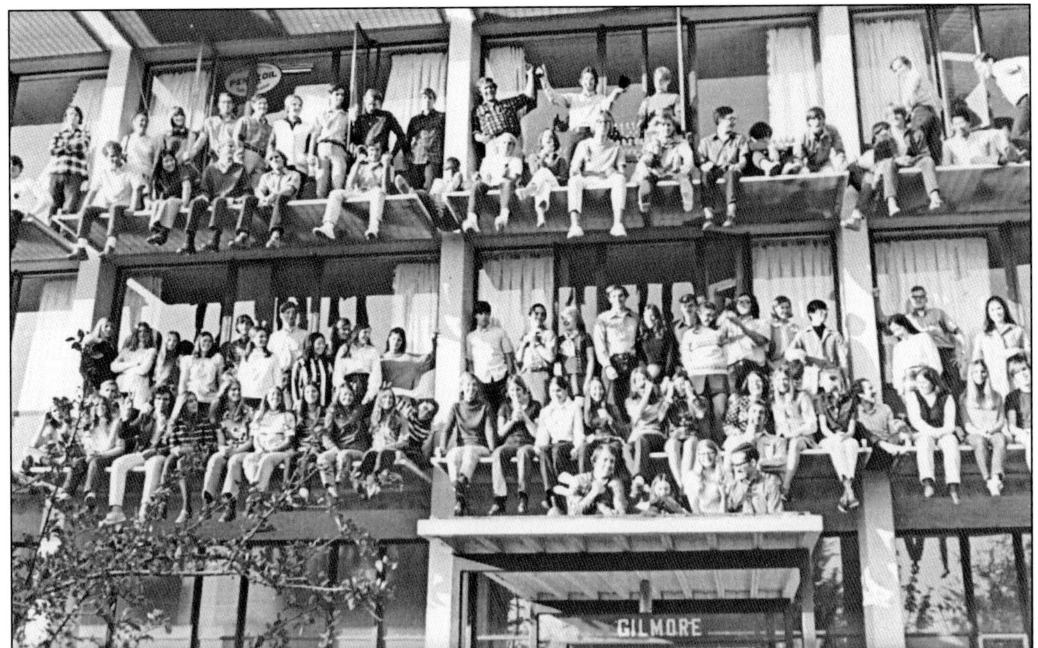

Gilmore Hall is the 1971 setting for a replication of the 1916 West Hall scene. One of four identical five-story buildings that made up the Segundo complex, it did not survive to be 50 years old (neither did West Hall). John Gilmore, for whom the hall was named, was a professor in agronomy from 1913 to 1942 and a respected organizer of activities for progressive-thinking students. (YB, JL.)

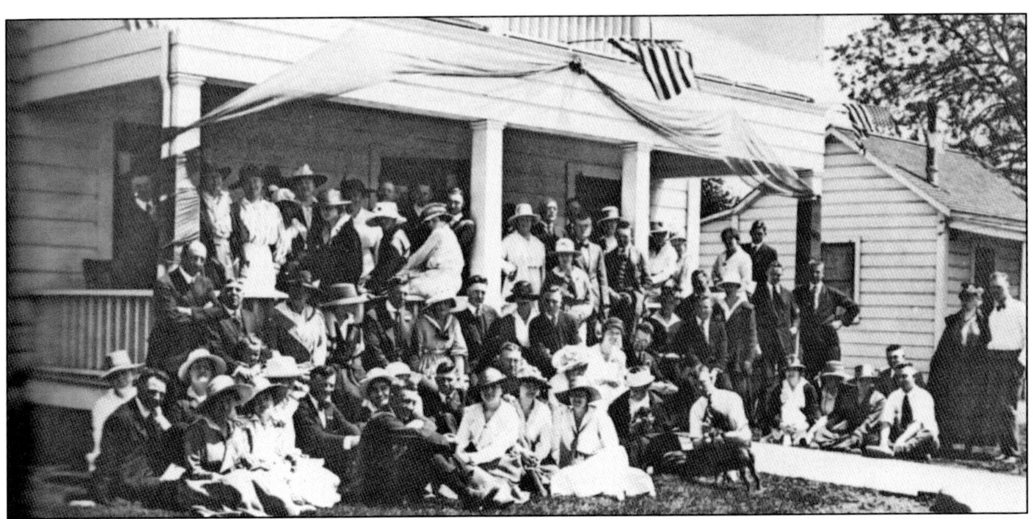

In 1914, one of the University Farm's original eight fraternities, Calpha, which later became Phi Delta Theta, bought one of the biggest houses in town. Here, at 336 C Street, the brothers gather for Picnic Day, probably in the 1930s, to see the parade go by within a block of their porch. The structure is a much-modified Presbyterian church from the 1870s. Colby "Babe" Slater was a Calpha. During World War II, the house served as an Army barracks. (YB, JL.)

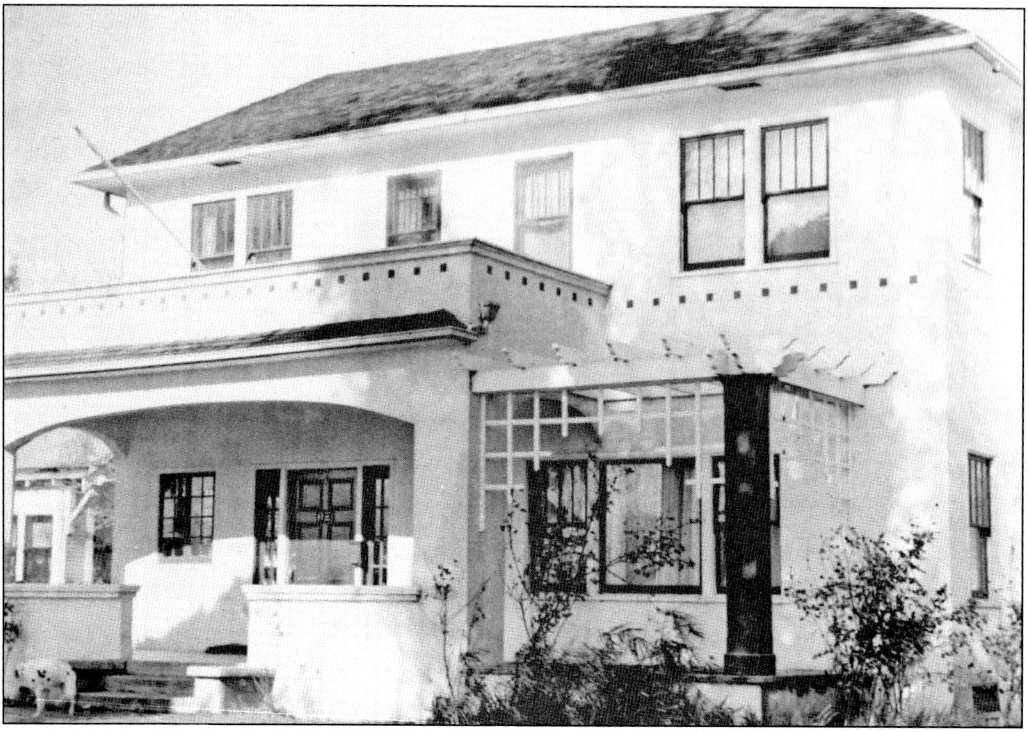

Founded like Calpha in 1912, Theta Xi owns this and two adjacent houses. The ensemble occupies First Street frontage between D and E Streets. It was the adopted fraternity of history professor W. Turrentine "Terpie" Jackson, who, for half a century, supported it in many ways. These houses, unlike most Greek venues at UC Davis, are among the first structures seen by most visitors coming into downtown Davis. (YB, JL.)

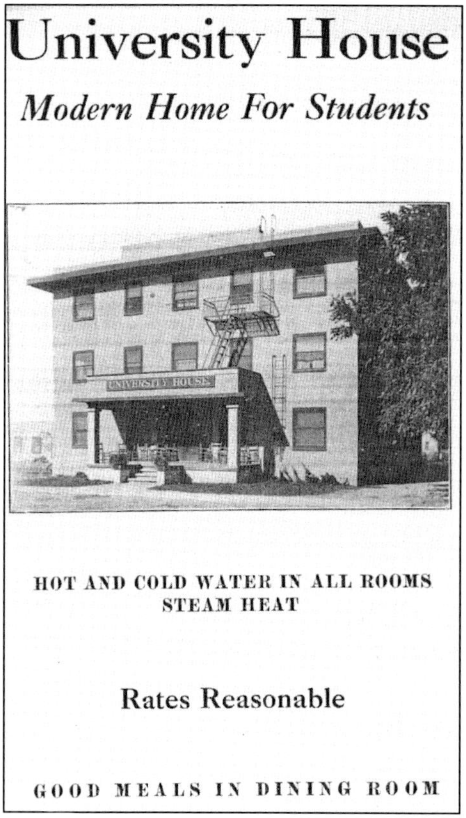

In 1920, an off-campus housing option was already in business at the northwest corner of Second and B Streets. University House, a three-story boardinghouse, was managed by the Schmeiser family. The building was advertised as having "steam heat." The interface between campus and B Street might well have become a fraternity row or a high-density student ghetto, but city government used zoning to prevent these possibilities after 1925. (YB, JL.)

A bygone tradition mourned more than most others is the Spring Sing competition. Here in the 1950s is an 80-voice women's chorus. Yearbooks of the time reported enthusiastic audiences for the choral performances put on by residence halls and Greek organizations. Venues were the Old Recreation Hall and then Freeborn Hall. (SCL.)

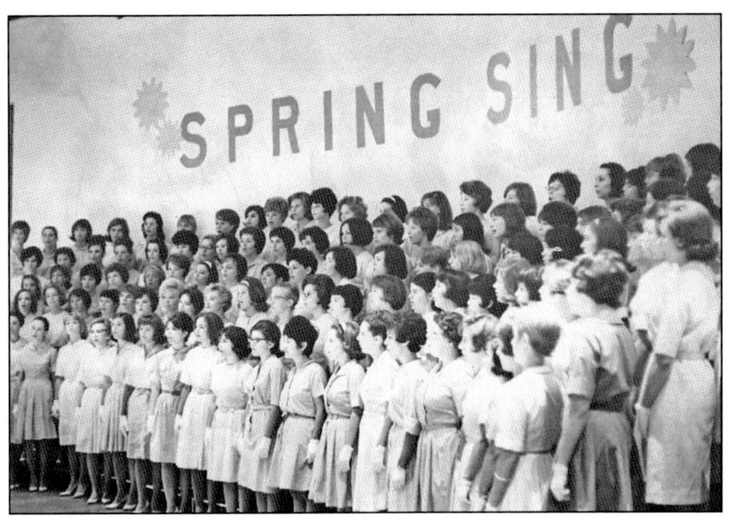

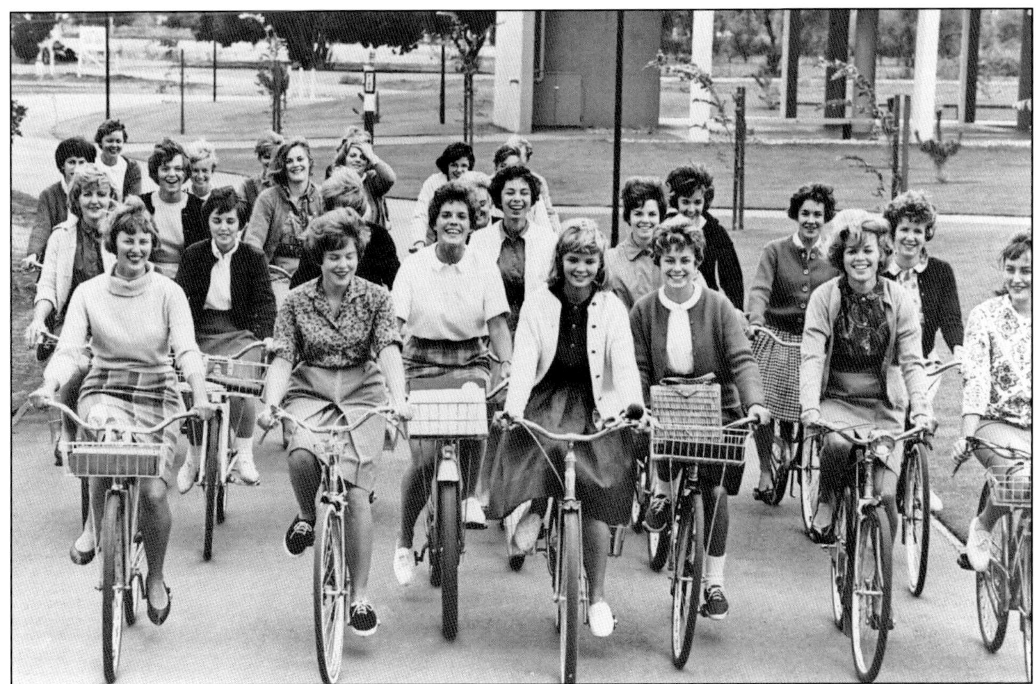

The first sign that "a bicycling campus" was an identity to rival farm or ranch themes came in the 1940s when student yearbooks began showing bike riders. This 1962 publicity photograph features women riding bikes equipped with book baskets on their commute to class. Chancellor Mrak directed his planners in the 1960s to create a supportive infrastructure for bicycles. (SCL.)

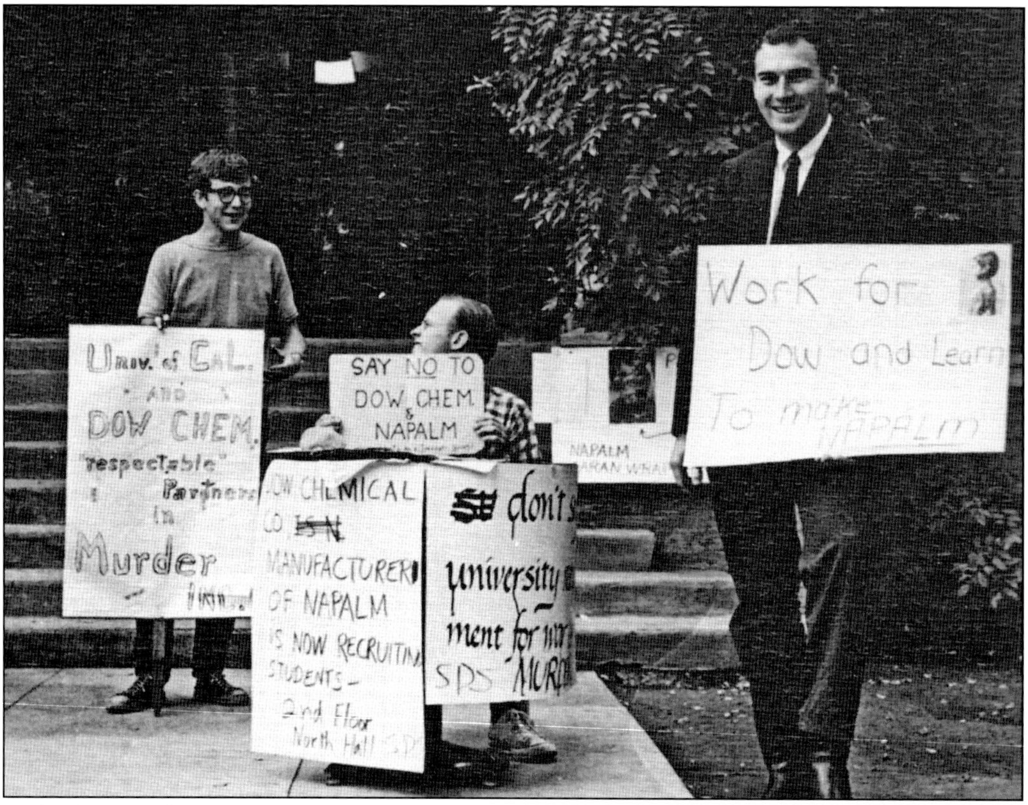

At the height of antiwar protests in 1967, while military recruiters met with prospects in North Hall, the Davis campus showed opposition to recruitment efforts. Dow Chemical, manufacturer of napalm, is said in the signs to be a "partner in murder." The signs mention Students for a Democratic Society (SDS), but the SDS was never well organized on the campus. (YB, JL.)

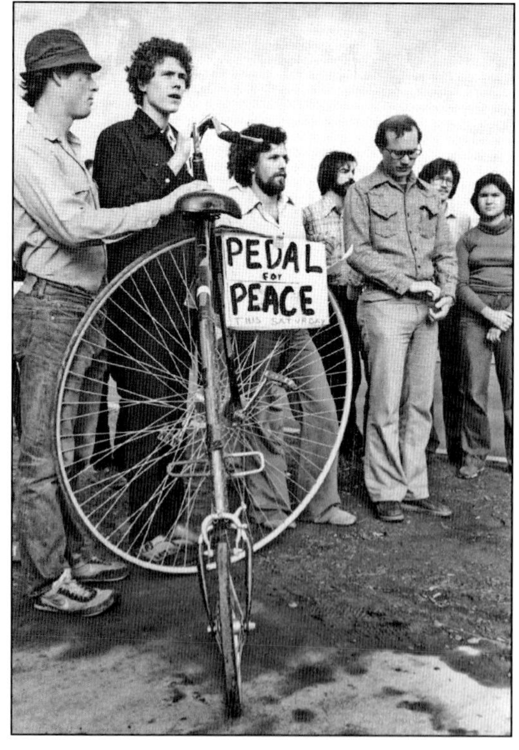

Among the students and student leaders gathered on the quad in this photograph from the era of antiwar protests is Bill Kopper, fifth from left. A law student, Kopper served on the city council of Davis for two terms from 1976 to 1984, which included a two-year stint as mayor. (YB, JL.)

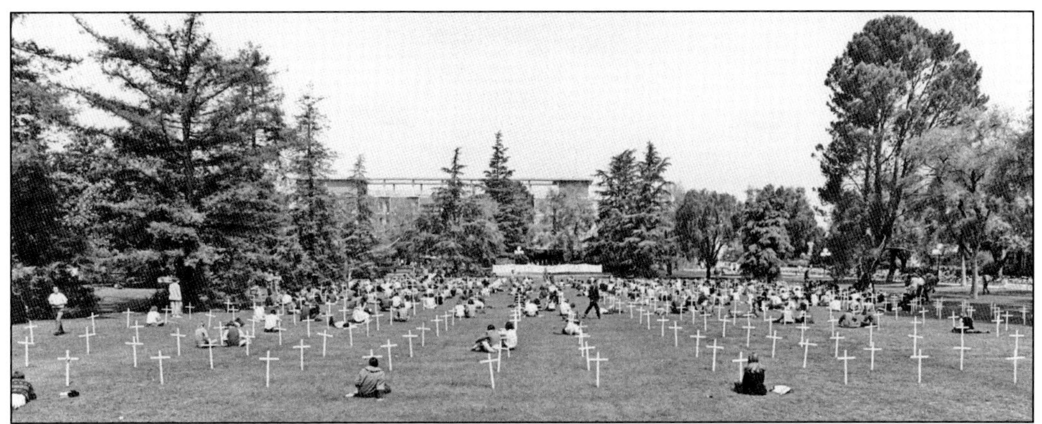

The campus experienced a three-day siege of protest in April 1970, which was part of a longer period of protest. During that event, a field of 500 crosses was planted in the grassy quad, making an eloquent statement. Another high point of protest was on May 26, 1969, when UCD leaders helped organize a state capitol gathering that was, at around 7,000 persons, one of the largest in California history. (SCL.)

The most dramatic event of the war protest era occurred in May 1972, when a splinter group of protesters broke away from the main group of 1,500 on the quad. They marched downtown, tried to stop traffic on the I-80 freeway, and then blockaded the Southern Pacific Railroad tracks by the station. Sixty-six individuals were arrested for sitting on the tracks and interfering with the train. (SCL.)

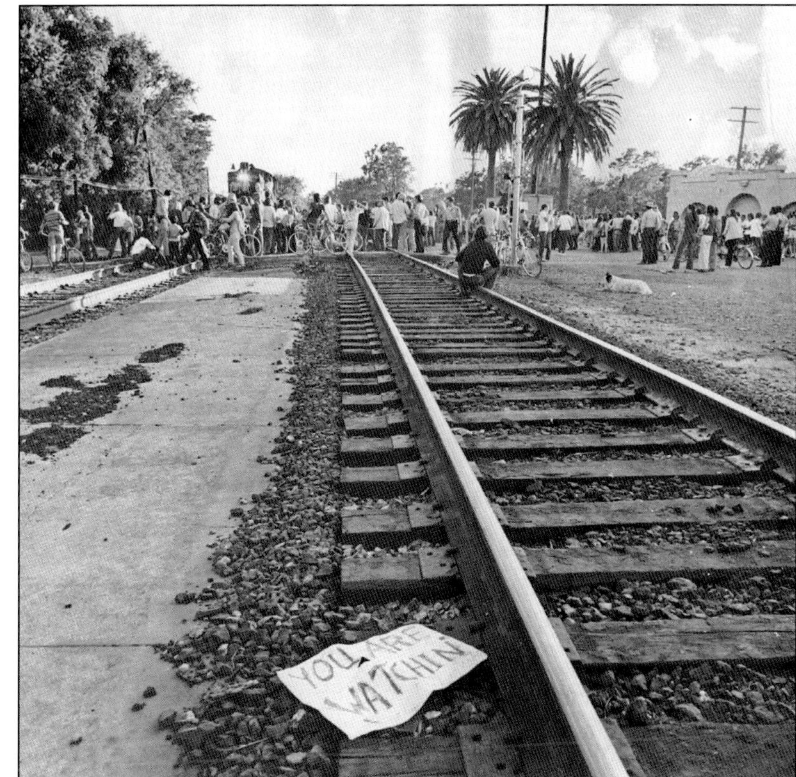

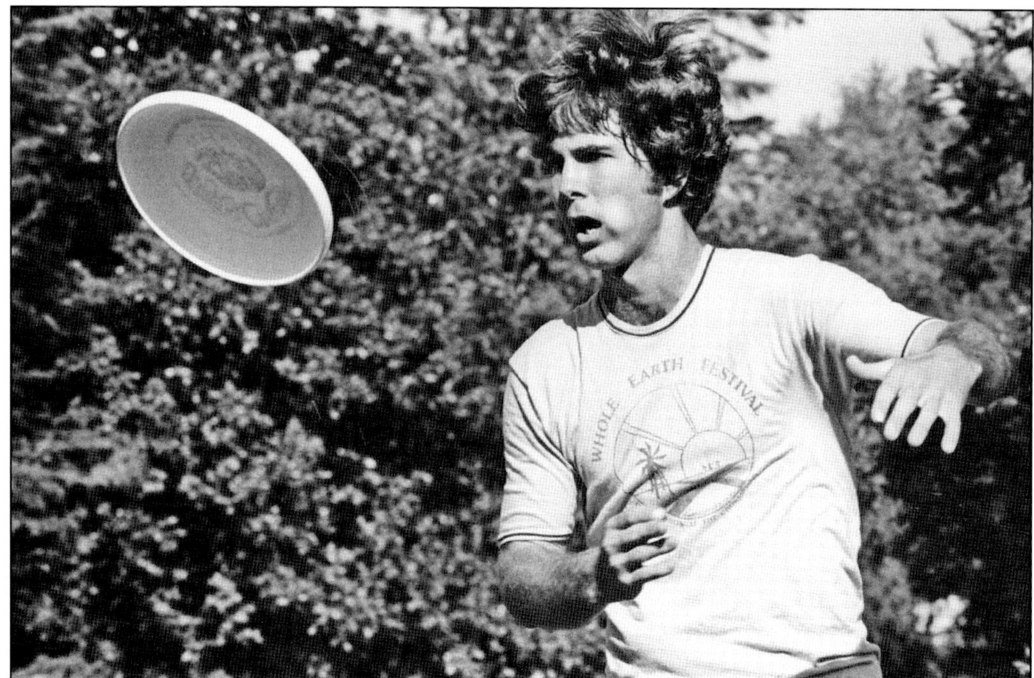

An annual spring festival with attendance that grew to rival Picnic Day began in 1970. The student groups that organized the Whole Earth Festival included an art class taught by Jose Arquelles. Pictured here at one of the early festivals, a Frisbee player enjoys the quad while the crowds groove elsewhere at musical performances or patronize the scores of vendors. (SCL.)

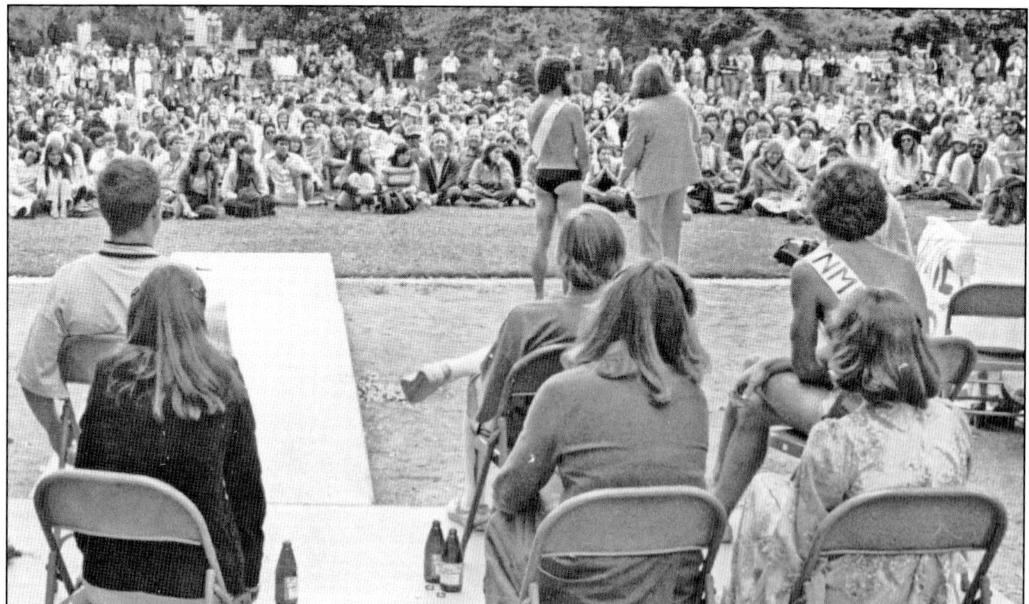

The students who, on Labor Day 1932, put in an irrigation system for a grass lawn on the quad gave the school a tremendous gift, for the quad is at the center of many campus events. Seen here during the 1970s is a male beauty pageant sponsored by the Women's Center, satirically objectifying men instead of women. (WC.)

Six

Athletics

Sports and Recreation

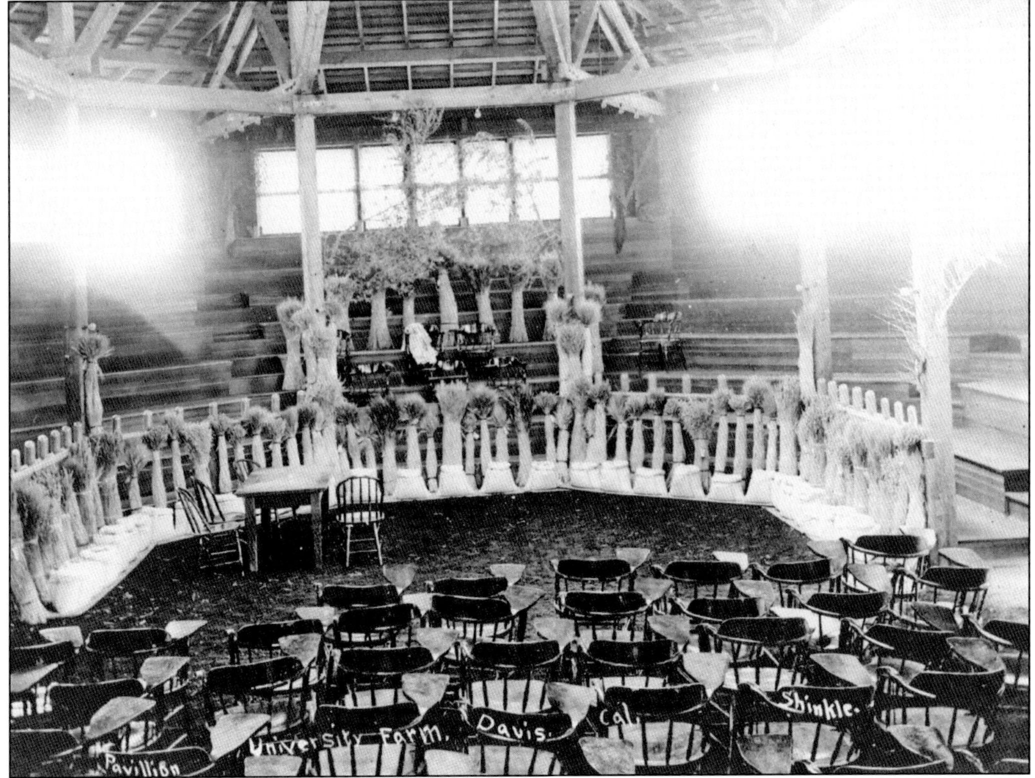

The first campus venue for recreation and sports was this livestock judging pavilion, shown here set up for an agronomy event. This postcard view by noted local photographer J.C. Shinkle has sunshine streaming in for deliberate dramatic effect. Decades later, theater replaced livestock judging as the main function of the octagonal pavilion. (HWM.)

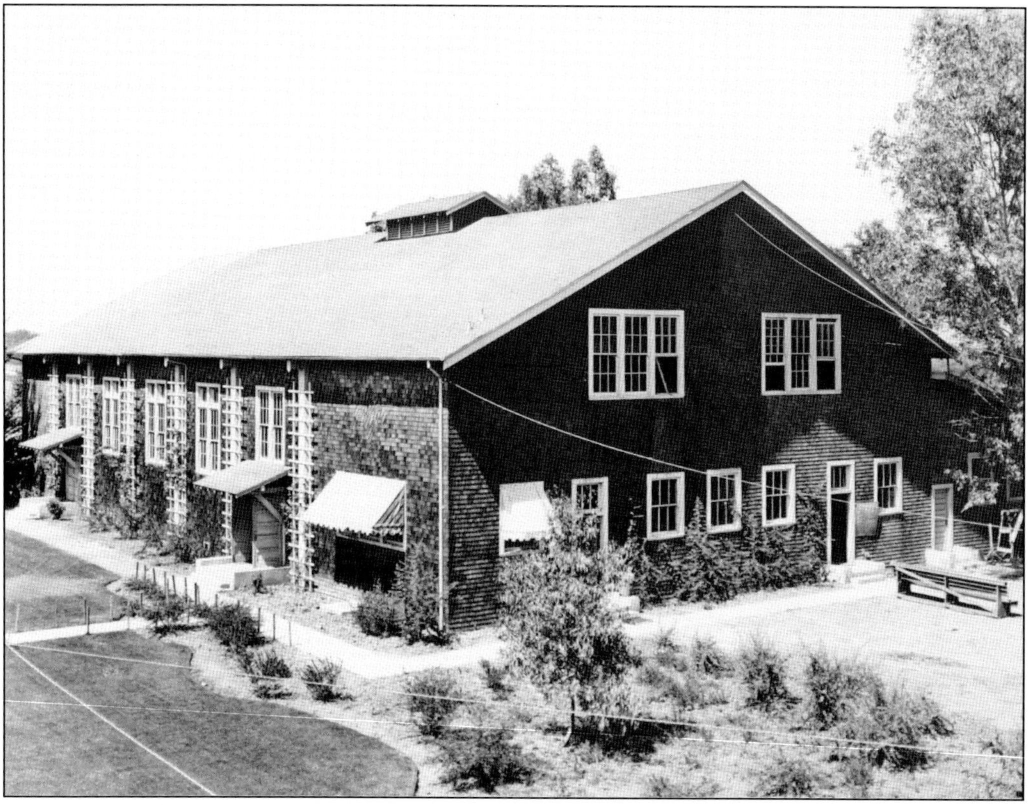

Built in 1921 for $7,500, Recreation (or "Rec") Hall was the first purpose-built gymnasium. Needing strong advocacy, its funding was a sign that the Davis campus was to be as much a college as a farm. Its shingled exterior was consistent with the design of other University Farm buildings, while its interior was simply a big box. Many nonathletic events were also held here before it was demolished in the 1950s. (SCL.)

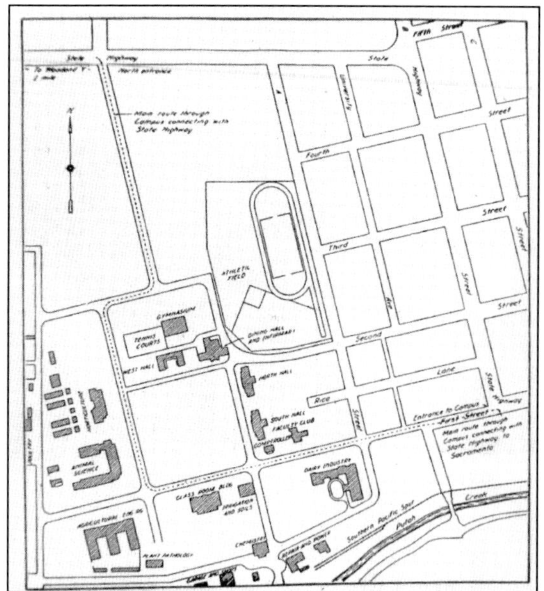

The cluster of athletic facilities at the northeast corner of campus began during the first decade of the farm. Tennis courts, a baseball diamond, football field, and track were here almost from the beginning. The 1921 Rec Hall is labeled as the gymnasium on this 1936 campus map. In 1938, a second Rec Hall was built northeast of the old one; the building still stands today and is known as Hickey Gym. That athletic facility was a beauty in its day, featuring a swimming pool and 83,000 square feet of space. (HWM.)

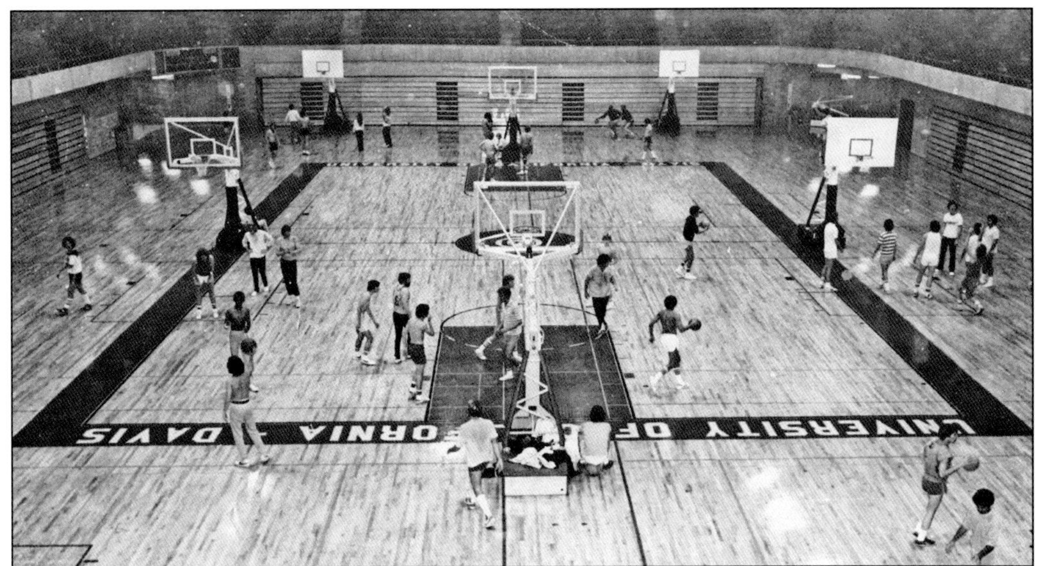

The third Rec Hall opened in 1978, and as a $5-million project, it provided more space for more diverse facilities. As with the two before it, a lengthy campaign was required before the project was funded and built. Situated on the west side of the main cluster of campus structures, it anchored a new cluster of subsequent facilities, such as the new football stadium and competitive pool complex. The main basketball court shown here also hosts events such as graduations and concerts. (SCL.)

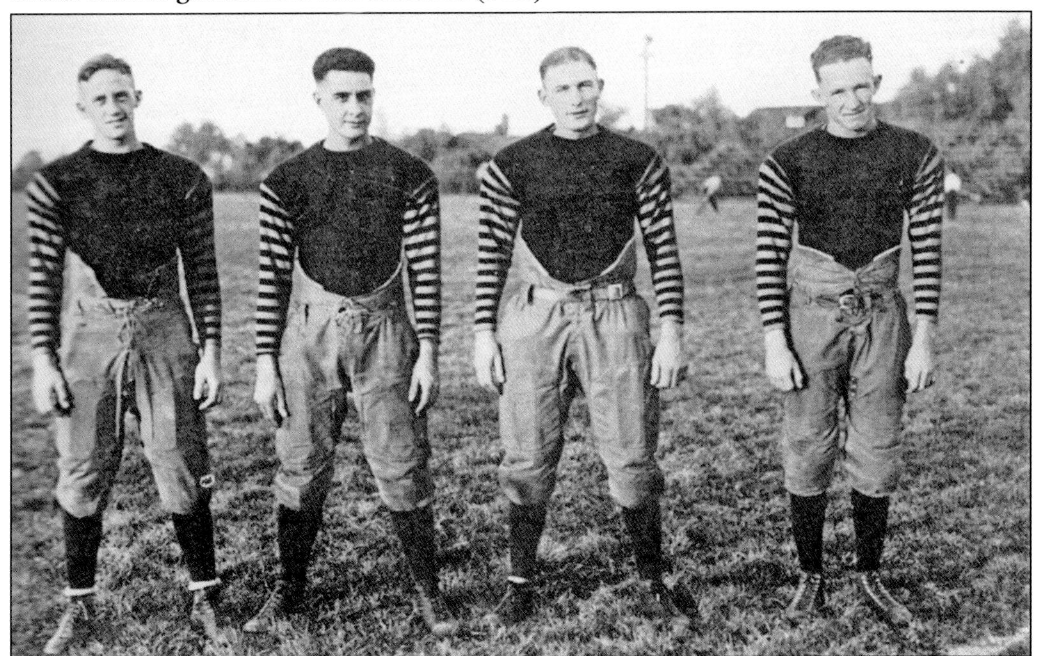

The backfield four from the 1922–1923 football team are seen here on the field located just east of Hickey Gym. With striking uniforms and rugged physiques, these student athletes fit the frequent portrayal of Farm School teams as toughened by their rural upbringing. Rugby (active from 1911 to 1914) and American football were initially the major fall intercollegiate sports. (YB, JL.)

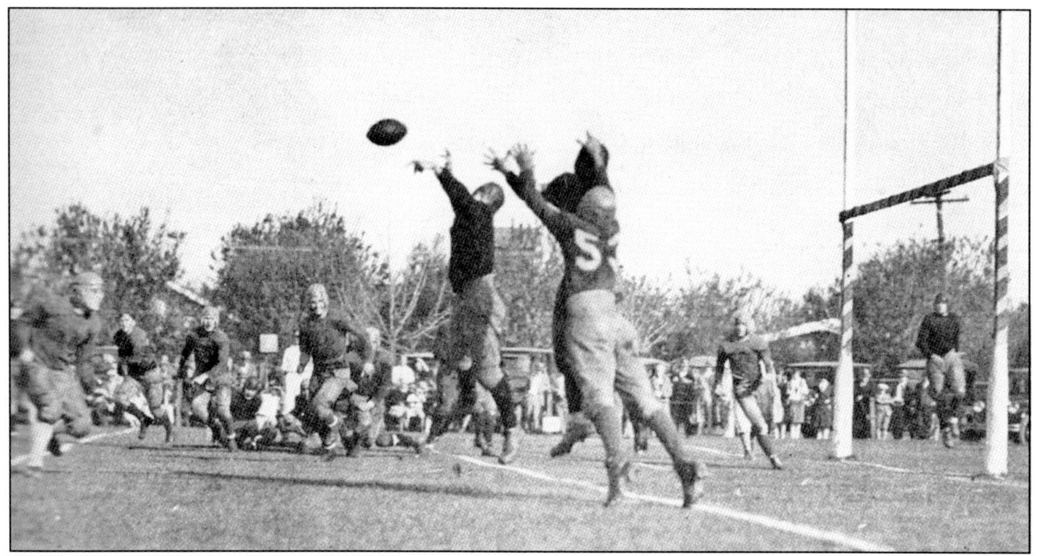

In the fall of 1926, the "big game" was against Navy, but the team was from the Bay Area and not Annapolis. It gave Davis one of its two victories in seven games that year. The grass turf of the field was a source of pride, declared by the school paper to be "the best in the state." This was the second year of the Far Western Conference. (YB, JL.)

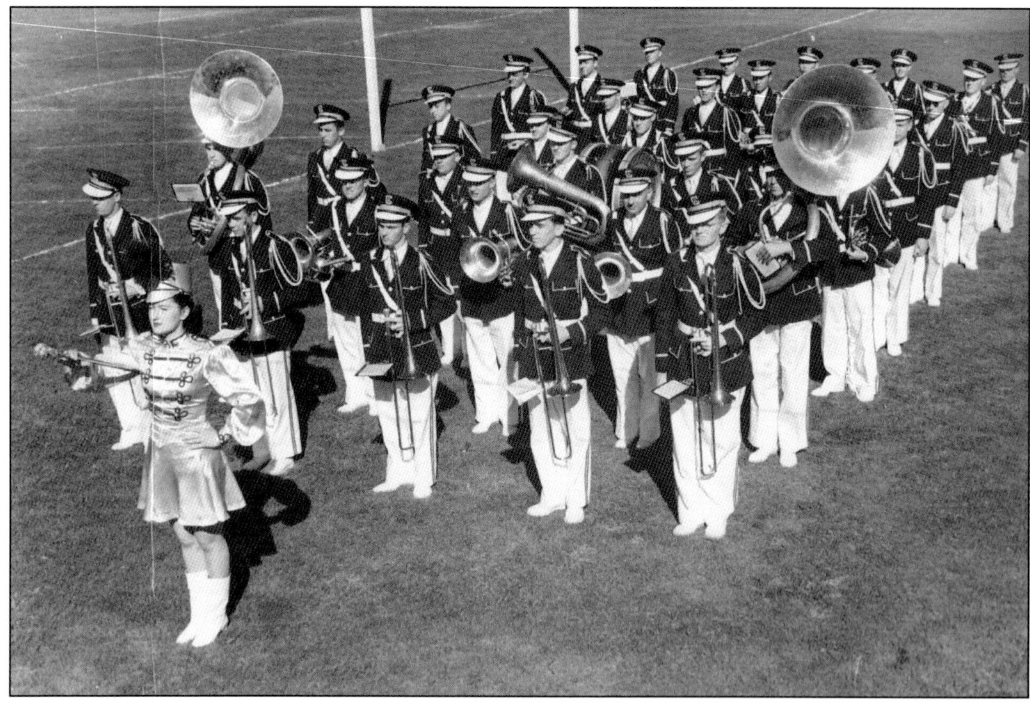

The Cal Aggie Marching Band practices on the quad in 1940. The striking drum majorette is Mary Jane Gilhooley. The band director is Price Gittinger, who founded the group in 1929. By the 1950s, the band was an accomplished musical unit and rare in being coed. Elaborate football halftime shows were its forte. "Every bit as good as Berkeley's" crowed the *Aggie* in 1958. A bit of a low point came 1961 to 1973 when women were banished from the band. (YB, JL.)

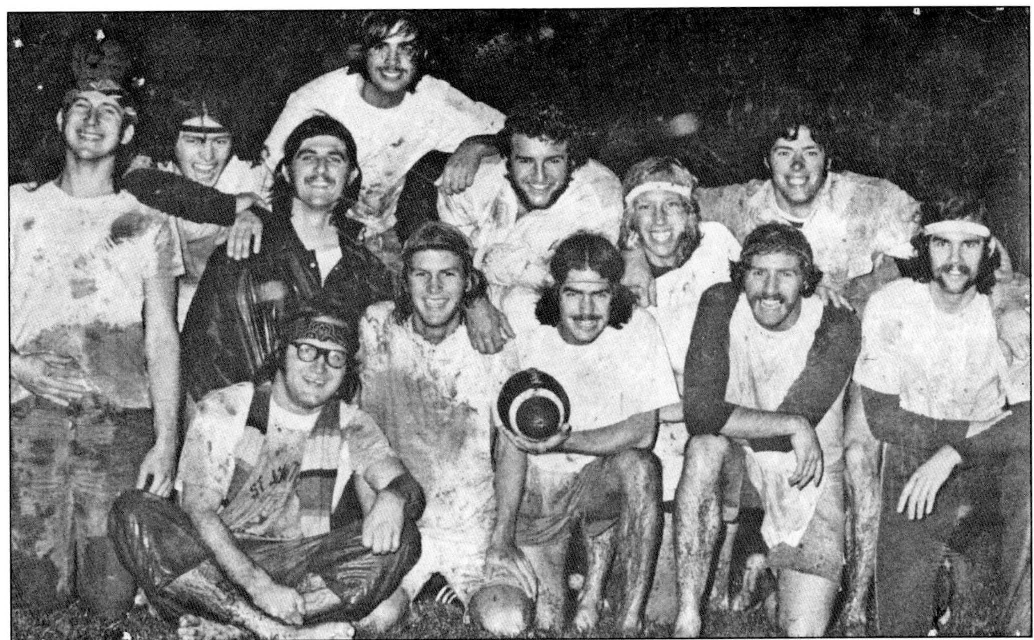

The term "intramural sports" was not in use until the 1930s, but activities of the intramural type were organized early and have thrived at Davis. Track and field competitions for non-varsity teams began in 1912, and a host of other intra-campus sports competitions followed. Here is an undated photograph from the 1960s of a team pleased with its intramural football experience. (SCL.)

In this 1968 image, powder-puff football is in action. The jerseys, with their play on words, suggest a light-hearted approach to the competition. The emphasis on intramural sports is reflected in the physical planning of the campus, where large open fields for these activities have fronted Russell Boulevard for decades. (YB, JL.)

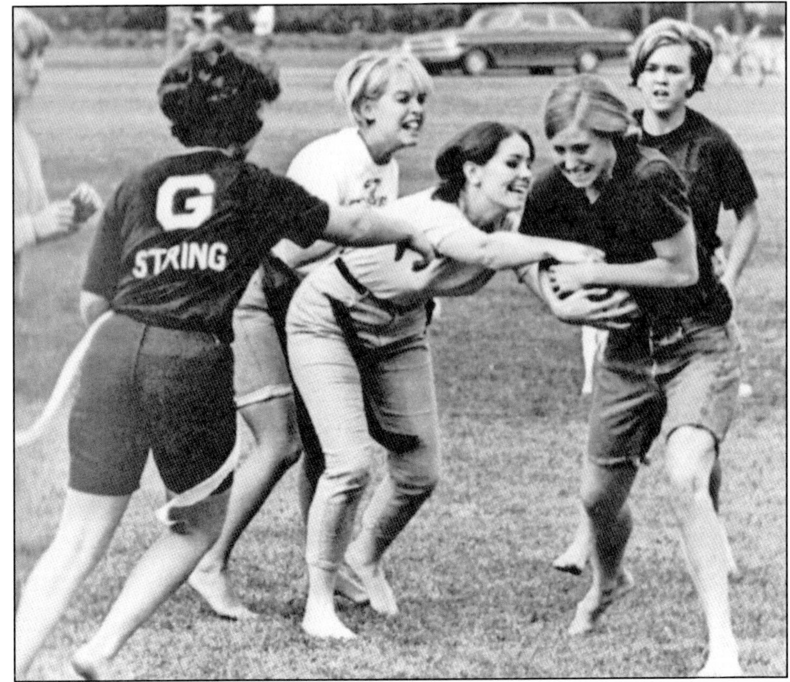

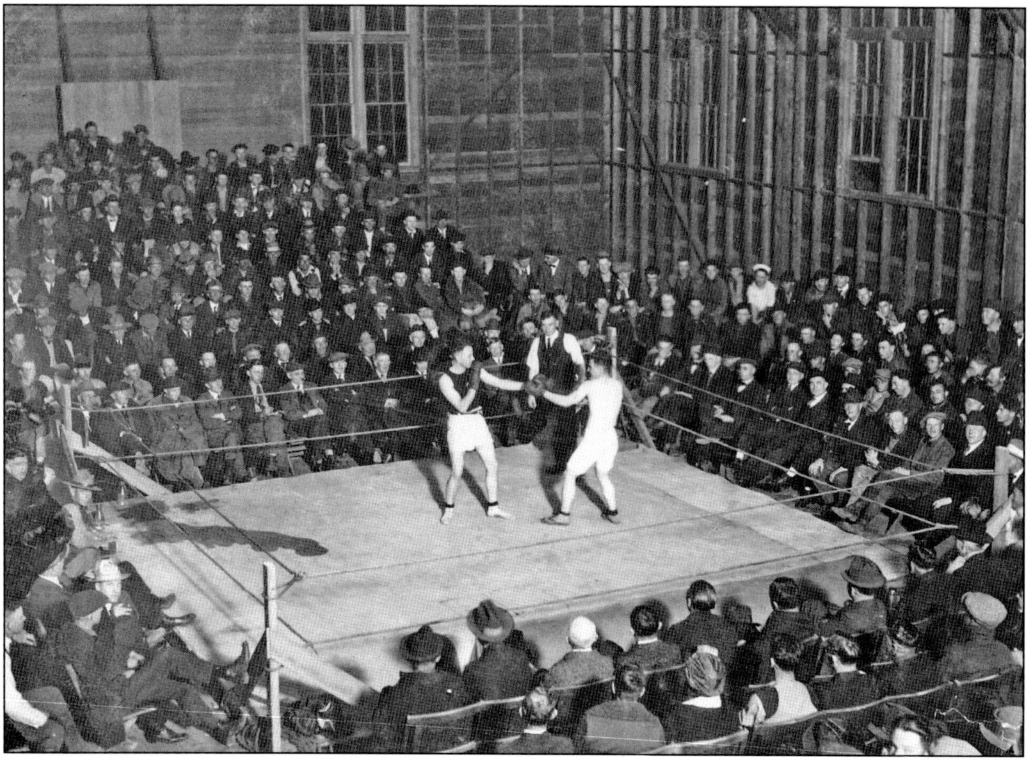

In 1921, on Saint Patrick's Day, the first Rec Hall hosted what might have been its first big event: a boxing exhibition involving a mix of intra-school matches and some against visitors. The gym's unfinished framing is visible. The crowd is large and formally dressed. (SCL.)

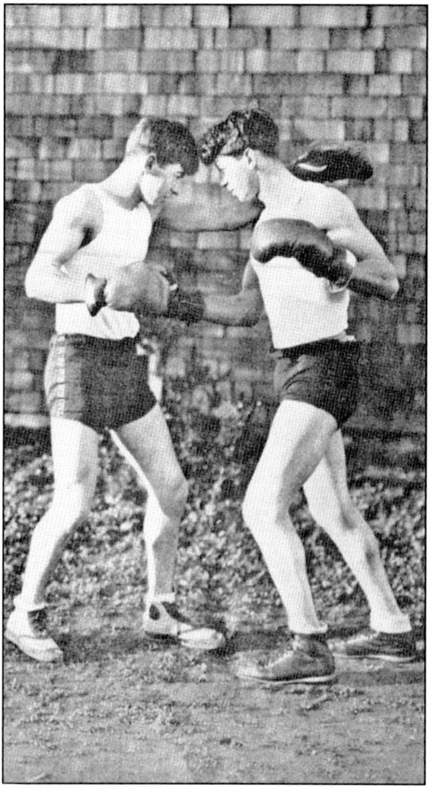

The caption under this 1926 photograph says these are the Gomez twins, and they are advertising interclass bouts. One of the twins, Al, was inducted into the Cal Aggie Athletics Hall of Fame during its first year in 1980. The boxing program at the intercollegiate level was then one of the most successful varsity sports at Davis. (YB, JL.)

Coach Myron Schall is seen here with his 1947 boxing team. Schall coached boxing and swimming and was assistant supervisor of physical education. Earlier, he spent 10 years on the athletics staff at Stanford. An inventor of athletic equipment, he was also the world champion endurance bag puncher. (YB, JL.)

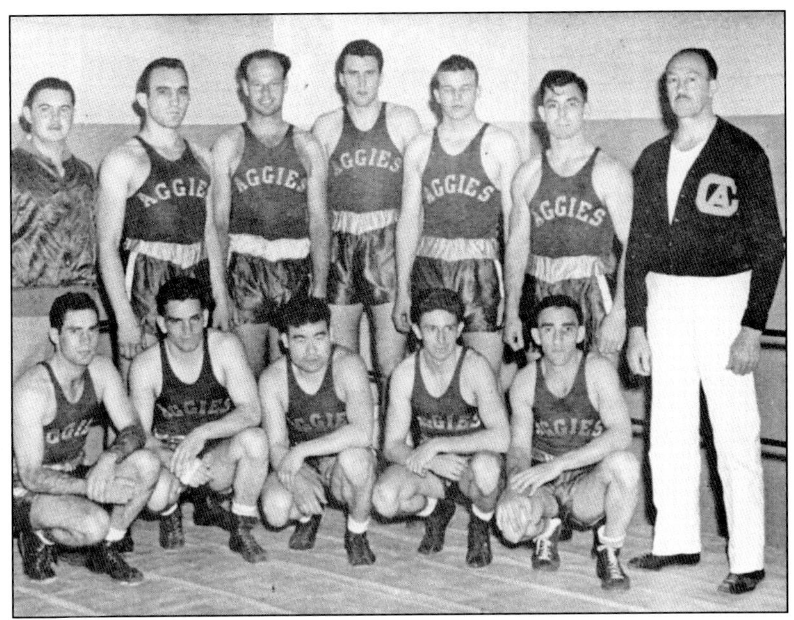

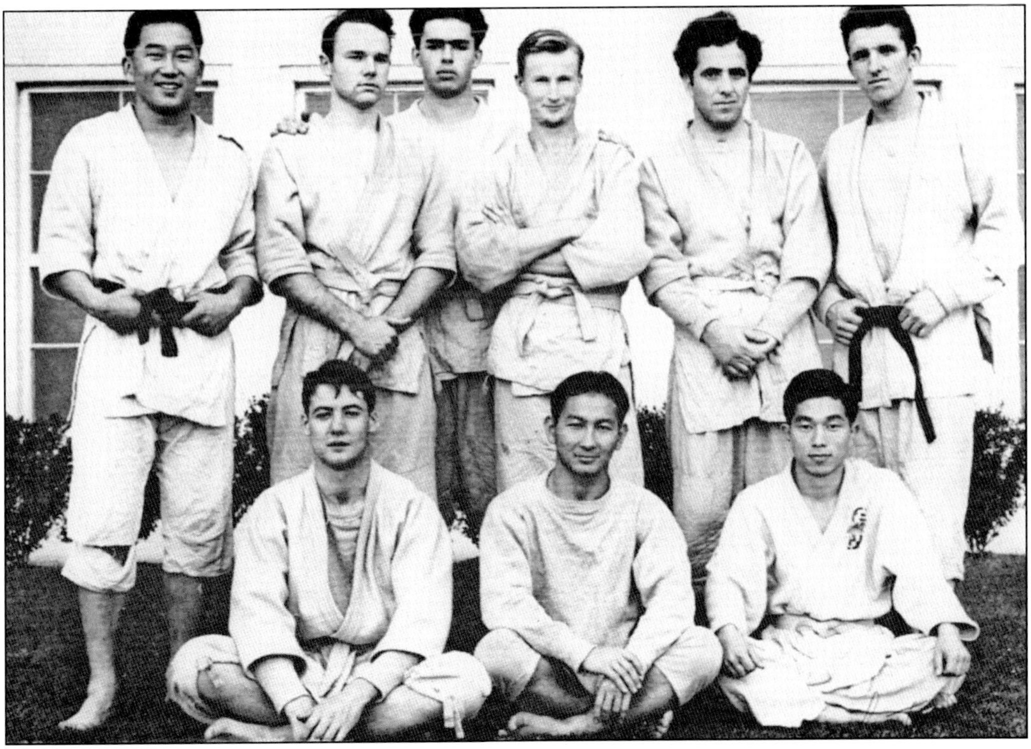

Pictured here in their third season as a competitive club team are the campus judo enthusiasts. Their coach and organizer was Bob Squibb (upper right), and his multiethnic crew included three with Japanese surnames. The 1940 yearbook reported that this club competed well against the best opposition in the state. (YB, JL.)

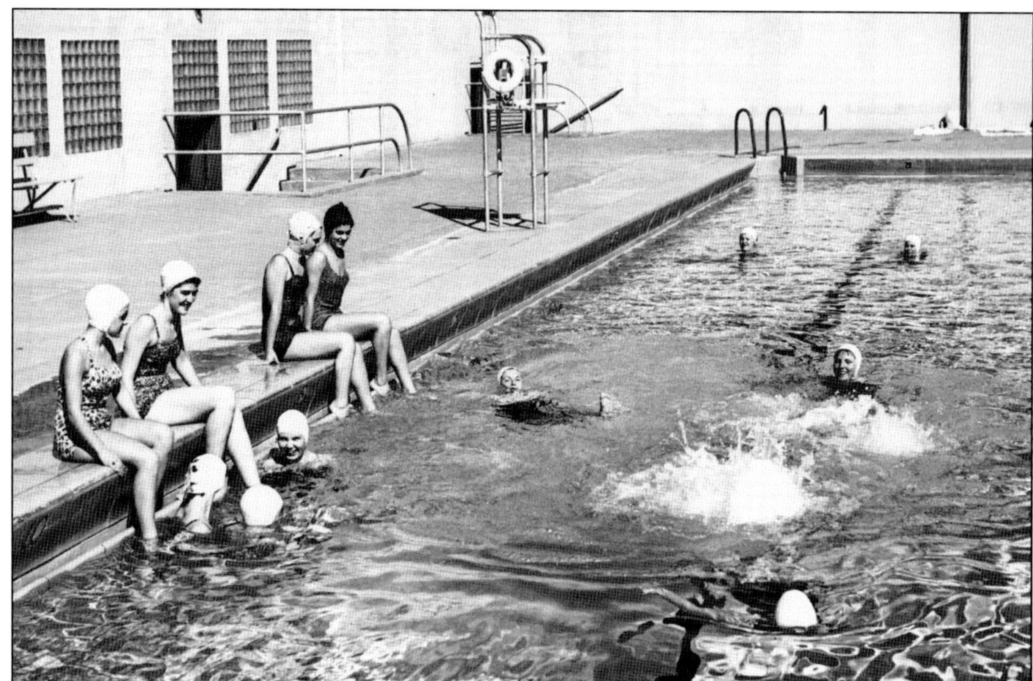

The second recreation hall, Hickey Gym, was built with a pool that served intercollegiate water sports teams as well as club teams, intramural teams, and recreational users. Various levels of men's and women's water polo, swimming, diving and other sports shared this very busy facility. Synchronized swimming was a particularly popular non-varsity women's sport, and Picnic Day was their moment in the sun. (SCL.)

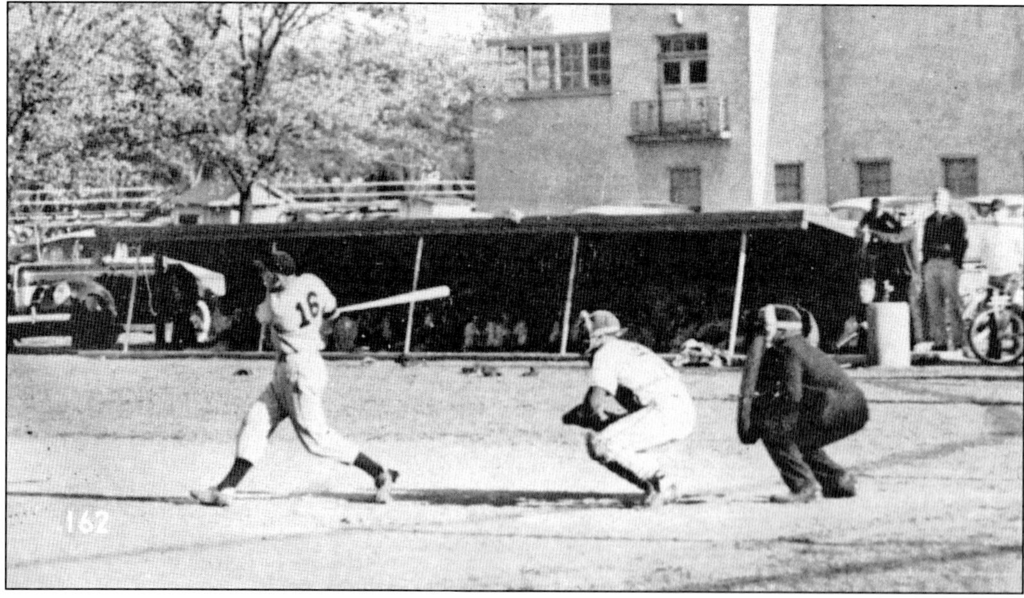

In this undated photograph, probably from the 1940s, the baseball team is at its old location; later, the field moved a short distance northwestward to Howard Way. The baseball field and football stadium both shifted to make way for the 1963 expansion of the gym, enabling the enlargement of their grounds and their stands. (YB, JL.)

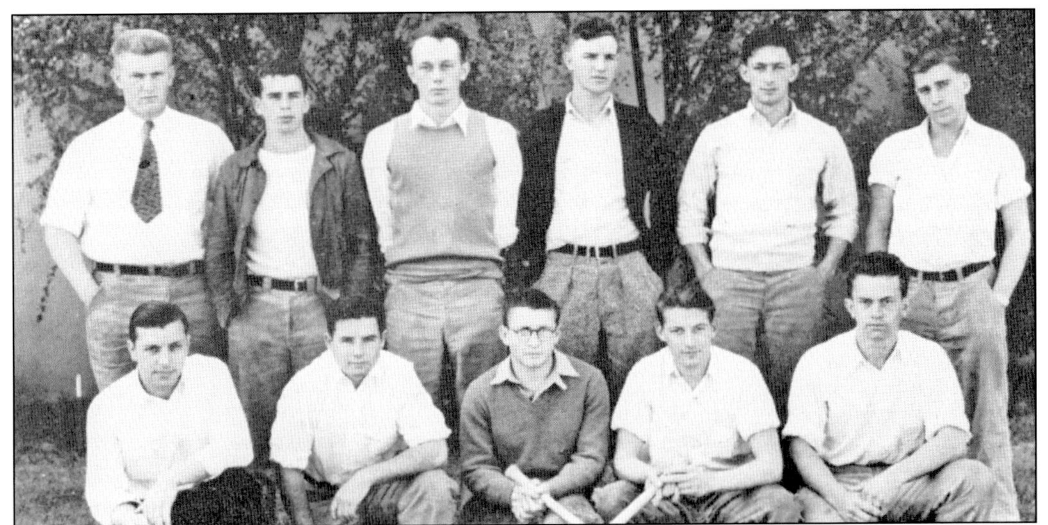

Baseball was the nation's pastime in 1932 when the Beta Phi intramural team was playing hardball, and it was no accident that a fraternity team won. Then as now, sports competitions are often serious matters for the Greeks. (YB, JL.)

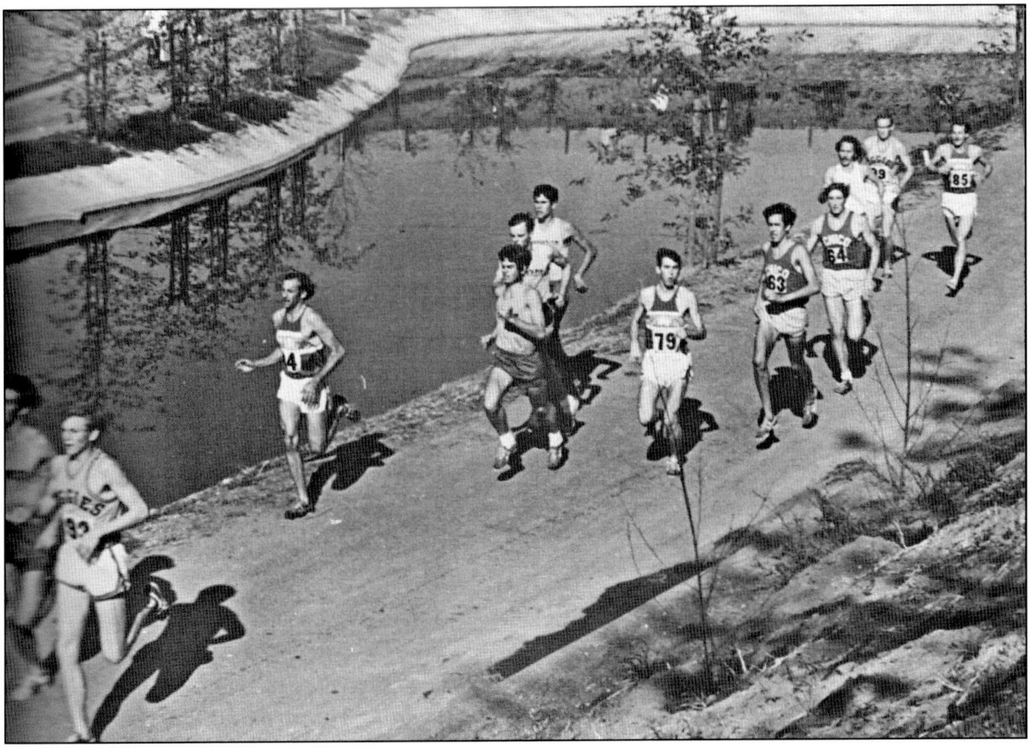

Here, the cross-country team runs competitively on the almost three-mile loop around the campus arboretum. By 1970, major amenities had been built along Old Putah Creek, but the vegetation had far to go to reach today's mature attractiveness. The arboretum remains a popular walking and running locale. (YB, JL.)

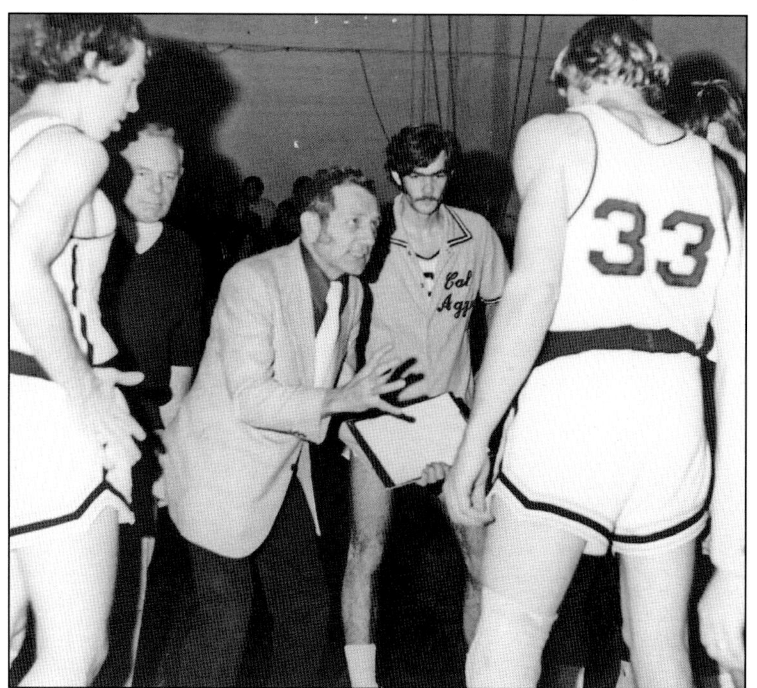

With his characteristic intensity, longtime basketball coach Bob Hamilton exhorts his team. This photograph was taken in Hickey Gym before the 1978 move to today's Rec Hall. Missing from the image is the towel the coach famously grasped, chewed, and threw regularly from the sidelines. Coach Ham took over the team in 1962, won seven conference titles, and saw all but two of his four-year players graduate. (SCL.)

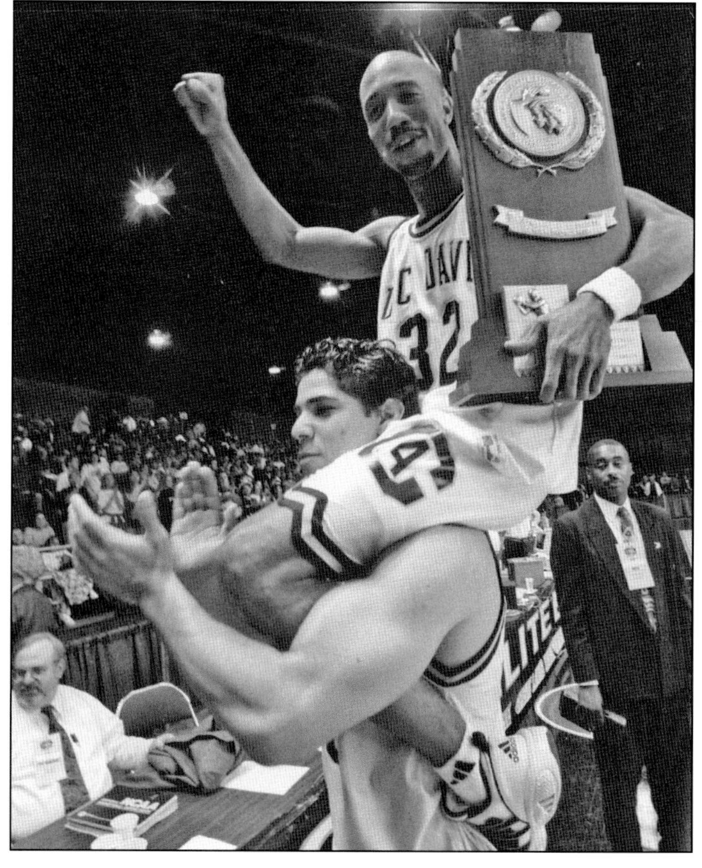

Surely, the greatest moment in UC Davis athletic history is seen here. Justis Durkee hoists Dante Ross after their team won the 1998 NCAA Division II basketball championship. Other national titles for Davis varsity teams came in tennis, golf, gymnastics, rowing, and softball. (Photograph by Mark Bullard, ICA.)

Here on the small stage of Lower Hickey gym, the intensity of intramural play is on full display as Sigma Alpha Epsilon tries to block Delta Sigma Phi's layup. For many years, UC Davis was known for having one of the best intramural sports programs in the nation. Having one's winning team's photograph hanging in the gym hallways? Priceless. (SCL.)

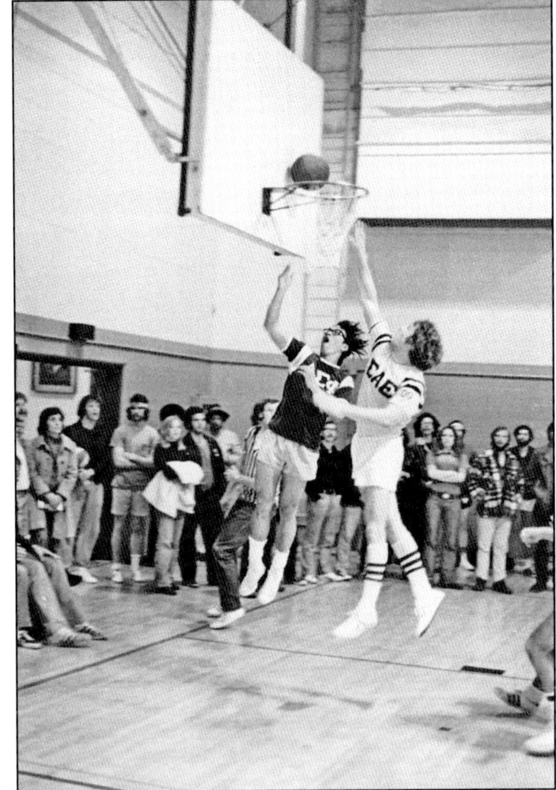

Almost unbelievable on several grounds, a basketball game in 1970 featured players riding donkeys. The damage by animal hooves to Lower Hickey, the problem of getting enough donkeys, and concerns over animal abuse would prevent any repeat today. It was an iconoclastic era. (YB, JL.)

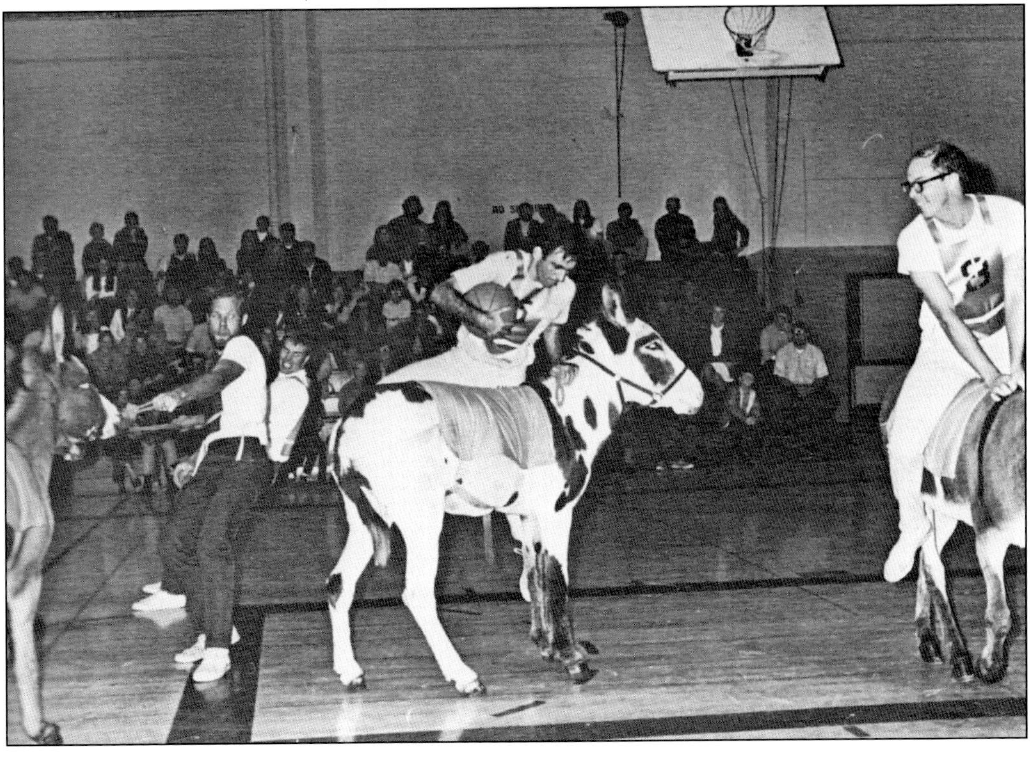

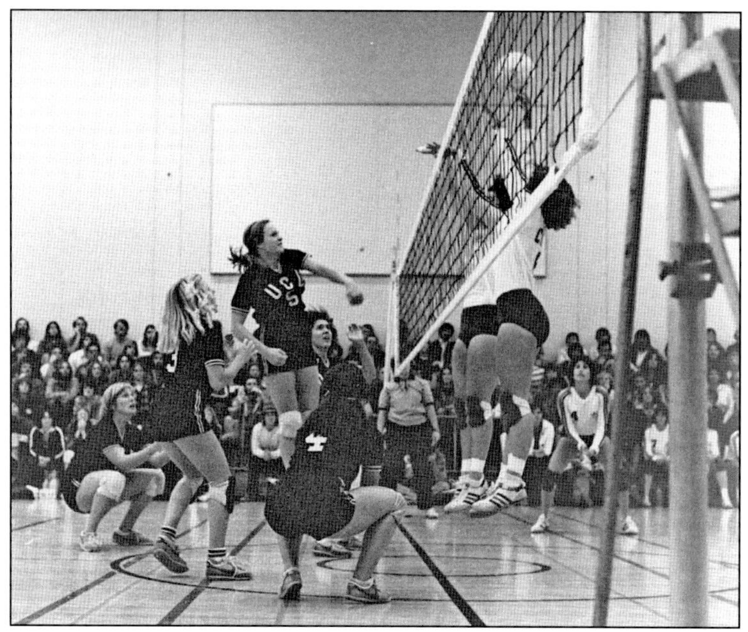

The intensity and athleticism of volleyball are captured here in a game from the 1970s. Women's volleyball first fielded a team in the early 1950s, but it had a low profile. The yearbook's first photographs of the team in action came in 1969 over the caption "WAA Chicks Displayed Beauty with Muscle." The first volleyball player in the Aggie Athletics Hall of Fame in 1987 was Lisa Kennedy, who played from 1979 to 1982. (SCL.)

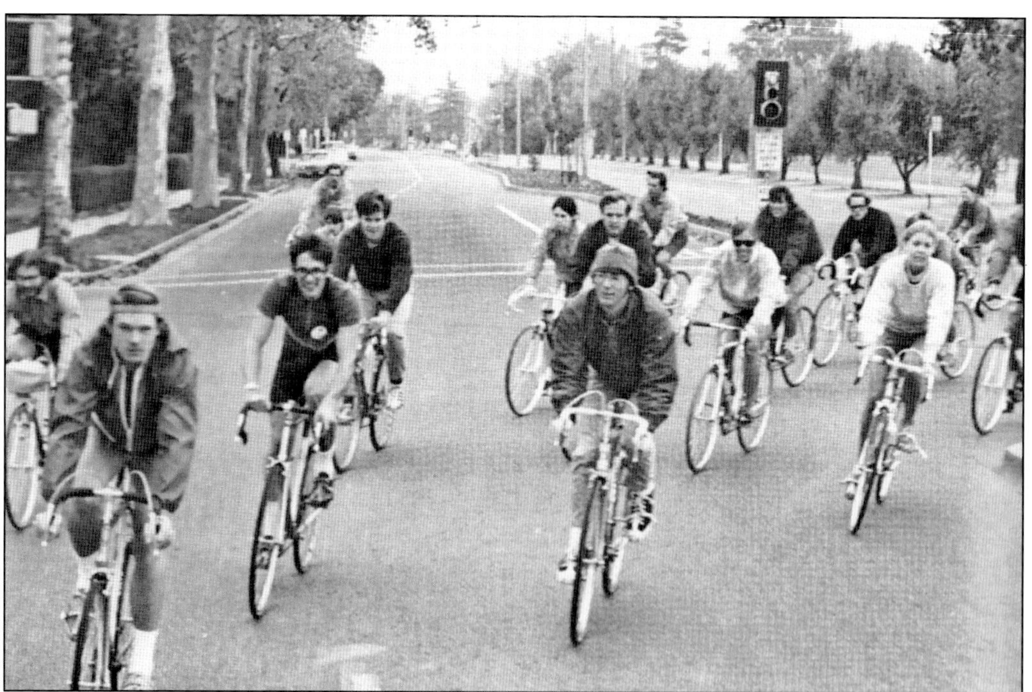

Here, a club's team of bike riders turns onto westbound Russell Boulevard from California Avenue in 1971. The road leads 15 miles to Winters and 30 to Lake Berryessa. Back then, these "California Wheelmen" unsuccessfully advocated for varsity team status. Instead, consolation came in the form of four national championships for the UC Davis Cycling Team, which operated as a coed sports club. (YB, JL.)

When golf became an intermittent campus sport in the 1930s, the team drove 20 miles to play at Sacramento's Haggin Oaks golf course. Now, three courses are within five miles of campus. The men's golf team was national champion in 1979. Non-team golfers used the Russell Boulevard athletic fields, shown here, for driving and pitching. Adjacent to this scene is the instructional putting green at the corner of Russell Boulevard and Howard Way. (SCL.)

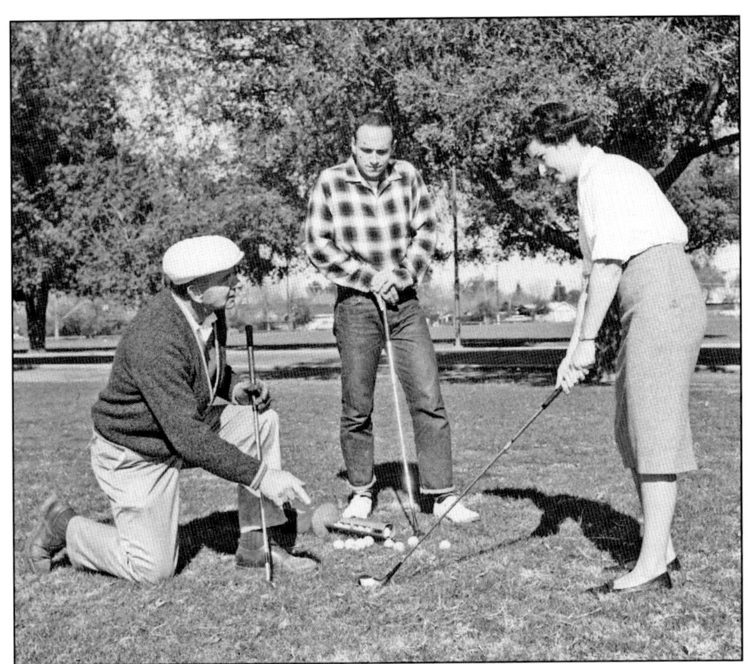

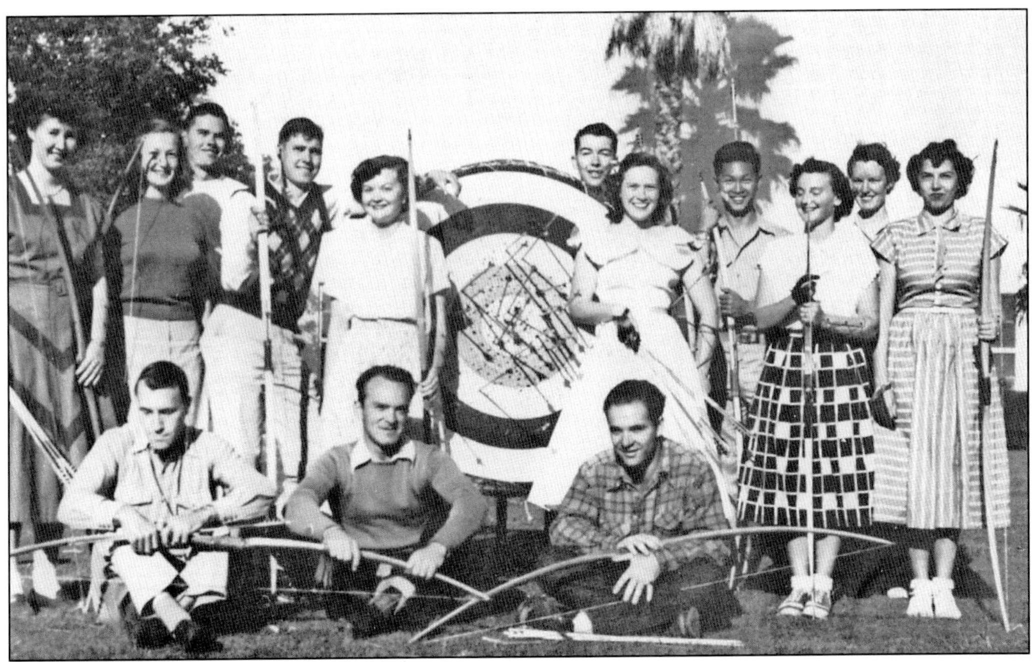

Never a varsity sport, archery enjoyed a rush of popularity when the country was watching Western movies starring cowboys and Indians. Pictured here in 1950, seven guys and seven gals pause after an impressive round of hitting bull's-eyes. Archery was one of the classes taught by Marya Welch during her five decades on campus. (YB, JL.)

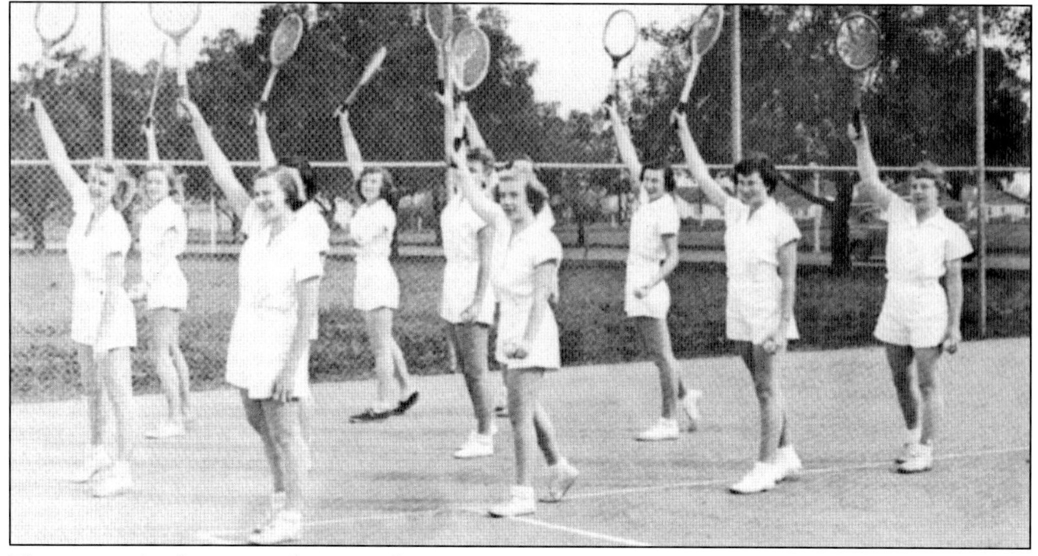

Eleven tennis players synchronize their warm-ups on the excellent tennis courts, well located just west of the gym in 1950 or 1951. Tennis courts appeared within a decade after students first enrolled at the University Farm. Recently, a generous donor greatly enhanced the cluster of courts. Between them, UC Davis women and men have won five national titles, with the women bringing home four of the five. (YB, JL.)

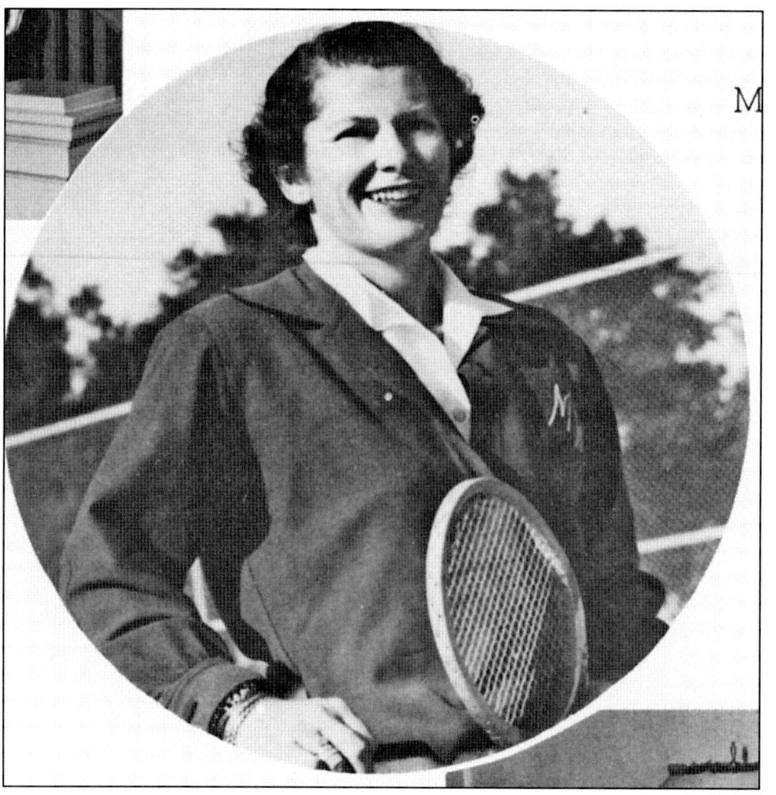

In 1947, Marya Welch arrived as the first female faculty member in athletics, when she was also the ninth female faculty member and there were just a hundred women students. She proceeded to do it all for women's athletics on campus. In short order, she had taught or coached archery, basketball, equestrianism, riflery, softball, swimming, tennis, track and field, and volleyball. (YB, JL.)

Seven

HALLMARKS

PICNIC DAY AND THE ARBORETUM

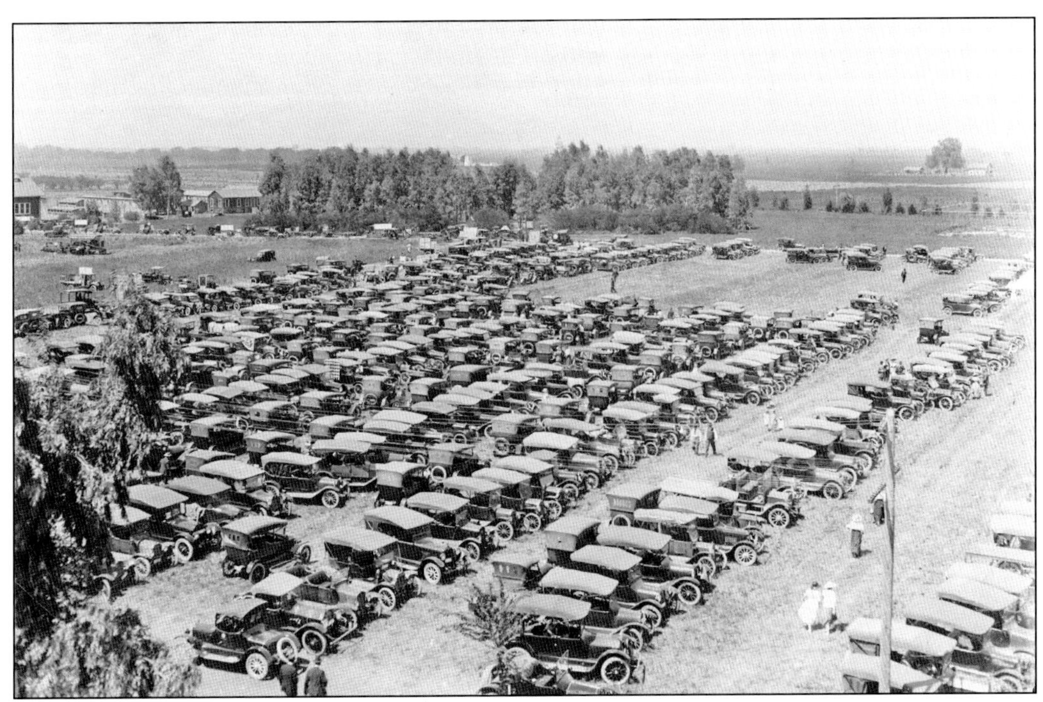

Picnic Day drew a crowd of 3,000 when first held in 1909 as a celebration of the new North Hall dormitory. It had been advertised statewide as a chance to see what taxpayers had supported, and a huge number of visitors arrived by rail, horse, and car. Pictured here a few years later, Picnic Day revealed California's flourishing automobility. It was a time to be entertained by a parade and educated by exhibits about good farming practices. (SCL.)

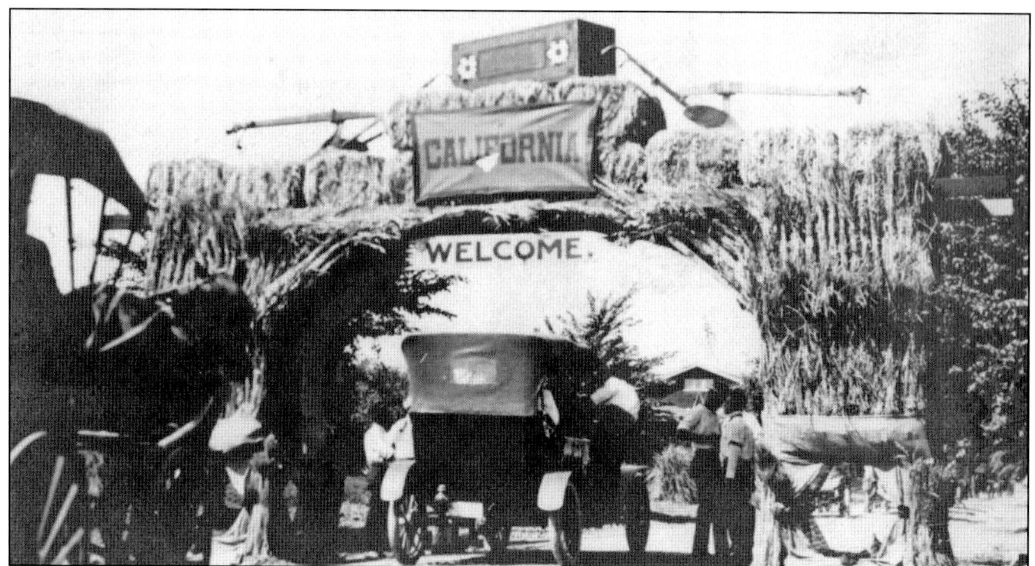

Another early Picnic Day had a welcoming entrance arch constructed on the east road into campus. As were many parade entries, this arch was decorated with sheaves of grain. Regional festivals and arches were popular during this era. The city of Modesto's permanent arch, for example, bragged about "Water, Wealth, Contentment, Health" while after 1919, a permanent arch in downtown Davis identified the city as the "Gateway to the University Farm." (HWM.)

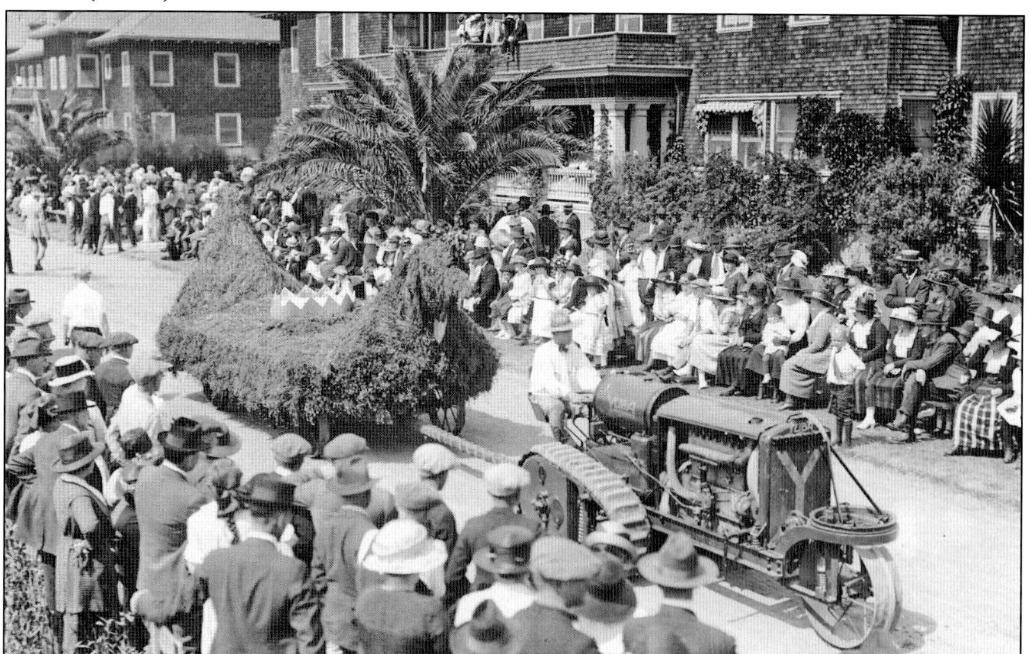

Machinery buffs then (and now) were treated to tractors such as this Yuba Ball Tread model with distinctive front steering. Less easy to recognize is the float it pulls, featuring a stylized chicken and newly hatched egg. The many well-dressed audience members have staked out prime positions for themselves. For a century, farm machines have rumbled along the parade route, then as the latest technology and now as historical agricultural artifacts. (SCL.)

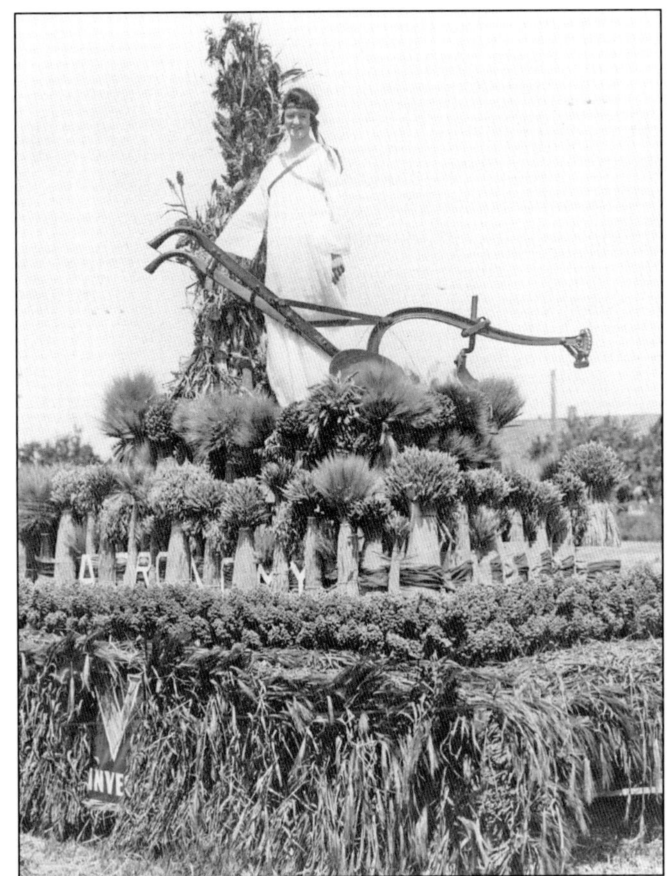

This Picnic Day float by the agronomy department won first prize and featured multiple grain sheaves, a heavy one-bottom plow, and a presiding classical figure. After her dramatic ride in 1919, Margaret Patricia Kelly went on to be a weed and seed botanist for the state and coauthor with Prof. W.W. Robbins of his multi-edition *Weeds of California.* (PSH.)

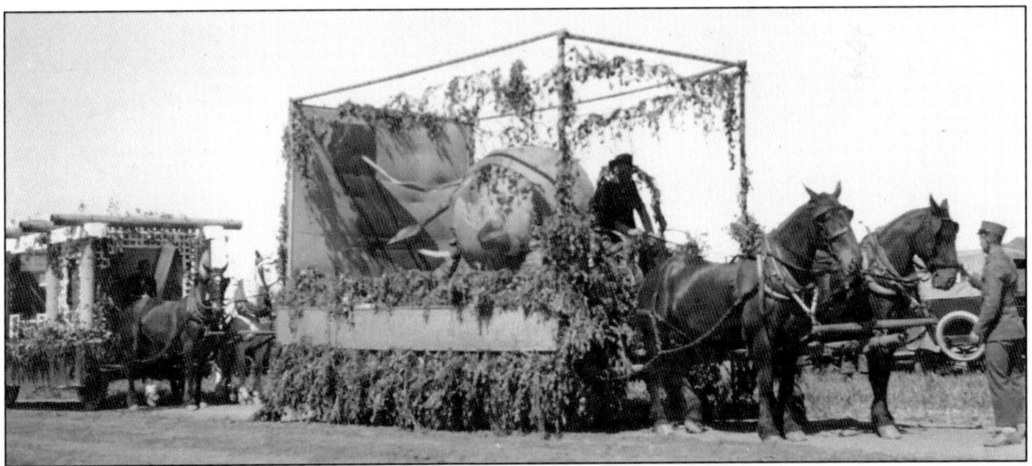

By 1917, approximately 18,000 people attended Picnic Day. From 1914 on, it was a student-organized activity, as it remains today. The Picnic Day parade began with a procession of livestock, but the display animals were quickly joined by other elements of the typical small-town parade. Bands marched every year, and comedic entries paraded. This early juggernaut of workhorses draws a huge decorated wagon carrying a globe. The float's label reads "California's Farm Market is the World." (SCL.)

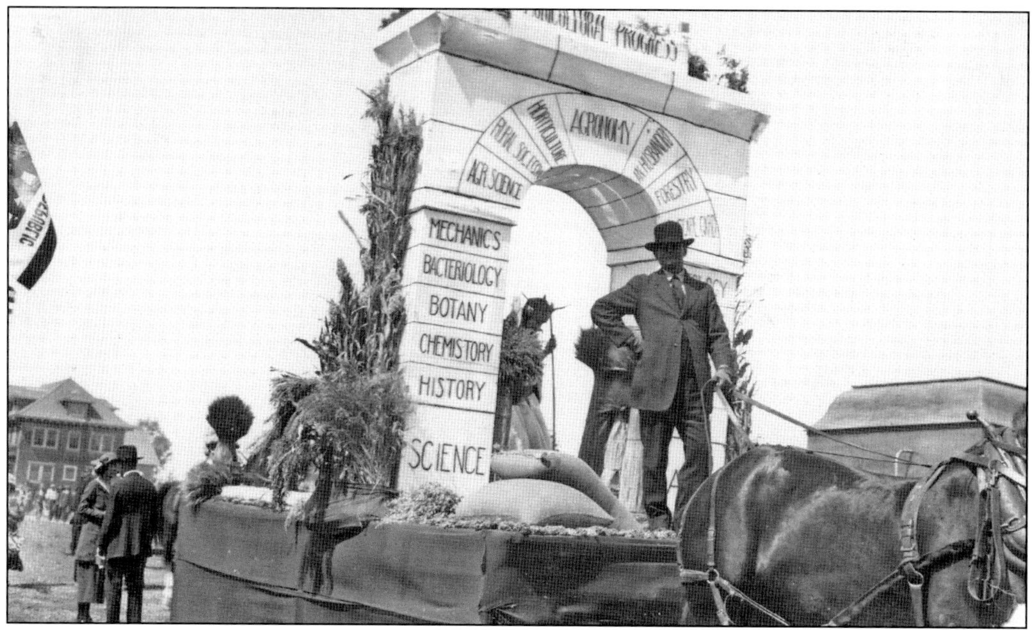

This may be another agronomy department parade entry. An old-fashioned team of mules draws this float, which celebrates a discipline as modern as bacteriology. A mark of the emerging diversification of the campus is the listing of history as an academic area of study. Perhaps the experience of the nation in World War I motivated the use of a Parisian triumphal arch as the float's core design element. (SCL.)

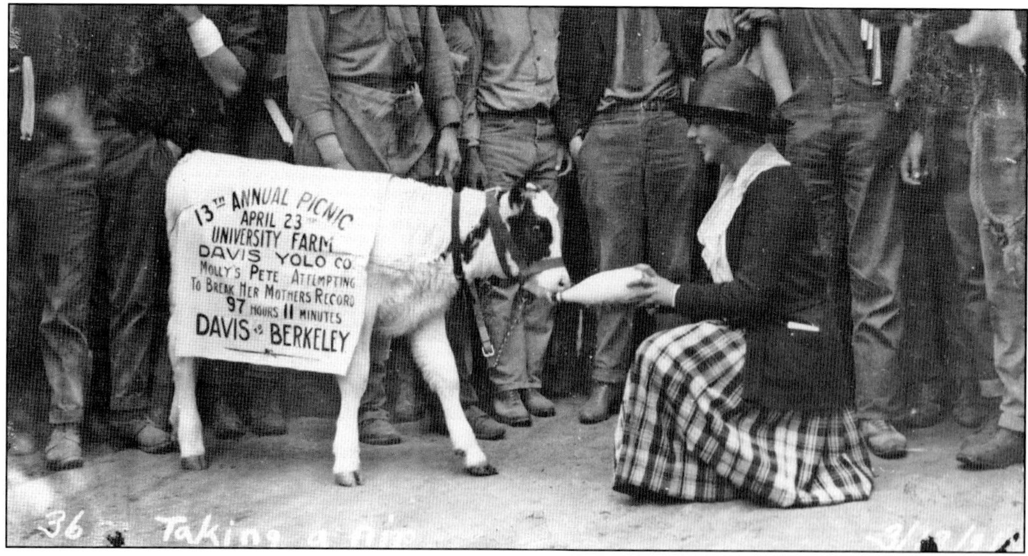

Animals have always been an important part of Picnic Day. This 1921 scene with a calf celebrates her mother, a cow that publicized a previous Picnic Day by walking between Davis and Berkeley over the course of four days. Another early Picnic Day saw livestock being taken by passenger train to the Bay Area for publicity. (SCL.)

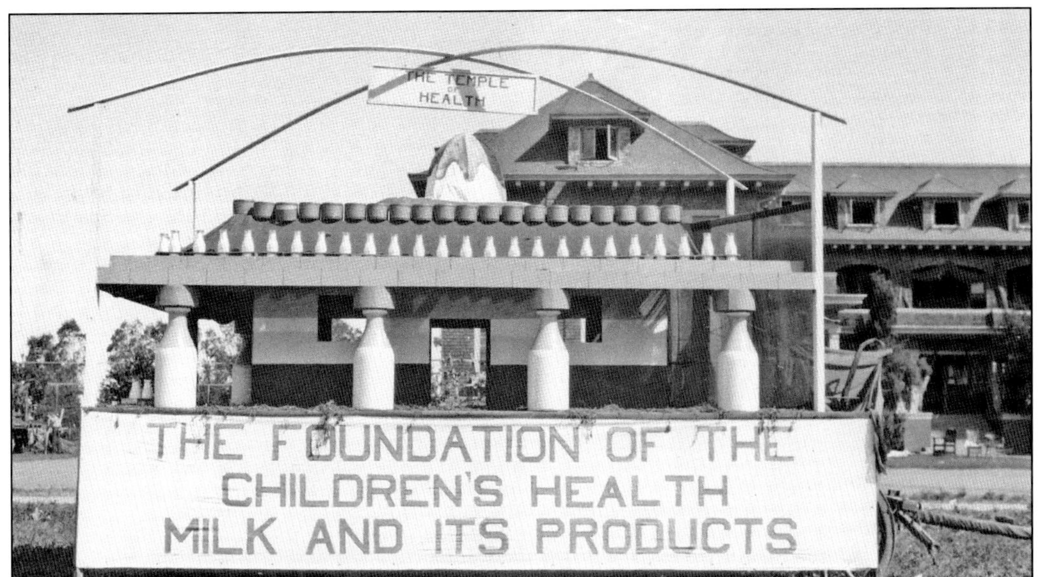

On a farm campus where the creamery was central to activities, Picnic Day extensively promoted the dairy industry. The top of this parade entry proclaims, "The Temple of Health," while the health benefits of milk products are touted below. The campus creamery made and marketed locally a wide array of milk products. During the 1930s, a near majority of students at Davis were studying some aspect of dairy and creamery operations. (SCL.)

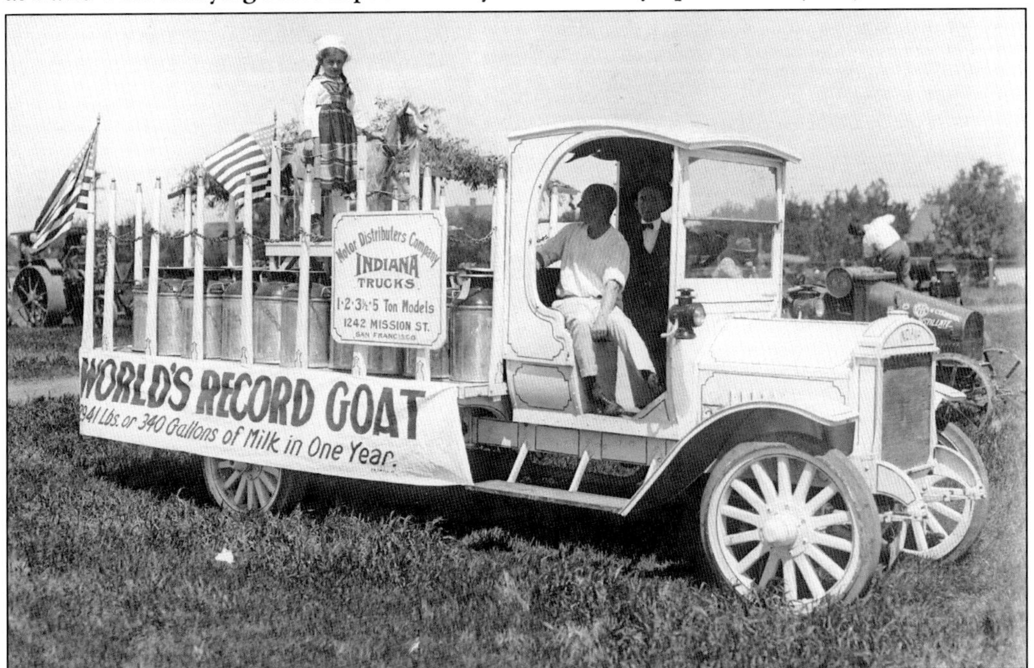

Here, a motor vehicle dealer from San Francisco advertises both his Indiana Trucks and the "World's Record Goat," which produced 340 gallons of goat milk in a year. The float's theme is appropriate for Yolo County, in which the school is located, because in 1920, one Yolo County cow named Tilly Alcaltra was at this time heavily advertised for holding the world record for milk produced annually. (SCL.)

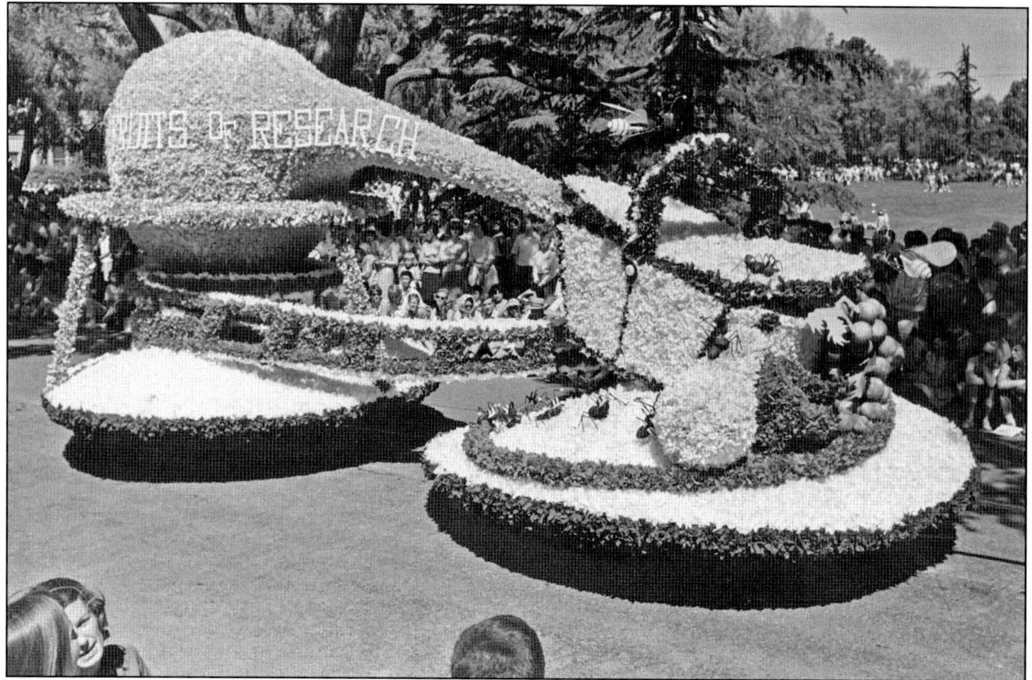

In the 1950s, the preparation of elaborate parade entries reached a creative peak. The "Fruits of Research" is the title of a celebration of pomology's progress on campus. This is not just a decorated farm wagon or truck; this is a specially built chassis comparable to the productions associated with the big-time Rose Parade, which the nation now watched on television. (SCL.)

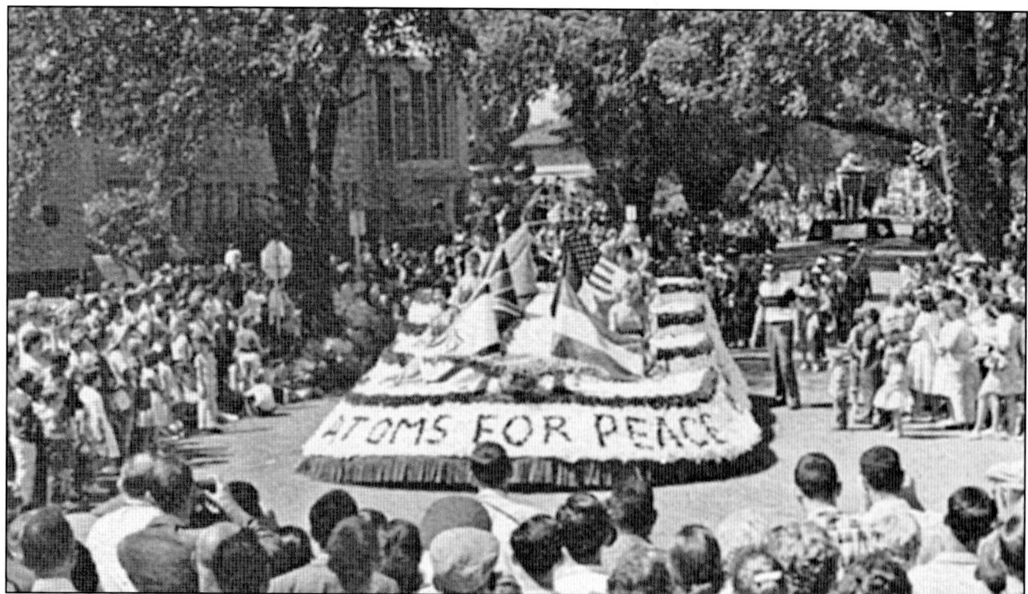

About the same time that the campus was getting its cyclotron and ramping up its research faculty in nuclear physics, this elaborate parade entry by a student organization celebrated "Atoms for Peace." The message of multiple flags is internationalist, but the float was overly optimistic about the contributions of nuclear power. (YB, JL.)

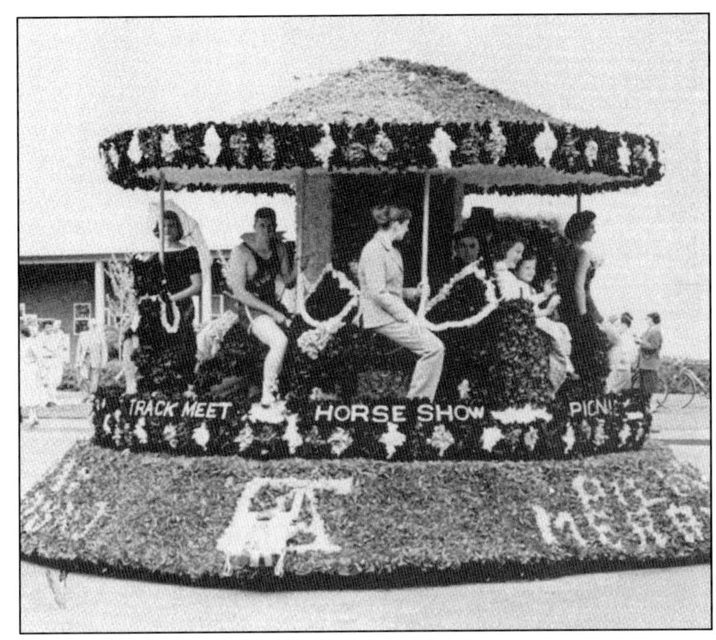

Another winner from this era is a 1957 carousel float. It advertises the great diversity of activities available on campus after the parade. A horse show and track meet were regular features of this decade. The campus had fairly complete rodeo grounds and a track in its football stadium. Baseball games, motorcycle races, fashion shows, folk dances, and dog races have been on the program. In 1950, the "Cal Aggie Cooners" showed the treeing skills of their 11 hounds. (YB, JL.)

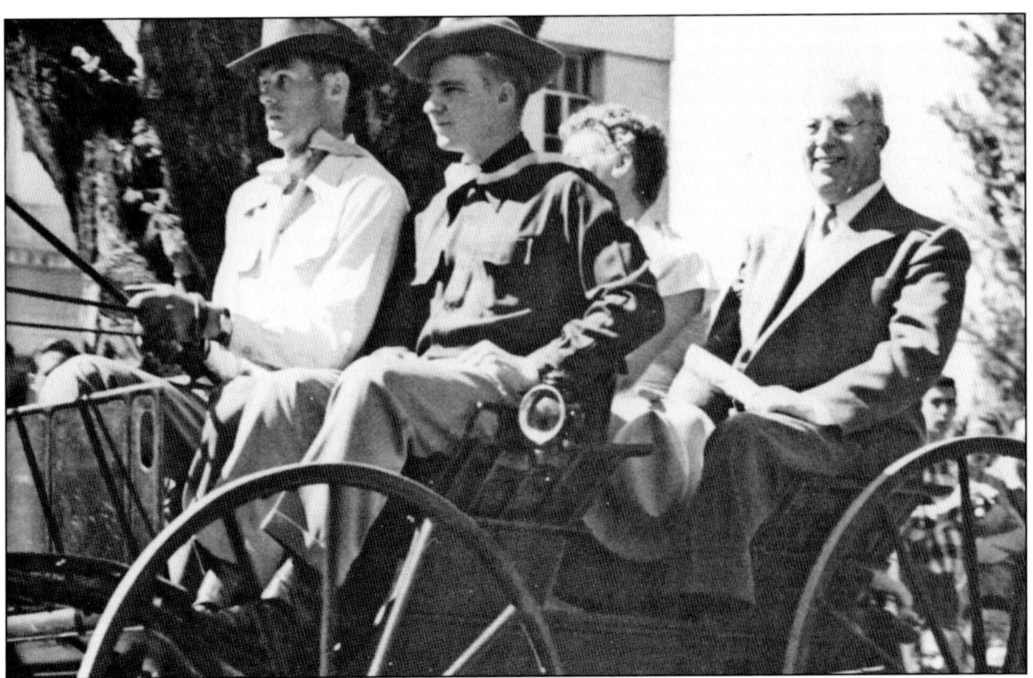

Governor from 1943 to 1953, Earl Warren is seen here being driven in the 1950 Picnic Day parade after having officially opened the event. A progressive, he raised taxes to improve the state's schools and roads. The postwar surge of enrollments by veterans was ameliorated by his measures to make room for them. (YB, JL.)

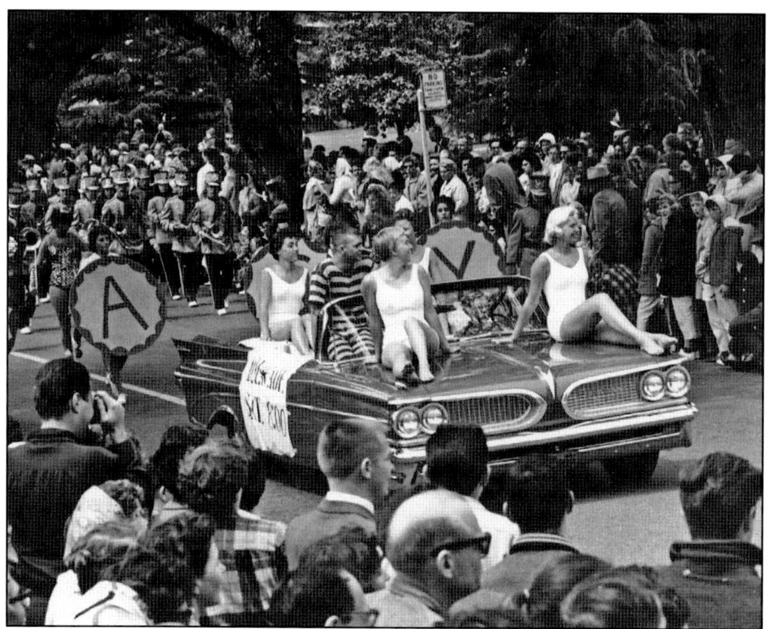

Not a big part of the Picnic Day parade tradition, here nevertheless is a classic small-town parade entry featuring young women on a convertible. These four bathing beauties ride on a c. 1962 Pontiac Bonneville. Five years later, heads really turned when the San Francisco strip club impresario Carol Doda rode in the parade in the back of a similar convertible. (SCL.)

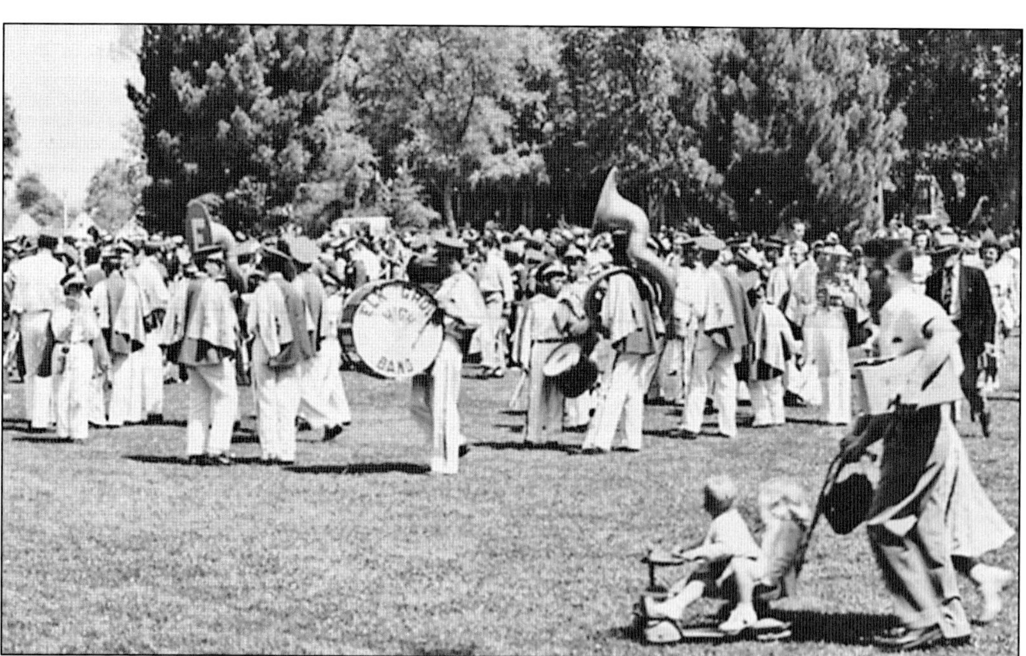

Marching bands are a big part of Picnic Day tradition, with a half dozen or more participating in most years. Pictured here in 1950 is one from Elk Grove, one of the 13 bands that year in the High School Band Festival. Picnic Day was, in a way, a recruiting event to attract future students to the campus. For the Cal Aggie Marching Band, this was a day for the best uniforms and most serious musical numbers because Stanford and Berkeley bands often were there as well. (SCL.)

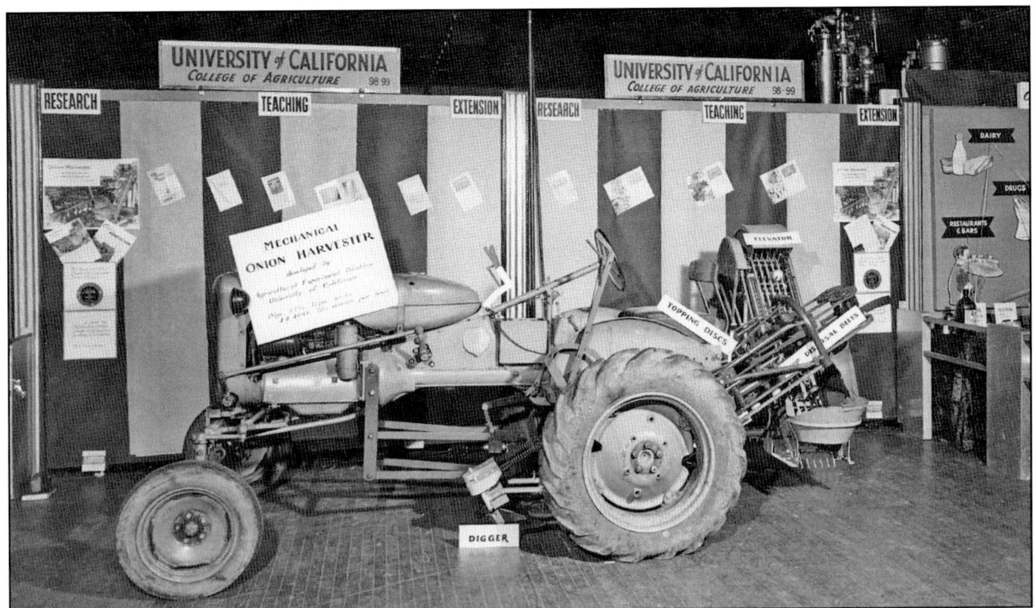

After the morning parade, most visitors head to the exhibits to learn about campus research. One distinguished alumnus, Jim Becket, recollects that his dad was at the first Picnic Day and a majority of all subsequent ones during his lifetime. The Becket family never left before spending serious time at the agricultural engineering displays. Pictured here in Walker Hall are details about a new mechanized onion harvester. (SCL.)

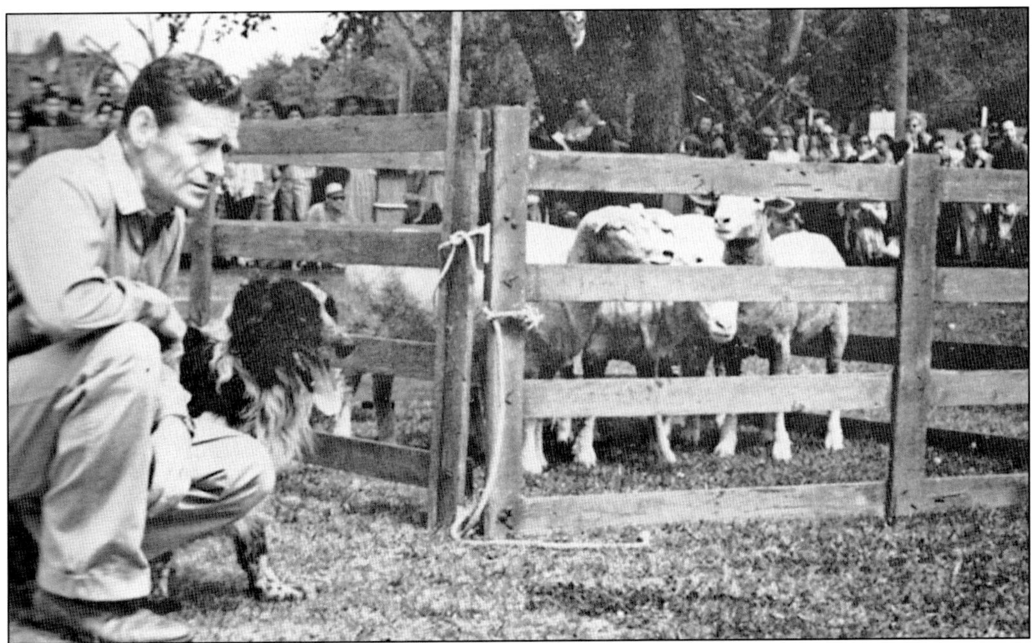

For decades, an immensely popular afternoon program has been the sheep dog trials or demonstrations. Competing teams of trainer and dog move a small group of sheep through something like an obstacle course. Speed and minimal signaling or whistling from the human earn a good score. Pictured in 1958 are some of the participants. (YB, JL.)

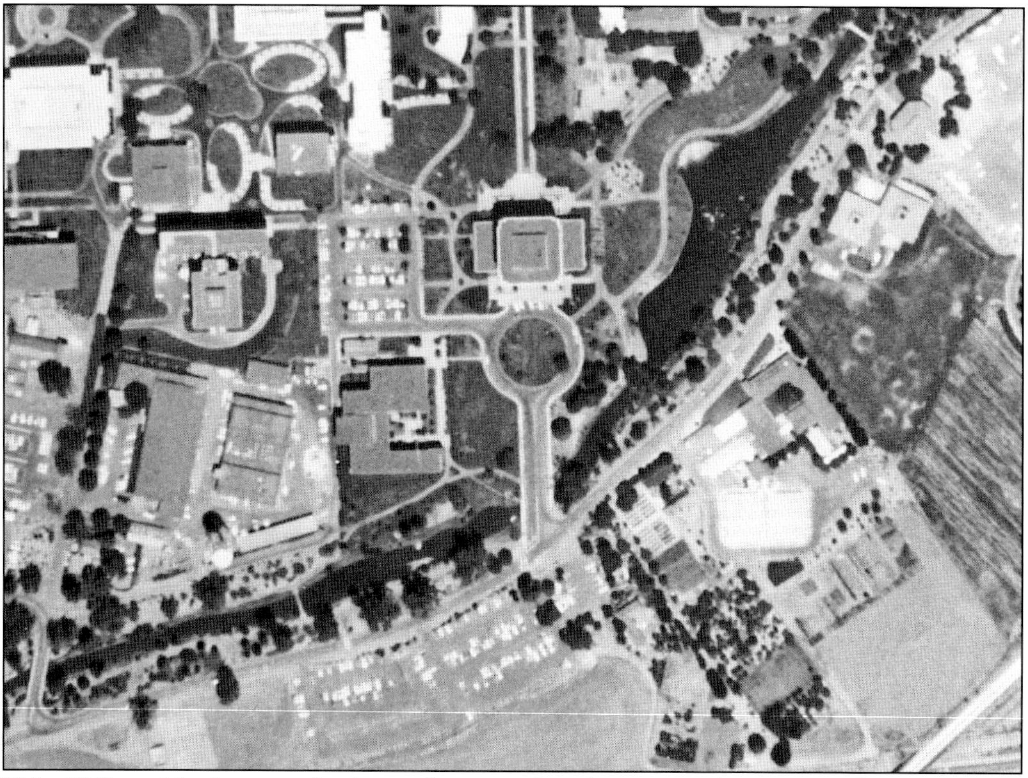

This 1972 aerial photograph shows the central and most-used segment of the UC Davis Arboretum. The full extent covers a mile and a quarter of Old Putah Creek. As a functioning waterway, the creek was made redundant by a rival channel in the 1870s. In 1948, the Corps of Engineers sealed off this old northern channel. Transformation into an arboretum began in earnest in the 1930s, and by the late 1970s, it was 125 acres in size. Just east of center is the widened segment now called Lake Spafford. (HWM.)

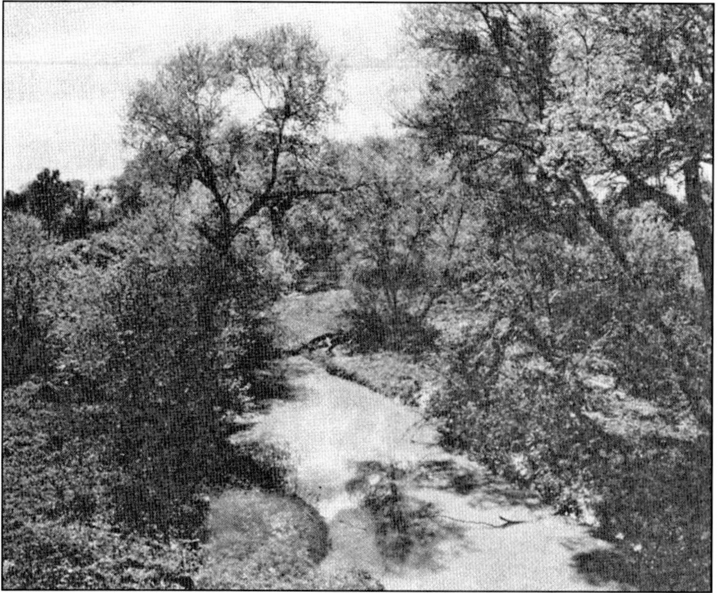

This photograph from 1927 shows Putah Creek in its pre-arboretum phase. Student yearbooks from the 1920s and 1930s published bucolic photographs and poetry romanticizing Putah Creek as a nature spot and campus amenity. Students used the area for passive contemplation of nature, swimming, and recreational use. Tiny as a waterway, it is still featured prominently on campus maps. (YB, JL.)

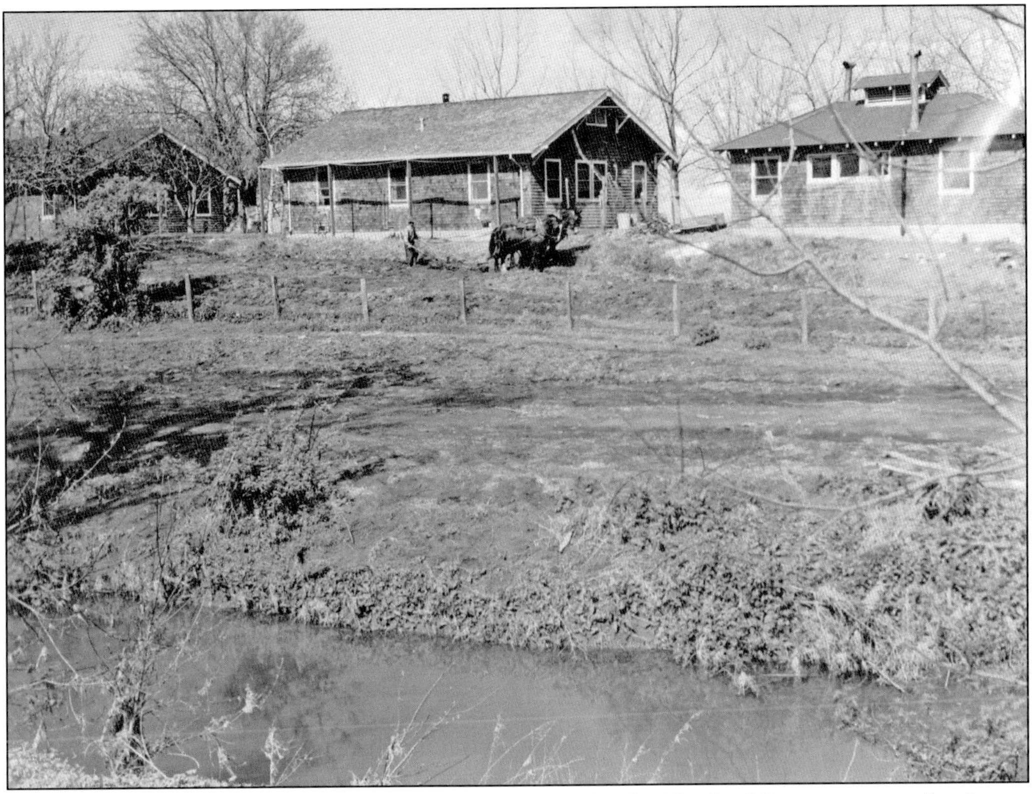

This 1920s photograph captures early use of the creekside. The buildings are part of a cluster of shingled cottages, including a bunkhouse and a dining hall, built in 1922 for campus employees. A brace of workhorses pulls the plow for a garden on the banks. The creek itself appears to be a springtime mud hole. Today, some of these buildings serve as arboretum offices. (PCA.)

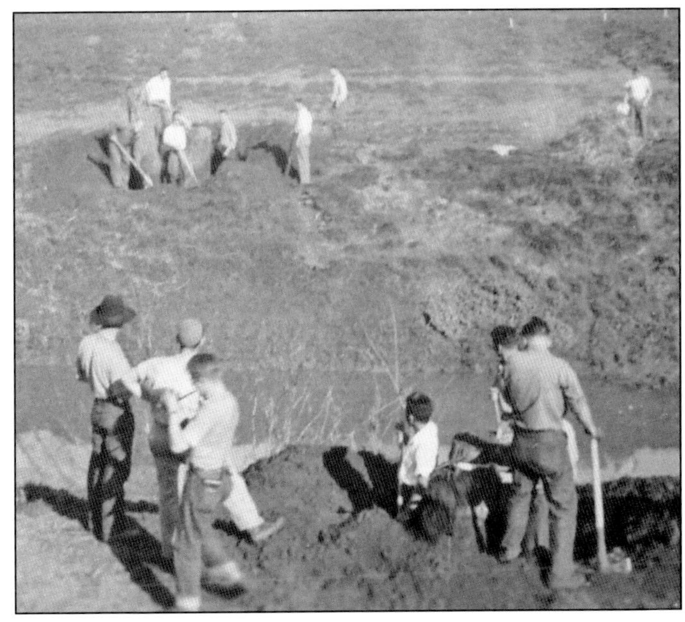

This is the earliest known photograph of the effort to create an arboretum along the creek. It shows a 1936 Labor Day crew of student volunteers who cleared vegetation and planted trees. That year, the redwood grove was established, which is today named for Prof. T. Elliot Weier, the botanist who organized this project. One of the largest concentrations of coast redwoods located away from the coast, the grove is a popular highlight among the arboretum's many nooks and niches. (SCL.)

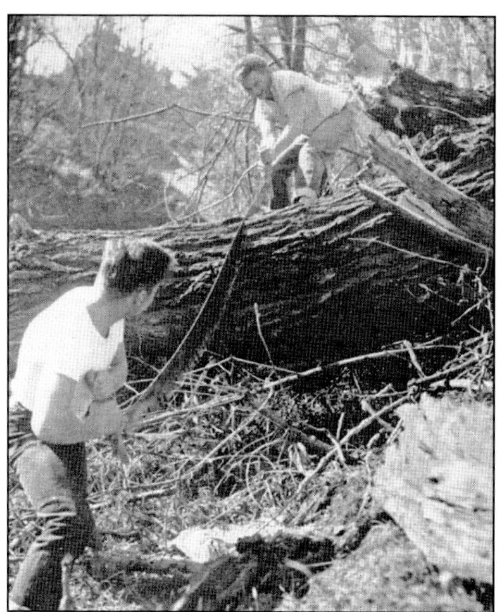

The budding arboretum got some serious attention from student volunteers on Labor Day 1948. A large cottonwood is sectioned the old-fashioned way, without a chain saw. Other photographs in the 1948 yearbook show dozens of brush trimmers and a large bulldozer at work re-contouring the banks. The groundwork was being laid for making Old Putah Creek home to a fantastic collection of plant communities assembled from around the state and the world. (YB, JL.)

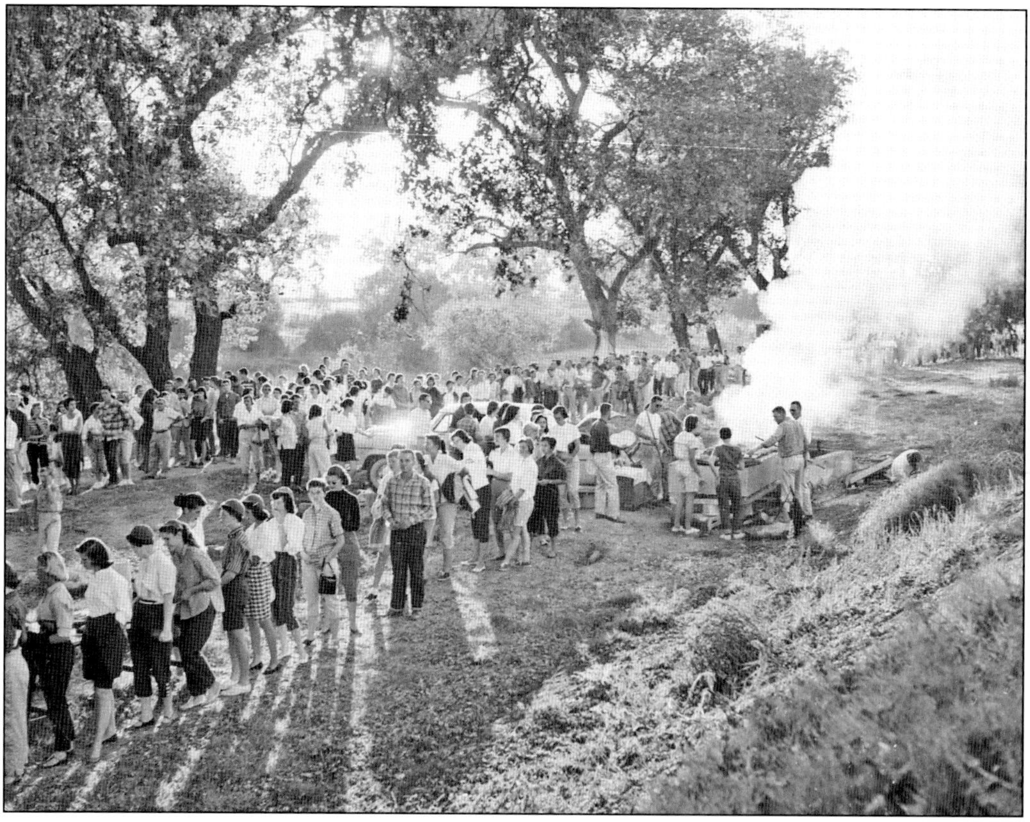

Pictured here in 1958 is a fall orientation week event known as the "steak bake." It takes place at Putah Creek's most remote picnic ground, known as Straloch Beach for the site's former farm owner. The site lies three miles upstream from the redwood grove and just south of the airport. For years, this spot was the setting for a youth summer camp. It remains popular for fishing and launching canoes. (SCL.)

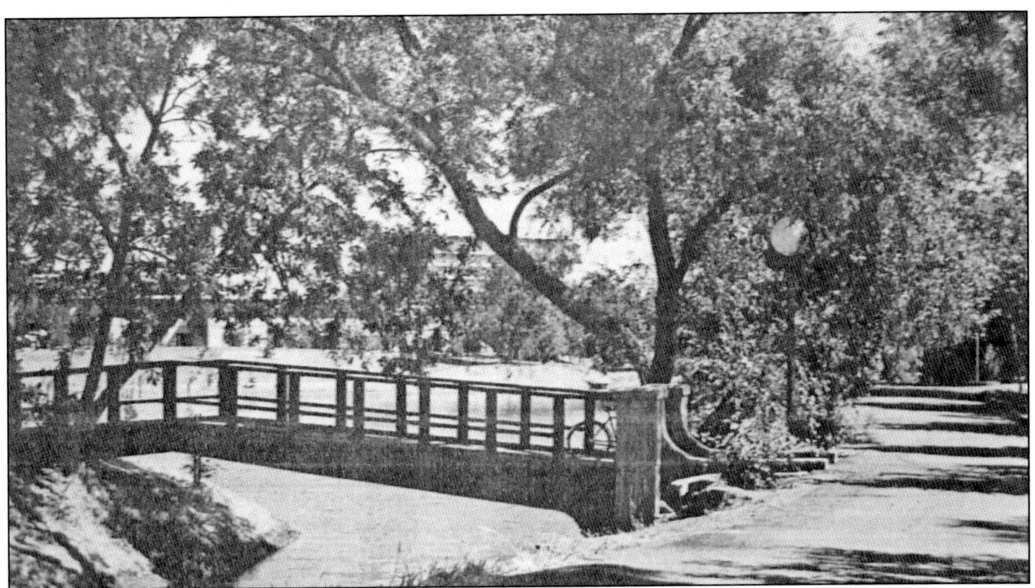

Arboretum pathways and bridges were planned and added over various years. A major building thrust came just before this photograph was published in the 1970 student yearbook. The 1963 Long Range Development Plan stipulated that the creek was to be an outdoor laboratory for educational purposes, as well as a recreational facility. Notable improvements came from landscape architect Theodore Osmundson, who laid out channel enlargements east of Mrak Hall and also at the west end. (SCL.)

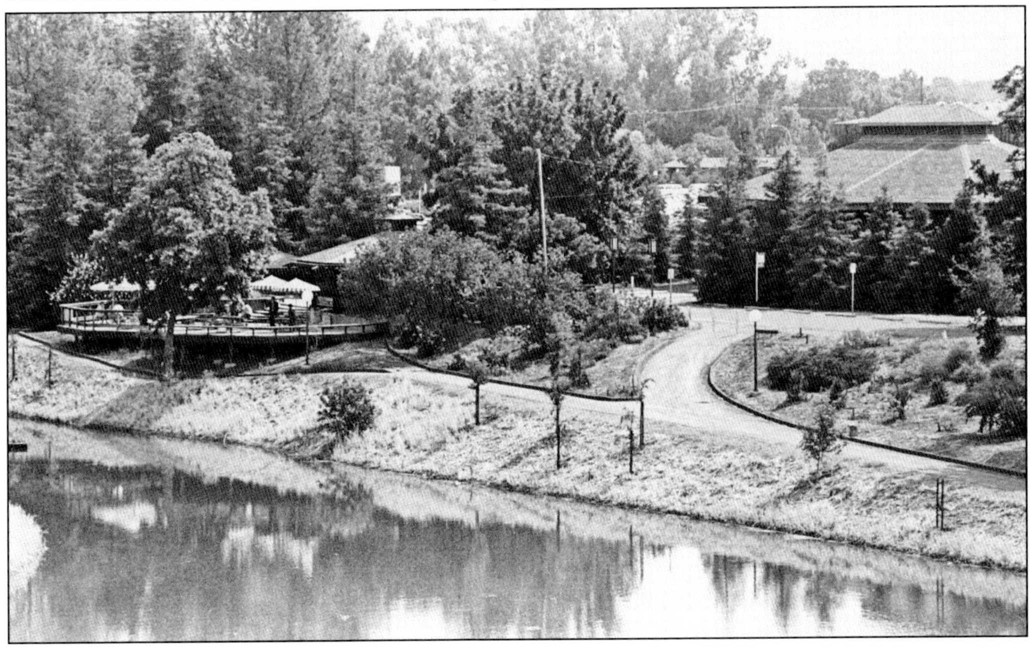

The flurry of construction during the late 1960s saw the old livestock-judging pavilion moved here to its third resting place on campus. The octagonal structure had been south of Haring Hall but now is east of Mrak Hall on the right bank of the creek. With funding from a generous former Aggie, it became known as Wyatt Pavilion. It has been rehabilitated to create a theater-in-the-round performance venue. (SCL.)

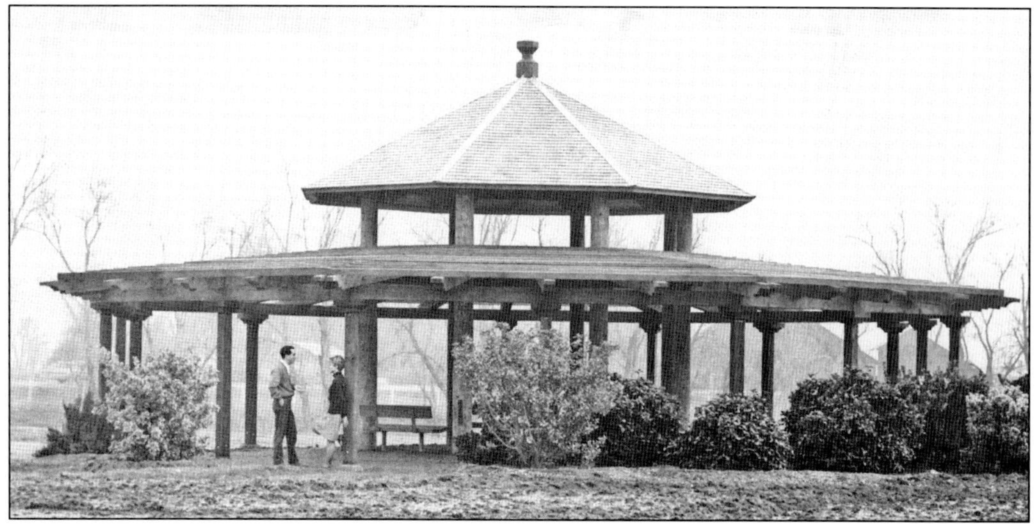

At the far west end of the arboretum is this gazebo, built in 1966 to adjoin three significant features: the Carolee Shields White Flower Garden, the Peter J. Shields Oak Grove, and the Ruth Risdon Storer Garden. The gazebo followed the building of Putah Creek Lodge, a more centrally located place for large groups to meet and eat. The oak grove is especially dramatic with its collection of 80 oak tree varieties spread over 15 acres, identified by descriptive ceramic plaques along the rambling paths. (SCL.)

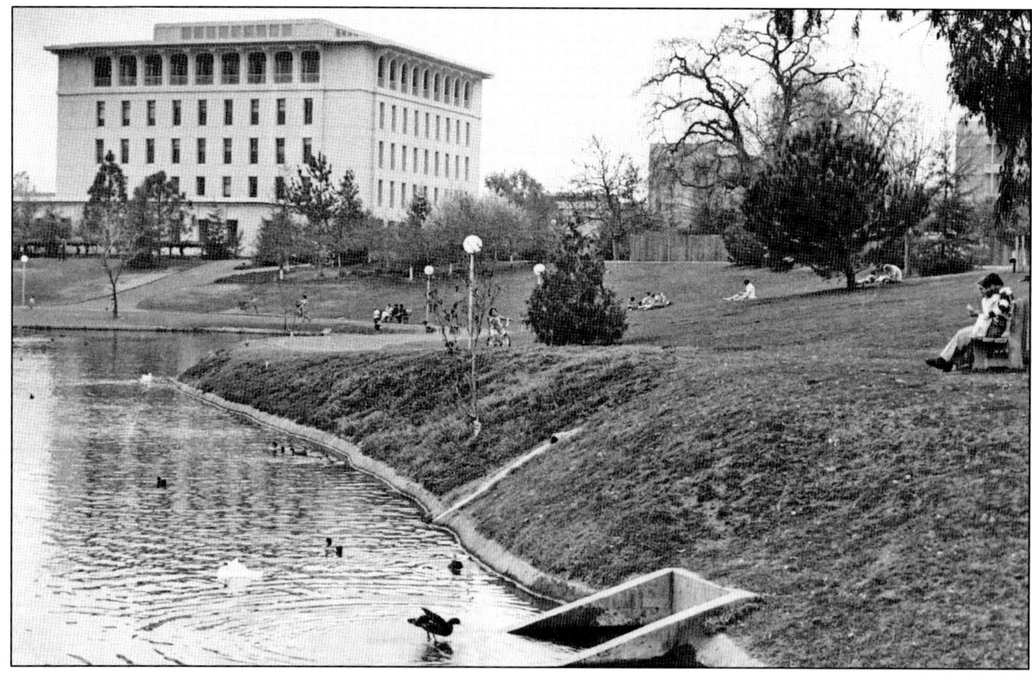

Lake Spafford was dug in 1968 as an artificial water feature to complement the Mrak Hall administration building. Named for Ed Spafford, longtime assistant to the chancellor, this is one of the most photographed spots on campus. Feeding the ducks has been curtailed, but watching wildlife is still common. Sculptures adorn the large lawn of well-kept grass. The Battle of the Bands, which takes place here on Picnic Day, can carry on into the evening. This spot rivals the quad for napping on the grass. (SCL.)

Eight

CONNECTIONS

UC DAVIS AND THE WORLD

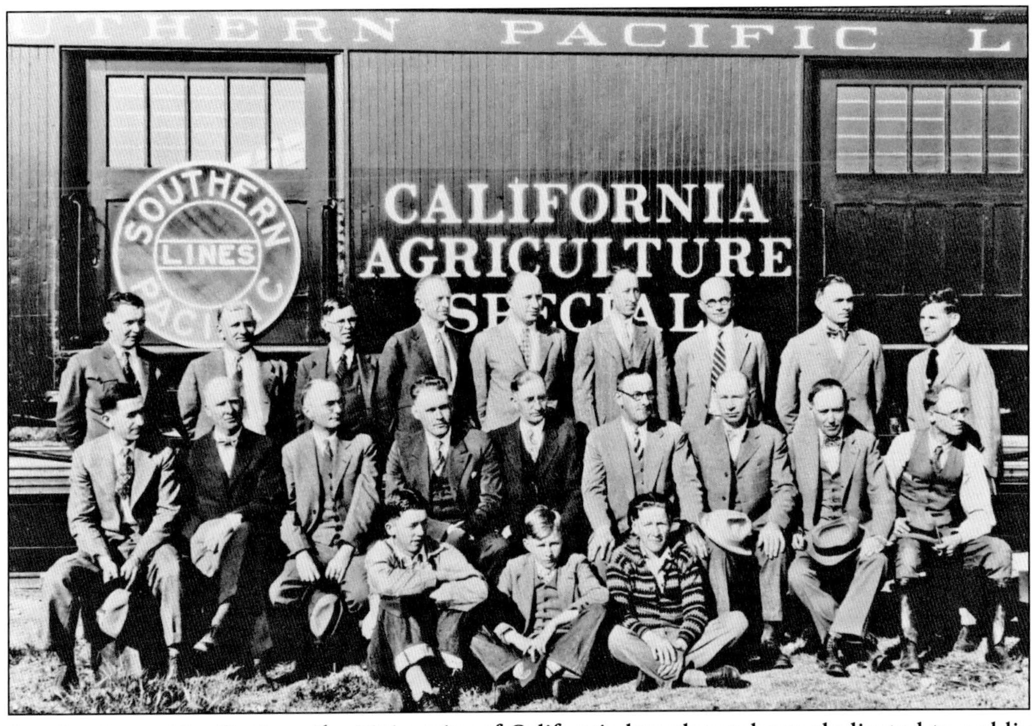

As a land-grant institution, the University of California has always been dedicated to public service, and since the Hatch Act established the Agricultural Experiment Stations in 1887, its College of Agriculture has been one of the largest and most active in the nation. Starting in the 1890s, college staff began extending the results of their research through State Farmers Institutes held in different locations. After the Smith-Lever Act started the Agricultural Extension Service in 1914, county agents continued some of this work, but in the 1920s, Berkeley and Davis staff also organized several traveling demonstration trains as a new form of outreach. This demonstration train of 1928 was one of the most successful, with a roster of 21 maintaining and explaining the exhibits inside the cars. Thousands of visitors flocked to see this train in locations all over California. (SCL.)

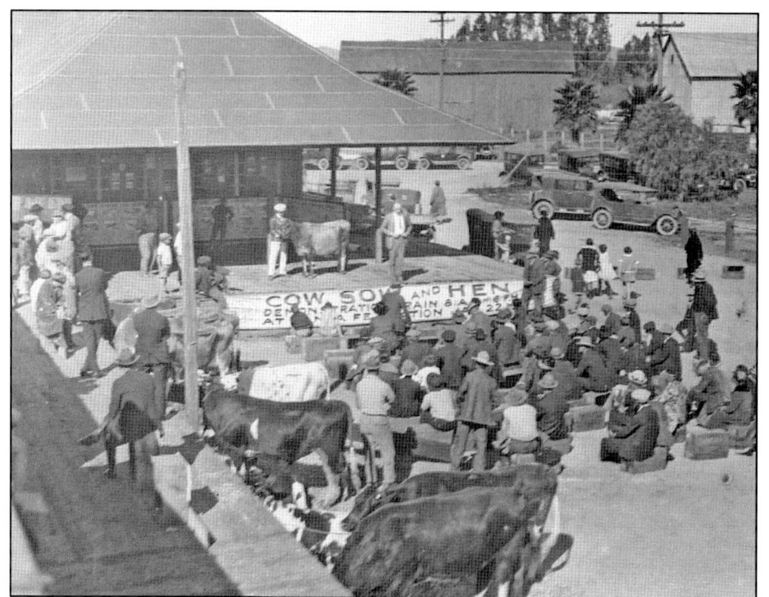

Outreach activities took staff specialists and animals from the Davis campus out to many small communities. They gave talks and offered demonstrations to farm families eager to learn the latest new findings in breeding and animal care. This kind of extension work was highly important in building more prosperous and stable rural communities. (SCL.)

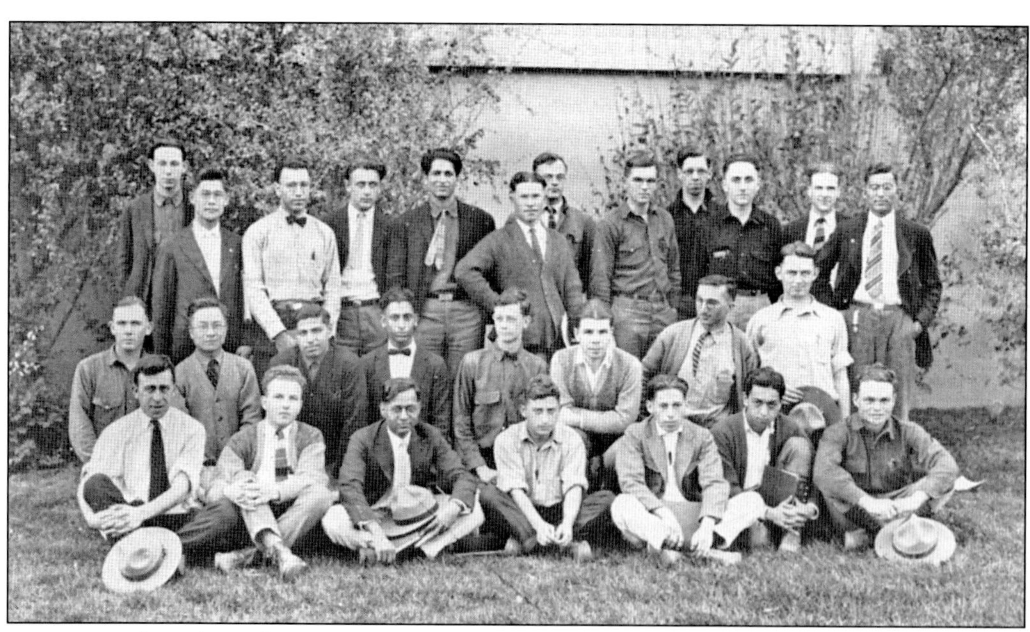

From its earliest days, the University Farm attracted foreign students. This picture from the 1924 student yearbook is of a club called the World Agricultural Society, which includes more than two dozen members representing at least half a dozen countries. Some international students stayed for only a year, but others completed academic programs and multiplied the impact of their education by going back to their home countries to spread the word about modern agricultural practices. (YB, JL.)

Max Kleiber, a Swiss-born scientist specializing in animal studies, arrived on campus in 1929 to spend a long career conducting research in animal metabolism. This photograph shows him with one of his prize constructions, which he called his "mechanical cow," also known as the California Respirator. It was used for modeling bovine physiological processes, especially involving simulations of lung/blood interactions. Kleiber's work after the war turned to studies using radioactive isotopes as tracers for chemical pathways. (SCL.)

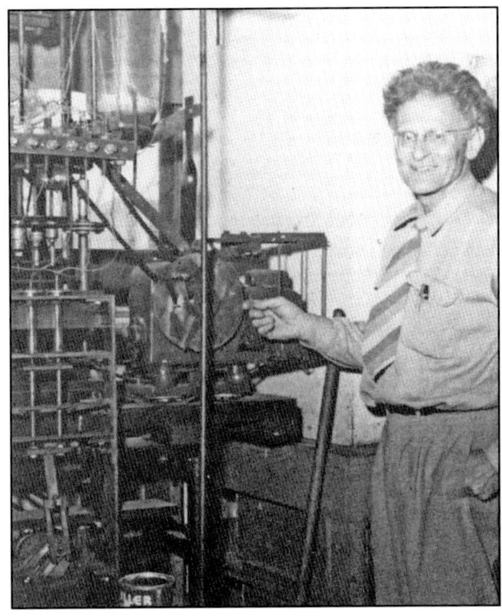

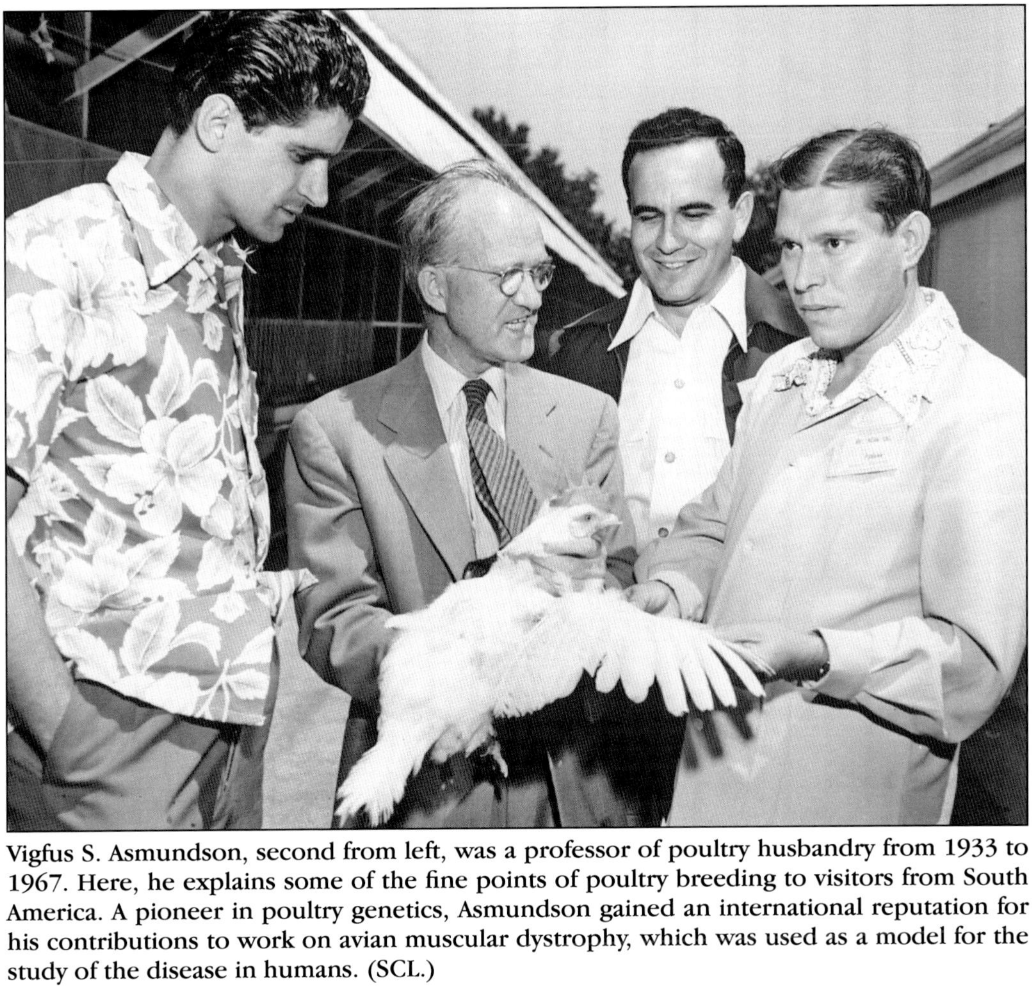

Vigfus S. Asmundson, second from left, was a professor of poultry husbandry from 1933 to 1967. Here, he explains some of the fine points of poultry breeding to visitors from South America. A pioneer in poultry genetics, Asmundson gained an international reputation for his contributions to work on avian muscular dystrophy, which was used as a model for the study of the disease in humans. (SCL.)

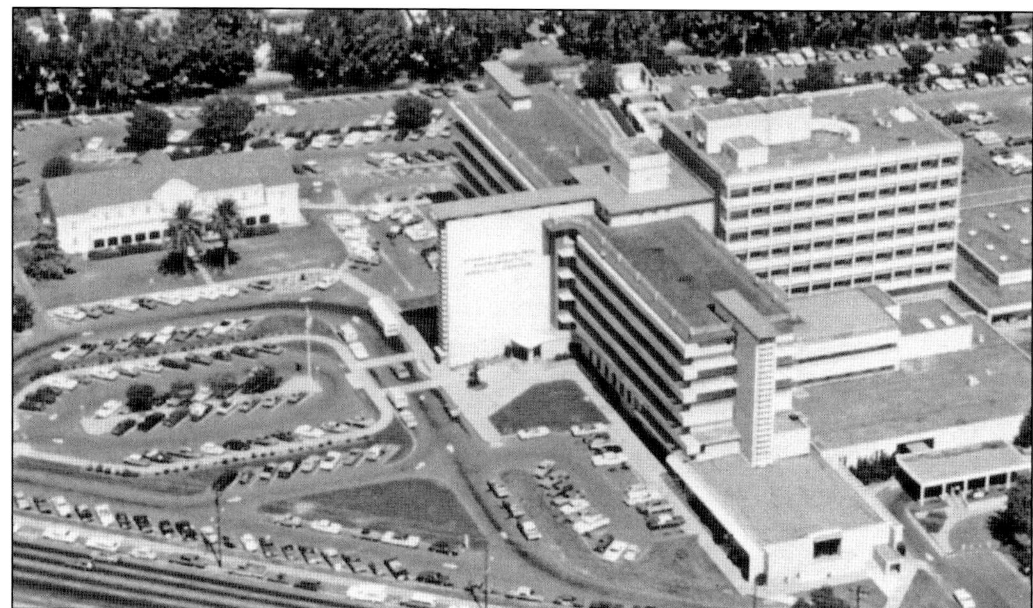

The Sacramento Medical Center, once a modest county hospital, became the new teaching hospital for the UC Davis School of Medicine in 1966. Over the years, it has been upgraded and expanded numerous times, has become a comprehensive care facility and been designated as the trauma center for all of Northern California, and, as the UC Davis Medical Center, has become a true health sciences campus encompassing many distinct centers of excellence. (MC.)

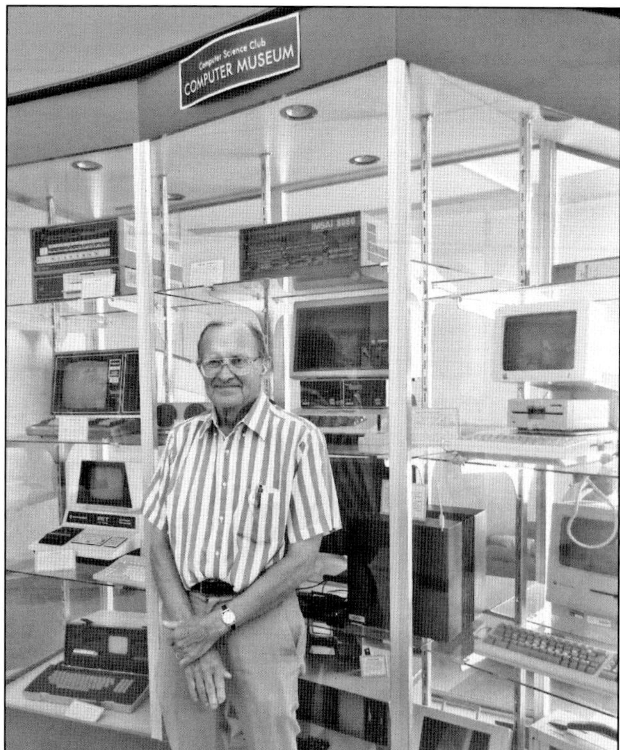

An expert in computer technology, Richard Walters joined the UC Davis School of Medicine in 1967 to set up computer programs in medical research and teaching. Over the years, evolving technology has revolutionized the ways in which medical data are collected and stored. Here, Walters stands in front of the campus computer museum he helped to create. (DJD.)

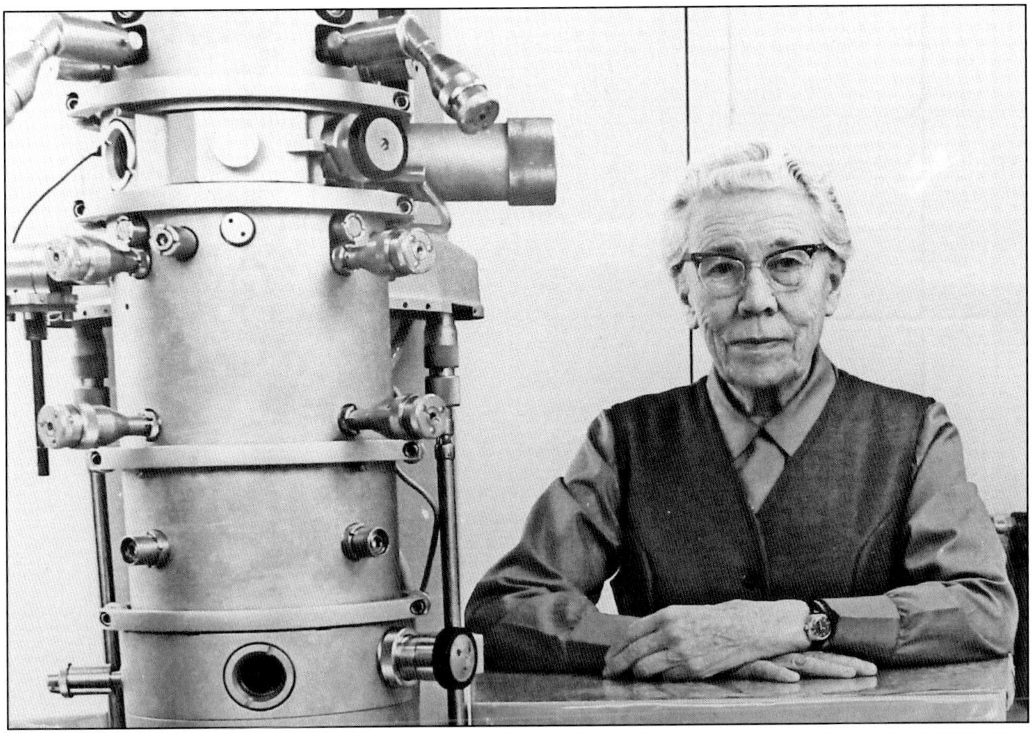

Katherine Esau, a brilliant plant anatomist, began her 30-year career at Davis in 1932. She studied plant diseases and plant structure and became a pioneer in electromicroscopy. Her encyclopedic books on plant anatomy have been key plant biology texts for four decades. In 1957, she was elected to the National Academy of Sciences, and in 1989, she was awarded a National Medal of Science. (TR.)

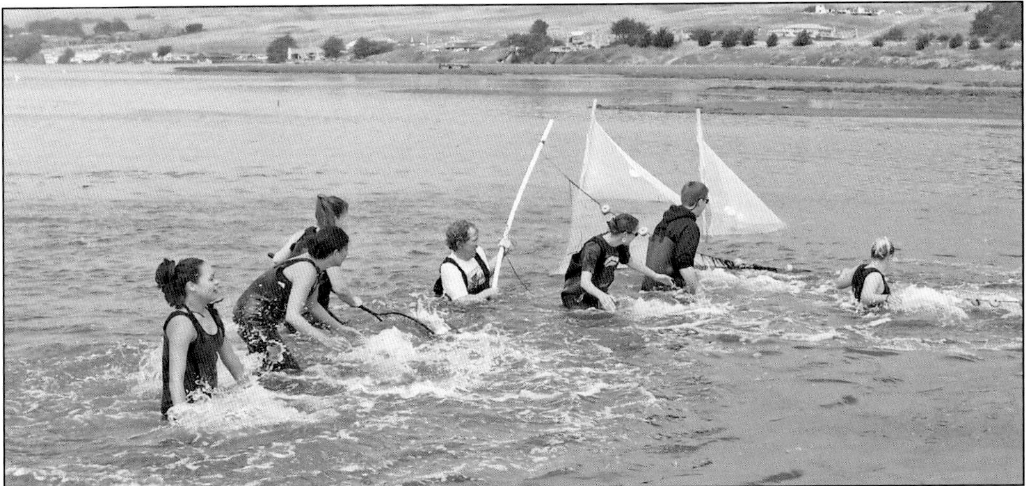

Bodega Marine Laboratory, which has been under UC Davis administration since 1983, is located on the biologically diverse Northern California coast on a 360-acre reserve. The facility draws researchers from all over the world for multidisciplinary studies on complex environmental problems in coastal ecosystems. Here, students operate a seine in Bodega Harbor to collect fish and invertebrates for population dynamics studies. (Photograph by Ely Huerta de Garcia, BML.)

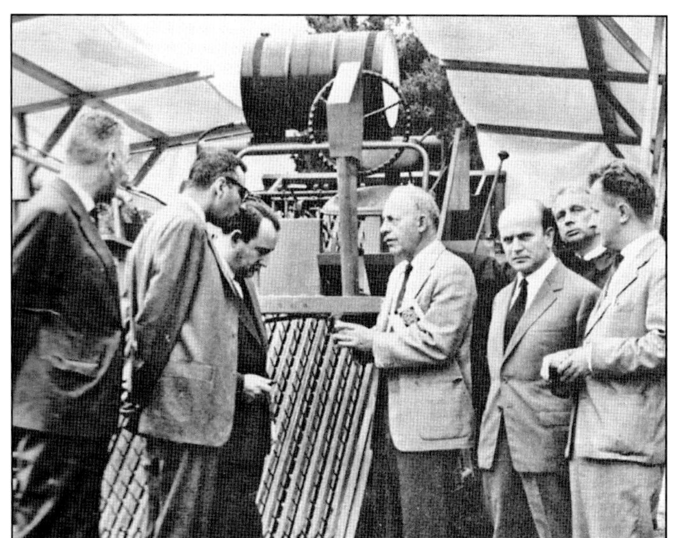

Coby Lorenzen of the Department of Agricultural Engineering shows several visiting Polish engineers some of the details of the mechanical tomato harvester that became famous during the 1960s. For a time, the harvester was controversial, but it proved to be highly effective, cutting down harvest costs and uncertainties. International engineers came to the Davis campus looking for ways to modernize their agriculture by mechanizing some of their labor-intensive tasks. (YB, JL.)

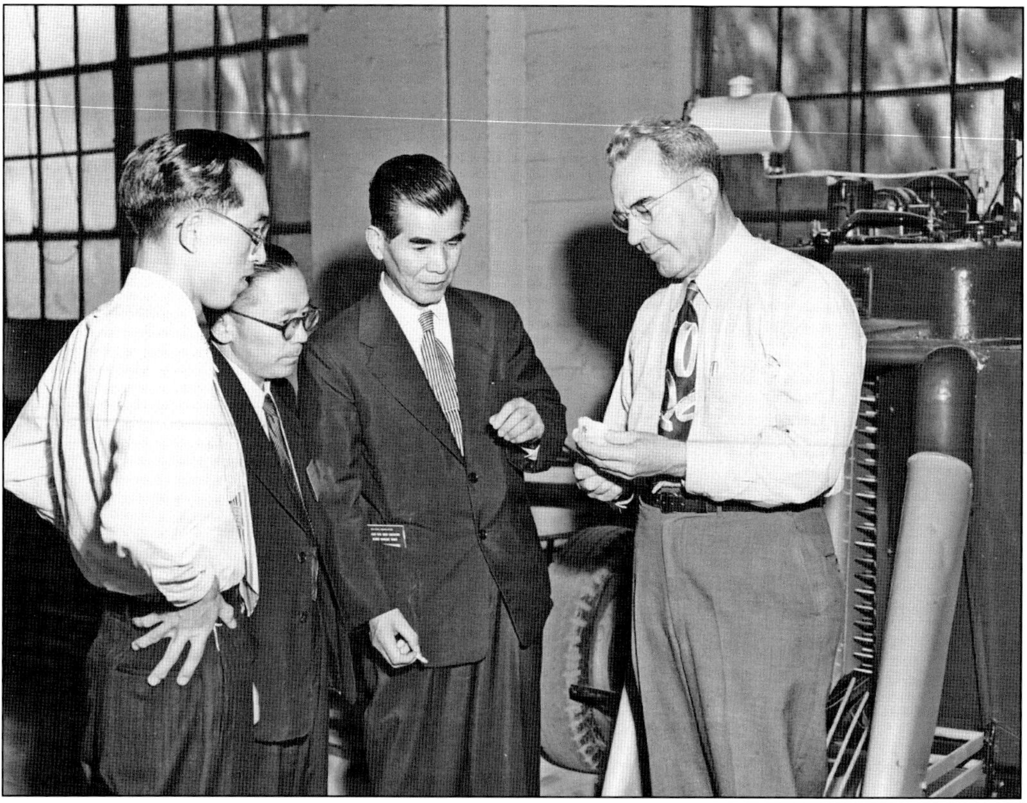

Roy Bainer, the beloved first dean of the College of Engineering, began his career at Davis in 1946 as an agricultural engineer working with Harry Walker. A friendly and outgoing man, he was always happy to explain the department's work to international visitors who were highly interested in what the Davis engineers were doing. *Time* magazine referred to the campus as "the wildly inventive center of the farm machinery revolution." (SCL.)

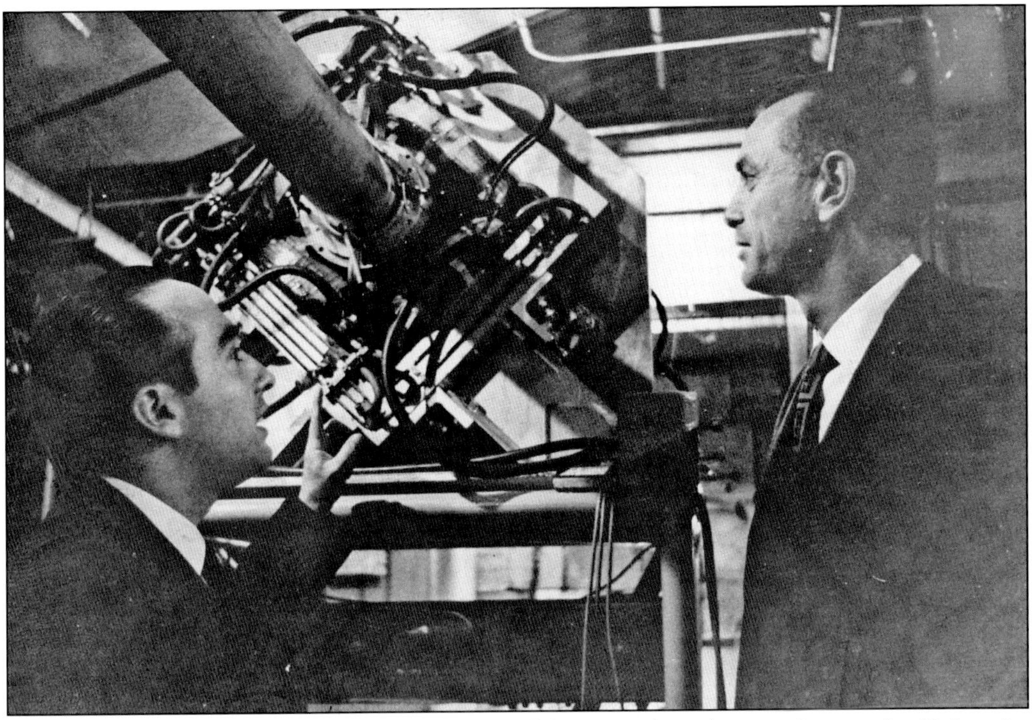

John Jungermann (right) discusses operation of the 22-inch cyclotron given to the University of Chile by the Davis campus in the late 1960s. A Convenio agreement then linked academic specialists at several UC campuses with those at the University of Chile. Funded by the Ford Foundation, Davis sent dozens of staff members to assist in upgrading education and research there until the project was halted after political upheavals in Chile suppressed academic freedom. (SCL.)

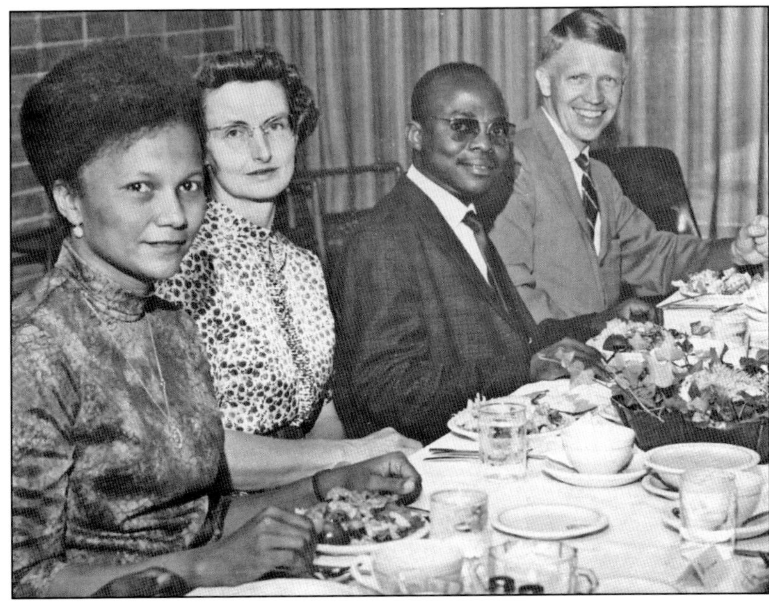

The founding dean of the School of Law, Edward L. Barrett (far right), hosts international visitors at a special dinner. Later, the school established an international law center at King Hall, as well as regular summer programs in international and American law specifically tailored for international legal professionals. Those programs continue today. (SCL.)

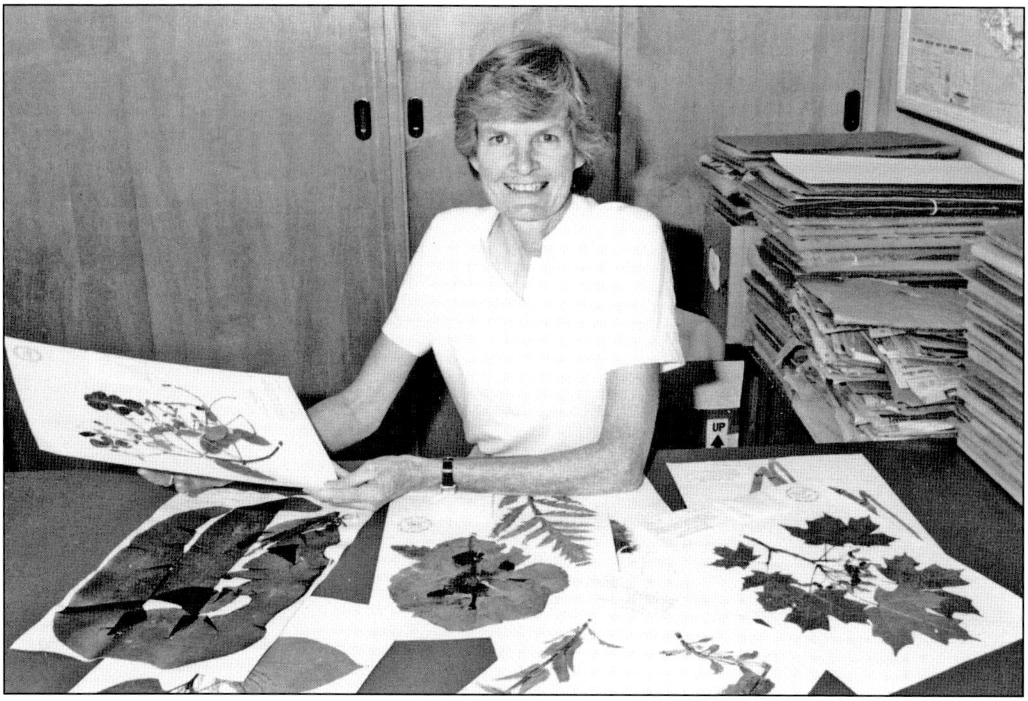

June McCaskill spent nearly 40 years as curator of the UC Davis herbarium, building a reputation as an expert in identifying weeds and advising veterinarians, farmers, and environmentalists, as well as aiding police investigations up and down California. She became affectionately known as "the Weed Lady," though her expertise was far wider. Hundreds of thousands of specimens of all kinds of plants are housed within the herbarium in today's UC Davis Center for Plant Diversity. (PSH.)

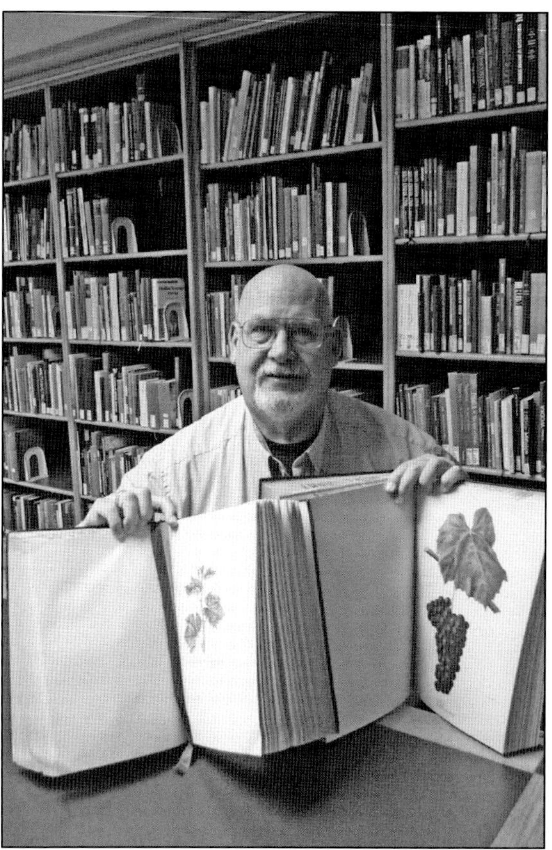

Axel Borg, a bibliographer and subject specialist at Shields Library, has charge of the university's viticulture and enology collection, which comprises some 29,000 holdings and is considered the finest such collection in the world, with a top ranking of five from the American Research Libraries Group. The collection is named in honor of Maynard Amerine, internationally famed for his enormous list of publications on grape growing and winemaking. (Photograph by Dana Welch, AB.)

Botanist John Tucker, seen here on a collecting trip in Sonora, Mexico, in 1958, pursued a lifelong interest in oaks. During the course of his long career, Tucker collected acorns from all species of oaks while on international research trips, then began growing them at Davis. He served as director of the Davis Botany Department herbarium from 1948 until his retirement in 1986, when it was renamed the J.M. Tucker Herbarium in his honor. (PSH.)

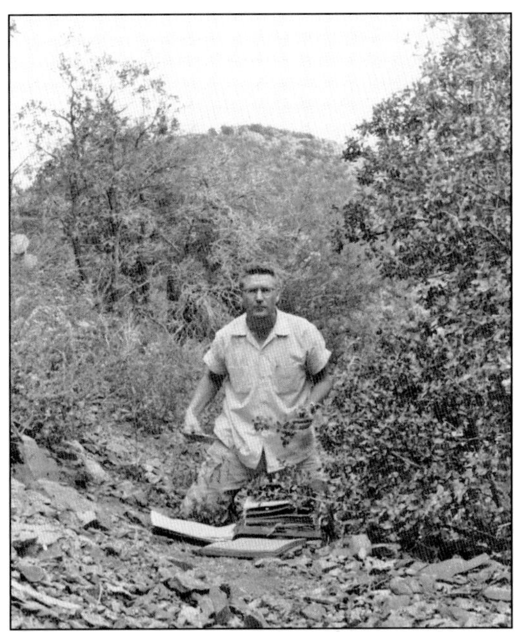

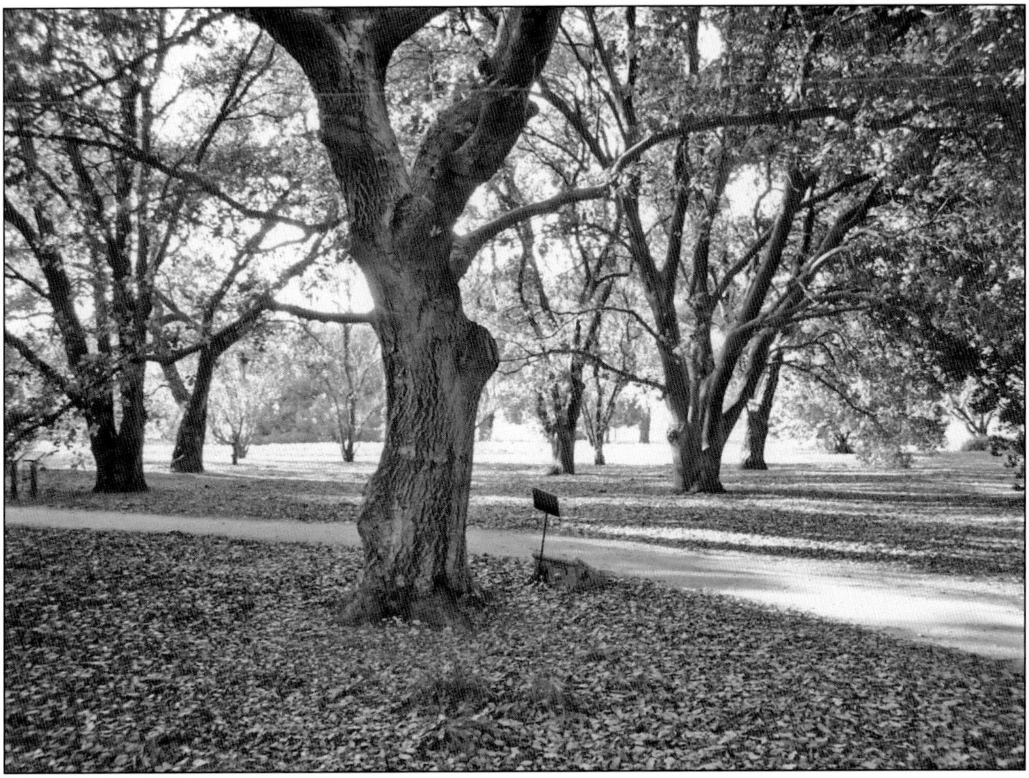

A crown jewel of the campus arboretum is the Shields Oak Grove (named for Peter Shields, who wrote the legislation creating the University Farm). It might well also be called the Tucker Oak Grove, as John Tucker established it in 1962 near the west end of the arboretum, planting the acorns he and others had collected. Today, the grove is home for 574 oak trees, including many native California species, and is a national resource. (DJD.)

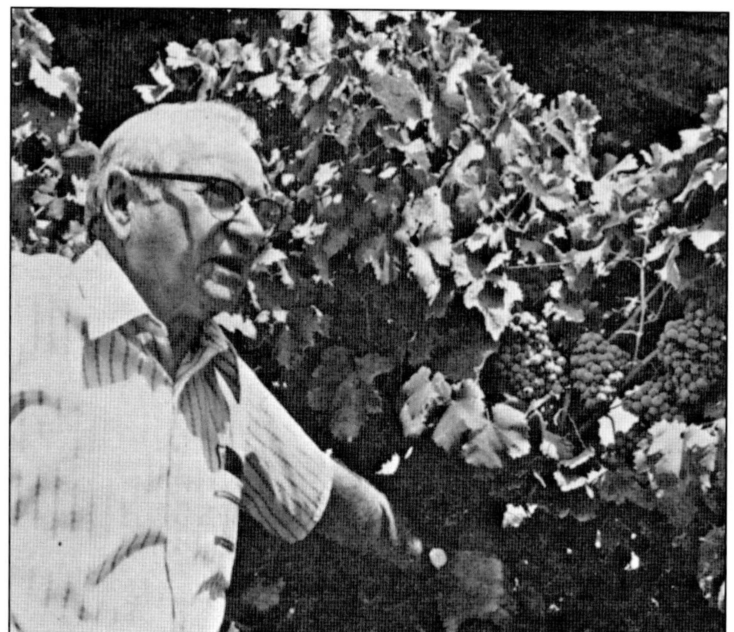

Once called the "Indiana Jones of viticulture," grapevine geneticist Harold Olmo amassed a collection of grape varieties from across the world. He joined a cadre of plant explorers in the 1930s, traversing the Afghan mountains by horseback and other remote areas in search of wild vines. At Davis, he released 20 varieties over his university career and formulated the first certification program to ensure clean and true-to-type plant material. (JO.)

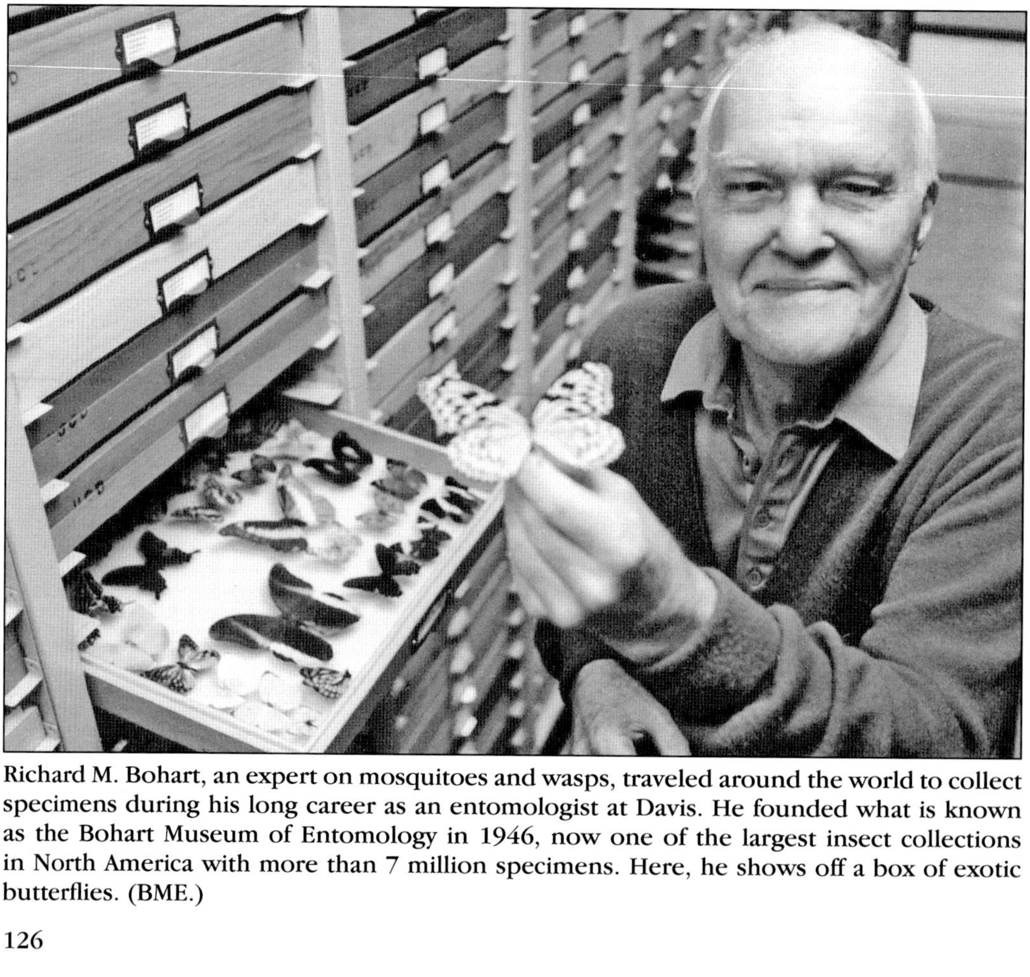

Richard M. Bohart, an expert on mosquitoes and wasps, traveled around the world to collect specimens during his long career as an entomologist at Davis. He founded what is known as the Bohart Museum of Entomology in 1946, now one of the largest insect collections in North America with more than 7 million specimens. Here, he shows off a box of exotic butterflies. (BME.)

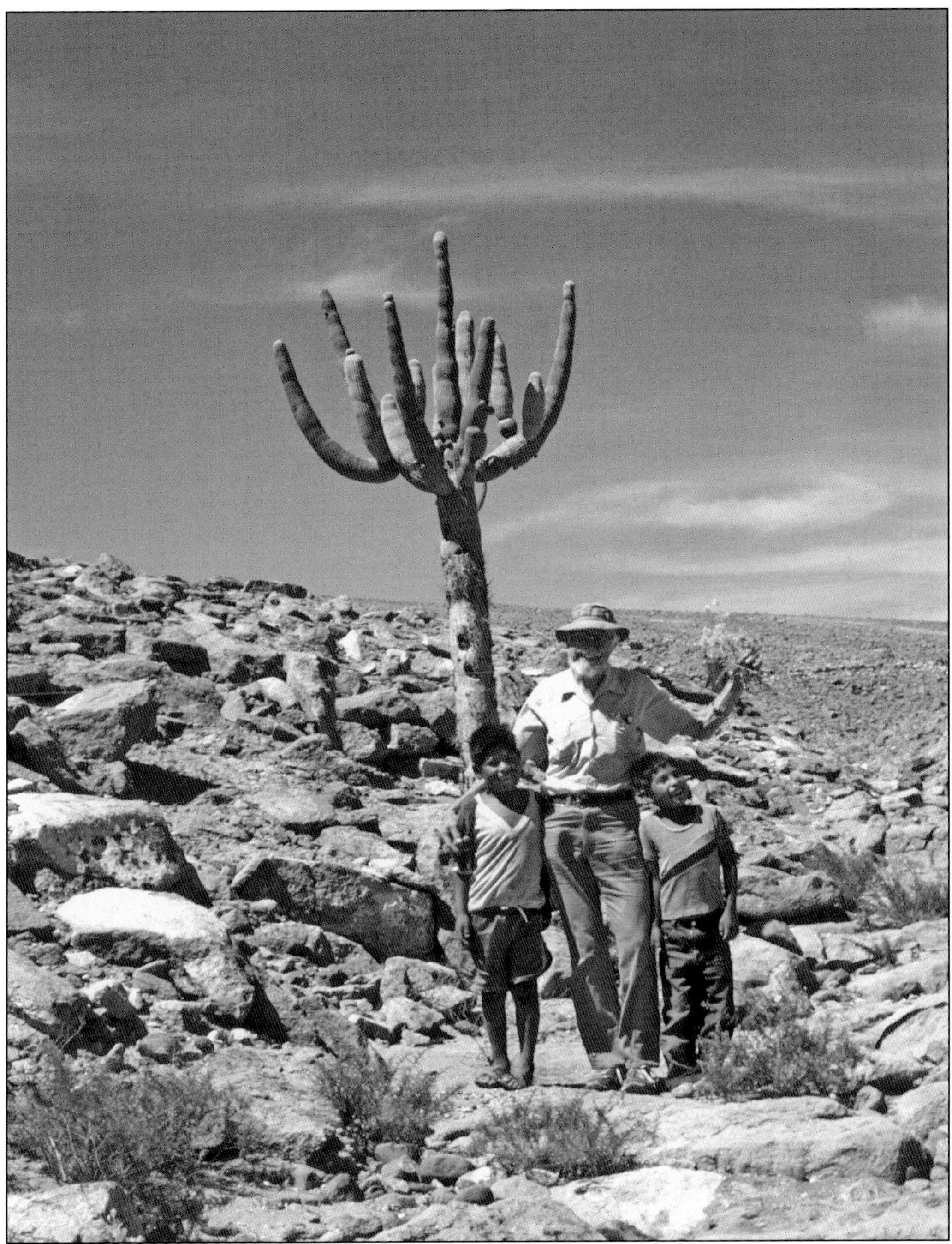

Charles M. Rick, shown with his assistant plant collectors—two local boys who led him to the site—holds a bouquet of the wild tomato species *Solanum chilense* near Chitita, Chile, in April 1986. Rick was famed for his collecting of wild tomato specimens all over the Americas, even at elevations like this one at 7,220 feet above sea level. Seed resources propagated from Rick's research trips are maintained by the center named for him in the Department of Plant Sciences. This photograph seems to show him toasting the future. (C.M. Rick Tomato Genetics Resource Center.)